ZOË BRÂN was born in Wales. Between university degrees she travelled extensively, turning her hand to all kinds of work, including teaching Buddhist monks in Bangkok; shaking cocktails for the US army in Bavaria; making new pictures look old in New York; and selling male strippergrams in London. Now a full-time writer and editor, her published work covers a wide range of subjects, from sexuality to poetry and jazz. Zoë's travel writing includes books on Vietnam and Burma, and she is a member of the Amazonians, the society of British women travel writers. Her first novel, *Some Increase of Brightness*, was shortlisted for the 1999/2000 Arts Council of England Writers Awards and was awarded a 1999/2000 Hawthornden Fellowship. Zoë lives in London.

After Yugoslavia

Zoë Brân

LONELY   PLANET   PUBLICATIONS
Melbourne • Oakland • London • Paris

After Yugoslavia

Published by Lonely Planet Publications
Head Office: 90 Maribyrnong St, Footscray, Vic 3011, Australia
                Locked Bag 1, Footscray, Vic 3011, Australia
Branches: 150 Linden Street, Oakland, CA 94607, USA
                10a Spring Place, London NW5 3BH, UK
                1 rue Dahomey, 75011, Paris, France

Published 2001
Printed by The Bookmaker International Ltd
Printed in China

Maps by Natasha Velleley
Designed by Simon Bracken

National Library of Australia Cataloguing in Publication Data

After Yugoslavia

ISBN 1 86450 030 1.

1. Brân, Zoë – Journeys – Croatia. 2. Yugoslav War – 1991–1995.
3. Bosnia and Hercegovina – Description and travel.
4. Brân, Zoë – Journeys – Slovenia.
5. Brân, Zoë – Journeys – Bosnia and Hercegovina.
6. Slovenia – Description and travel. 7. Croatia – Description
and travel. I. Title. (Series: Lonely Planet journeys.)

914.971

For Rochelle Bloch and Rivka Micklethwaite Bloch,
the people upstairs.

Contents

Acronyms

BiH – Bosnia-Hercegovina

EU – European Union

HDZ – Hrvatska Demokratska Zajednica

ICTY – International Criminal Tribunal Yugoslavia (the Hague)

JNA – Yugoslav National Army

NATO – North Atlantic Treaty Organization

OHR – Office of the High Representative (Sarajevo)

OSCE – Organisation for Security and Co-operation in Europe

PHR – Physicians for Human Rights

RS – Republika Srpska (Bosnia)

SFOR – Security Force

UN – United Nations

UNHCR – United Nations High Commission for Refugees

UNPROFOR – United Nations Protection Force

Acknowledgements

With special thanks to:

Jim Pett, Andrej Blatnik, David McIlfatrick and Nataša Hrastnik, for all their invaluable help and advice.

Thanks also to the following:

Enes Ališković, Jennifer Anderson, Oksana Antonenko, David Austin, Belma, Juliette Cole, Ken Corlett, Alex Cowan OBE, N. Dervisbegovic, Robin Evans, Steve Fallon, Quentin Hoare, Geraldine Hodgson, Nidzara Horozovic, D. Huic, Graham Inett, Rok Klančnik, Klara Koltaj, Elma Kovačević, Branka Magaš, Rusmir Mahmutćehajić, Jasna Marić, Eva Marn, Aleksij Mekjavić, Jeanne Oliver, the Rijeka City Tourist Office, Janet Rogan, Miranda Sidran, Shahbaza Sidran, Alenka Suhadolnik, Mela Telalbašić, the Travaš family, Flora Turner, General F. Viggers and Vladimir.

Many of the people I met on my journey asked me to change their names. There were many different reasons for this request. Some people wanted to protect themselves, their families, or their jobs. One or two names I changed for my own reasons. You all know who you are.

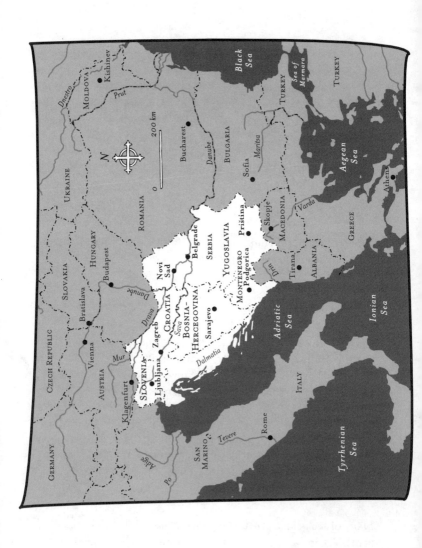

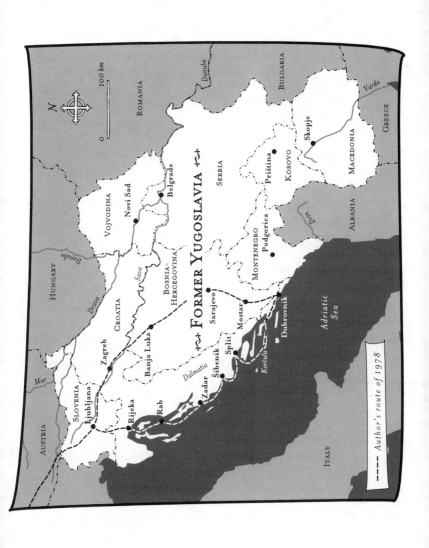

N

100 km

0

AUSTRIA

HUNGARY

Danube

ROMANIA

Mur

Drava

Sava

SLOVENIA

Ljubljana

Zagreb

CROATIA

VOJVODINA

Novi Sad

Belgrade

Danube

BULGARIA

Varda

Rijeka

Rab

Banja Luka

BOSNIA–
HERCEGOVINA

✦ FORMER YUGOSLAVIA ✦

SERBIA

Priština

KOSOVO

Skopje

MACEDONIA

GREECE

Dalmatia

Zadar

Šibenik

Split

Sarajevo

Mostar

MONTENEGRO

Podgorica

Drin

ALBANIA

Korčula

Dubrovnik

Adriatic
Sea

ITALY

––––– *Author's route of 1978*

Introduction

I N THE EARLY autumn of 1978, I made the short train journey
from Munich to Ljubljana. I was twenty-one, a student living
part-time in Bavaria, and there was almost a month before I had
to return to university in Scotland. Yugoslavia was close, cheap
and required no visa. It was the smiling face of Communism.
Having spent the summer on an American military base, it offered
the thrill of opposites.

In 1978 Josip Broz Tito, father and protector of the nation, still
lived in a palace in Belgrade. His Yugoslavia was large, prosperous, and geographically and culturally diverse; yet it was easy to
travel through Slovenia, Croatia and Bosnia, as I did that
September, believing you were in one country. Compared to
provincial Britain it was paradise. Locals and tourists alike
enjoyed good food and drink, and cheap public transport. For
Westerners, there was the added *frisson* of lifting the hem of the
Iron Curtain.

Yugoslavia had everything: high mountains and long coast-
lines; turquoise rivers and emerald forests; romantic castles and
classical ruins; ancient churches and mysterious stones . . . and
the place where the history of the twentieth century changed for
ever. Where else in the world could state so categorically that
here on this very spot, in the time that it takes to lift an arm and
press a trigger, the direction of the world was knocked off course?
The Gavrilo Princip Bridge in Sarajevo became my destination

in 1978, not from ghoulish sentiment but because the assassination of Archduke Franz Ferdinand by the Serb nationalist Princip, the inciting incident of World War I, was almost the only thing I knew about Yugoslavia back then.

Tito died two years after my visit, in 1980, to live on in the popular imagination, a symbol of the past and of possibilities. His death marked the beginning of the end of federal Yugoslavia as his complex political constructs and economic deals began to crumble. By the late eighties what had seemed stable proved illusory. Centralists vied with federalists, Communists with nationalists, as the divides between Slovenia, Croatia, Bosnia, Serbia, Montenegro and Macedonia widened.

Like most Westerners, I was unaware of what was happening on Europe's edges. It was only when war started in 1991, and the names of the cities and villages I'd visited were repeated daily like a litany of horror on TV and radio, that I recalled details of my journey and of Yugoslavia as it had been, or rather as it had appeared.

It requires a leap of the imagination for the generations born in the West after 1950 to grasp the nature and scale of the conflict experienced in the Former Yugoslavia in the 1990s. Not because it was more horrific or more widespread than, for example, Vietnam, Afghanistan or Rwanda, but because it happened in Europe, in the West itself. Now, in a new millennium, the conflict seems likely to continue, in some form, for years to come. Kosovo, merely the most recent tragedy in a region fraught with them, has been described in the foreign media as 'tribal, savage', as though such emotions were unknown to Europeans. When the Bosnian war finally ended in 1995, mediators from 'stable' Western countries preached at the participants about the unacceptable hazards of nationalistic violence, forgetting the cost of their own stability – a twentieth century of blood and violence on a scale previously unknown in human history.

2

War distorted the Yugoslavia that I had known briefly in 1978; it also distorted my own memories of the country. Each evening, as I watched the TV news, I tried to recognise towns, landscapes, roads – and could not. While Sarajevo was still besieged, I planned to return one day to rediscover what was lost and, more importantly, to try to make sense, for myself at least, of what had happened in the twenty intervening years, and why.

It was obvious that grasping the Yugoslav nettle would be impossible without some understanding of the region's history. All histories are complex, and as those of Slovenia, Croatia and Bosnia are more complex than most, they are frequently the subject of academic and lay disagreement. What follows may not accord with everyone's notion of events, but it is not intended as a history of the Former Yugoslavia, or even an attempt at one. It's nothing more than my own effort to make sense of past events in order to better understand the present.*

Every country has *histories*, rather than *a history*. Depending on the time, the need, these histories vary. The Celtic tradition of north-west Europe, for example, awaits the return of Arthur, Once and Future King, though whether he'll be Welsh, Scots, Cornish or Breton when he does return is a matter of continuing dispute.

Since the middle of the nineteenth century, when Europe was swept by nationalistic fervour, the area later called Yugoslavia, the land of the South Slavs, has been a creator of histories second only to Germany in the 1930s and '40s. Subjected to the rule of vast, foreign empires for many hundreds of years, the Balkan peoples' need for histories was particularly strong. No nation in this region is without its myths, its distortions. Since the mid-nineteenth century, Bosnians have been told by Croats that they are Croat and by Serbs that they are Serb, all in the interests of Croat and Serb expansion. In 1942, during the occupation of Bosnia, a group of Bosnian Moslems wrote to Hitler informing him that they were descendants of the Germanic Goths, and therefore a 'superior' people. Hitler, surrounded by master mythologisers, was

* There are many excellent books on the region's history for those who want to read further.

not impressed. In 1525, a Croat Dominican friar protested at the lowly status occupied by the Croat nation, claiming that most of the great men of the past, from Aristotle and Alexander to Diocletian and numerous popes, had actually been Croatian Slavs. The Serbs have carefully preserved the over-arching myth of the role they played at the Battle of Kosovo Polje in 1389, which they continue to celebrate as a glorious defeat in which the flower of Serbian nobility perished at the hand of the vile Turk. More accurately, Kosovo Polje was a stalemate which the Serbs initially interpreted as a victory despite the capture and execution of their leader, Prince Lazar. The army facing the Ottomans that day included Croats, Hungarians and Bosnians; among Lazar's forces were followers of Islam. But on the myth of Serbia's proud defeat rests its claim to modern Kosovo.

When asked what 'the Balkans' currently means in geopolitical thinking, a foreign diplomat in Bosnia told me it means 'a pain in the arse for the rest of the world'. What the West perceives as 'the Balkan problem' had its earliest origins in AD 293, when the Roman Emperor Diocletian decided that imperial territory east of the Adriatic was too large and difficult for a single administration to manage, and divided it. One hundred years later, Emperor Theodosius divided the entire Roman Empire into two: the Western Roman Empire (including Slovenia, Croatia and Bosnia-Hercegovina) and the Eastern Roman Empire (including Serbia, Kosovo and Macedonia). In this way the seeds of future discord were sown. When the Roman Empire collapsed in the fifth century, the north-western part of what would later become Yugoslavia saw waves of invaders including Asiatic Huns and Iranian Alans. Germanic Langobards and Ostrogoths swept through modern Slovenia, northern Croatia and into Italy. In the sixth century, two more tribes appeared: Turkic Avars and Slavs.

Ultimately, it was the Slavs who stayed. Settlers and farmers, they headed south through modern-day Serbia and parts of Bosnia, moving down the Balkan peninsula to the furthest shores of Bulgaria and Greece. Under pressure from the Avars, other Slav tribes pushed west into Slovenia, southern Austria and the

Friuli Plain. By 626, the Slavs of this western region had united to defeat the Avars and create the Principality of Karantania, which included present-day Slovenia and centred on Krn, today called Klagenfurt, in Austrian Carinthia.

Soon after these earliest settlements had been established, a second wave of Slavs – the Croats and Serbs – appeared from their respective kingdoms in what is now south Poland and the south Czech region. The Croats were apparently invited by the Byzantine Emperor to assist in pushing out the Avars; the Serbs seem to have accompanied them. As with the earlier Slavic peoples, the origins of the Croats and Serbs are not fully established. Some scholars suggest that the Croats could be of Persian descent, as the origin of the word for Croat – 'Hrvat' – is thought to be Iranian; others hotly dispute the notion. What is certain is that the two groups were connected from earliest times, although this link has, since the upsurge of nationalism in the nineteenth century, been denied, altered and exploited for territorial and ideological reasons. Significantly, the Croats and Serbs were not, as each often claims, the 'original' Slav inhabitants of the region, having arrived into what was an already-established Slav culture.

The history of the Balkans after this time and until the eleventh century is even less clear than the Dark Ages of Western Europe. The major contemporary power, the Byzantine Empire, retained only nominal authority in the region, and in the late eighth and early ninth centuries, northern Croatia and northern Bosnia were conquered by Charlemagne and subsequently ruled by the Catholic Franks for almost one hundred years. The administrative divisions of Diocletian and Theodosius were consolidated in 1054 by Pope Leo IX and the Byzantine Patriarch, Michael Celularius, when they ex-communicated each other, completing the division of Christendom which had been threatening for centuries and finalising the religious divide between the Western Roman Catholic and Eastern Orthodox Churches in the Balkans. As a result, the Byzantine-ruled Serbs identified with Orthodoxy; the Croats, dominated by Catholic Franks and then by Catholic Hungarians, with Rome. The Bosnians, in their remote and mountainous country, developed a distinctive, schismatic Church of their own.

As the power of the Byzantines waned, the region experienced shifts between national independence under charismatic leaders such as the Croat King Tomislav and over-lordship by more powerful local rulers such as the Hungarians. The Hapsburg star began to rise in the late thirteenth century, closely paralleled by that of the Ottomans. The clash of these two great empires on the fault line of the Balkans would directly affect the fate of the entire region until after World War I, seven hundred years later.

The revolutions that swept Western Europe in 1848 were reflected in Ottoman and Austro-Hungarian territory by the rise of Slav consciousness, expressed predominantly through Orthodoxy and the military in Serbia, and through literary and intellectual development in Slovenia and Croatia. Moderate Slovenian intellectuals called for reform within the Austrian empire, rather than independence, but their ideas were rejected; Bosnians, like Slovenes, hoped for greater autonomy from their Ottoman rulers, also without success. Some Croats began to look towards Serbia and consider a pan-Slavic nation, while others envisaged a Greater Croatia which would include Slovenia and much of Bosnia-Hercegovina. The Serbian Church urged the Serbs to form their own national identity based on Orthodoxy. It was during this period that people who had previously referred to themselves as Orthodox or Catholic began to think of themselves as Serb or Croat.

The four decades up to 1918 saw the decline of first the Ottoman and then the Austro-Hungarian empires, both being weakened by nationalist movements within their territories. In 1918 the Kingdom of Serbs, Croats and Slovenes was set up to prevent neighbouring powers such as Italy taking advantage of the Balkan power vacuum to seize land. The new king belonged to a Serb dynasty, and the Kingdom of Yugoslavia, as it quickly became known, was from the outset closely identified with the Serb nationalist movement and seen chiefly as the result of Serbian military achievement. Problems between Serbs and Croats started immediately, as the Croats wanted a more federal system and the Serbs, who viewed themselves as the upholders of Slav unity and survival, wanted increasing centralisation based on Belgrade. Slovenia, although reduced to a province by the two larger powers, managed to increase both its cultural and linguistic freedoms. In Bosnia, the tensions between Serbia and Croatia were reflected in the Moslem population, who began to identify themselves as Moslem Croats or Moslem Serbs. Not until the early 1960s would Moslems be able to identify themselves ethnically as anything other than Serb or Croat, and it was another decade before 'Moslem' was allowed as 'nationality'. Being 'Bosnian' was not an option for anyone, of any faith.

The King of Yugoslavia was murdered in 1934, and in 1937 Communist groups formed throughout Yugoslavia, completing the wartime triangle of the Croat Fascist Ustaše and the Serb pro-Royalist Četniks.

World War II was particularly bloody and vicious in the Balkans, as the suspicions harboured by Serbs and Croats against each other surfaced. Then, as later, it was less a question of 'ancient hatreds', as the Allied media liked to imagine, but more a question of recent power disputes allowed to surface under the sanction of war. Ultimately, it was the Communist Partisans of Josip Broz Tito who gained the support of the Allies and who, with continued Western support, formed the new government of Yugoslavia after 1945.

Since the 1980s the Western media, closely followed by politicians and international organisations, have used the word 'ethnic' in preference to the loaded word 'race'. This change contributed negatively to the West's reactions to the war in the Balkans, and confused onlookers and negotiators alike. The Greek word '*ethnos*' can mean 'race', 'nation', 'sense of nation' or 'community', but the conflicts in the Former Yugoslavia have been, with the exception of Kosovo, between peoples of the same 'race' – the South Slav race. Ethnicity certainly did play a part in distinctions of community and sense of nationhood, but if history reveals anything, it is that ethnicity, even in its sense of 'community', is at best an amorphous construct in a land of migrations and mixed marriages.

I visited Yugoslavia in 1978 as a tourist hoping for a good time; I returned twenty-one years later to a changed land. But I too had changed. I revisited the region hoping for the clarity and charity to observe without undue prejudice or favour.

On leaving the Former Yugoslavia in October 1999, I reflected on the answers to a question that I'd asked men and women throughout the journey: 'What does it mean to you to be a Serb/Croat/Moslem today?' In almost every case, the answer was not religion or nationality: the answer was 'tradition', '*ethnos*' in its sense of 'community'.

In the Krajina region of Croatia, an elderly Serb man, home after enduring four years in a refugee camp in eastern Serbia, gave this answer:

'We went to school together and married each other and then we fought. For what? For this?' He pointed at the almost empty landscape around him. 'No, it was for tradition . . . for traditions we hardly remember the beginnings of any more.'

1   Ljubljana

A N AUGUST afternoon. The sun beats down on the maize
fields that line the road between the airport and the city, and
upon the car travelling along it. The road is wide and straight; a
good, European road. Overhead, a hawk hangs on a current before
dropping into invisibility among the long grass. The rear-view
mirror reflects the barbed peaks of the Savinja and Julian Alps.
Beyond the maize and grass, the Sava flows wide and deep.

'What's changed in twenty years?' The driver twitches his
shoulders. 'Nothing much, except now things are more expensive. The prices here are the same as in Austria or Germany, but
our income isn't the same.'

After a silence he remembers another, small change. 'Also,
now I can say "Fuck you!" to the government.'

'And do you?'

'No. The government's OK.'

At first glance, Slovenia looks much as it did twenty years
ago; but the changes, though small, are there. This new multi-
lane toll road owes nothing to Communism, and the traditional
hayracks, a national emblem, are now steel and concrete as
often as wood. What hasn't changed at all is the ordered beauty
of the place.

Beyond the farmland, dense, multi-hued forest reaches in
all directions, into the suburbs and Ljubljana itself. There are
surprises in this city, things I'd forgotten about, like the view

of trees from almost every street corner. And the odd density of traffic.

'The rush hour starts at two and finishes at seven.' The driver waves companionably to a woman sitting in the car beside us at some traffic lights. 'That's because people start work at different times, some at six in the morning, some at ten. This is meant to help the traffic, but as you see, it doesn't.'

In a country with a population one quarter the size of London or New York, the traffic problem is a mystery, but quickly forgotten in the adventure of arrival.

In September 1978 I reached Ljubljana from the north-west, having travelled by train along the valley of the Sava, between mountain ranges, through the industrial city of Jesenice and past the tourist destination of Bled. The station was quiet; the city was quiet. After London and Munich, this capital of a small Yugoslav republic seemed sleepy and provincial, with an air of Central Europe touched by the Mediterranean.

My main memory of Ljubljana in 1978 is of red-tiled houses and a river crossed by many bridges. Today, it's still hot and sunny when I leave my hotel in the early evening and wander the short distance to the river, looking for the bridges and red roofs of memory.

Ljubljana's history is a record of arrivals. The Barje marshland, south of the modern city, was inhabited four thousand years ago by bogmen who lived in houses that swayed on stilts over the wet earth. Tribes such as the Celtic Noricii, Illyricii and Venetii, searching for fertile land, settled on the shores of the Ljubljanica River, beyond the marsh. Emona, the first major settlement on the site of modern Ljubljana, was built by the Romans, a critical point on the military map linking Roman Pannonia with northern Italy.

Like most of the Empire, Emona fell to the barbarians – to Huns, Ostrogoths and, in the sixth century, the earliest Slavs. By AD 620, Slavs had formed the Principality of Karantania, encompassing an area much larger than modern Slovenia. In the eighth century Karantania was dominated by Charlemagne's Franks, who brought the Christian religion which would, ironically, preserve the individuality of what became the Slovenian language. By the late ninth century, Karantania was 'drowned', as Slovenian tourist information puts it, 'in the Empire of the Franks and their German successors for a millennium'.

Modern Slovenes are very conscious of what they are *not*. That they are not Balkan, historically, ethnically or culturally, was made very clear to me before leaving the UK, when I informed the Slovenian tourism authorities by email of my planned visit and its purpose. The response arrived within five and a half minutes.

> *The problem is that Slovenia is* not *Former Yugoslavia. Yes, it was a Republic of what was Yugoslav Federation, but 'Former Yugoslavia' is a synonim* [sic] *for eternally troubled countries where there are no neighbours only foes, where you can not go to bed without a gun, where you wake up at 4 a.m. scared of being beaten (but found yourself only having nightmares) etc. etc. As soon as one mentions Former Yugoslavia, the listener, wherever in Europe says 'Oh God, no! War, fire, nationalisms and refugees!' Slovenia is – as I know that you know – different. Much closer and comparable to any Western European countries than to Balkans. A comparison between Slovenia and say, Bosnia, Serbia, even Croatia is absolutely not legitimate comparison. Comparison between Slovenia and Austria, no problem. But . . . there is a huge gap on the southern border of Slovenia. In the Middle Ages they called countries like that 'Hic Sunt Leones'.*

Evidently, the colonisers of the past have become the standard by which Slovenia wishes to be measured, its more recent confederates relegated to 'lion land'. But if Slovenes are not Balkan, neither do they see themselves as being related to Austria or Italy (despite those Holy Romans and Austro-Hungarians, and the desire for comparability with Europe), though aspects of both cultures are evident throughout Slovenia. Driving from the airport, I'd found myself looking for points of reference and thinking, 'It's like Italy, like Austria, like Switzerland.' But it's soon clear that Slovenia is like all and none of these places. It's like itself, and Slovenes are very much themselves, whether they know it or not.

'Now you're here, you can *see* it isn't the Balkans – this is Western Europe, it always has been.'

Over the telephone, Jelko Ertl, author of the 'lion land' email, persuades me that when we meet for dinner I'll know him by his aura. We meet in the early evening; his aura is distinctive and resembles cologne.

'We're a romantic people,' he says, as we walk slowly along deserted cobbled streets that have little evidence of the cars and buses of a few hours ago. 'We're romantic like the Italians, but also cool-headed like the Germans.' He waves a hand at Slovenia. 'We've taken pieces from all the cultures around us and made them our own. That's what small nations have to do.'

It's a Monday, and everyone must be at home relaxing after work because the city seems empty and suddenly large; the occasional strollers and shoppers are notable for the space between them. Ljubljana is the largest and most populous city in Slovenia, the place where everything of importance starts and finishes; but things happen, it seems, at a certain time, and nightlife starts late and finishes early.

We reach Prešernov Trg, a small yet spacious Baroque square and the heart of modern Ljubljana. This is where I came earlier in the evening to look for bridges and red roofs. And there are plenty of both here. The square, bordered by the earthy waters of the Ljubljanica, is an elegant confection of architectural styles and colours, and, of course, trees.

On the steps below the statue of national poet France Prešeren and his Muse, a few young people smoke and chat. Taxis wait with their doors open, the drivers sitting, one leg in, one leg out, gossiping. The cars point at Tromostovje, the Three Bridges, ready to whisk their passengers across the river to the castle on its hill above us, or maybe to the forested suburbs. At first sight, the three parallel bridges crossing one narrow stretch of river seem strangely cluttered, an architectural affectation.

Jelko and I sit in the Old Town, under the walls and flaming bollards of the Church of St Florian, patron saint of fires. Above our table in stone relief, Florian is being submerged upside down in the Ljubljanica. Beside our table a large oak tree spreads its branches above what was until the nineteenth century the main Ljubljana–Zagreb highway. The modern road is little more than a lane, which our waiter, who looks like Brad Pitt, must cross in order to feed and water us. Elegant and handsome in a floor-length white apron, he produces a fifth variety of wine with a flourish; the label sports a naked man dancing to celebrate a very considerable erection. My host offers a toast to Slovenia in Slovenian style, gazing directly into my eyes. It's faintly unnerving, but less so than the declamation of erotic poetry which follows. This is a man of many parts, and poet is only one of them.

'You won't believe it perhaps, but I was a punk when I was a kid.'

'Really?'

'Well, a sort of punk. Young Slovenes liked what it stood for, that way of opposing authority. Punk was part of that, maybe. We were always too small to fight for ourselves as a country, so we had to become intellectual fighters. Our conflicts have always been about books and language and religion, not military things. This is one of the reasons our separation from Yugoslavia was almost painless for us, our language being different.'

'And the other reasons?'

'That our population is almost entirely Slovenian, that was the main reason. Nearly 90 per cent of us are Slovenian by birth. And then the Serbs, Croats and Bosnians who were living here in 1991 were happy to be here. This was always the best place in Yugoslavia, they didn't want that to change.'

'Was there no support from inside Slovenia for a federal Yugoslavia?'

He laughs as if I've missed a joke. 'We thought we *were* part of Yugoslavia, most Slovenes wanted to be . . . but look what they did to us!' He grasps the air. 'So in the end, no, there was no support here for Yugoslavia.'

'Why do you think things happened differently in Croatia and Bosnia?'

'They had mixed populations, Bosnia particularly, and they had bad governments. We had a good government, we were lucky with that.'

It's odd being in a country with a well-liked government.

Listening as Jelko talks, it strikes me that perhaps the most remarkable thing about this country is that it seems to have created itself in less than a decade. 'Seems', because despite the lack of a state, its fluctuating geo-political boundaries and only the most minor of national mythologies, Slovenes managed to create their own unique identity in the face of what must at times during the last twelve hundred years have seemed overwhelming odds. Between 1990 and 1991, Slovenia freed itself from Yugoslavia, from the Balkans and the 'nationalisms' so anathema to Jelko.

Slovenia as a political entity didn't exist until the mid-twentieth century. The Socialist Republic of Slovenia was created in 1945 after Tito's Communist Partisans took power. Borut and Cheitmar, the eight-century Karantanian principalities which roughly corresponded to modern Slovenia, left no traces. And the medieval Counts of Celje, viewed with pride by many modern Slovenes for defending Slav rights against the Hapsburgs, may in fact have been Germanic warlords. Slovenia's national consciousness was historically strongest among the peasantry and intellectual bourgeoisie, who had little contact with the imperial court in Vienna. Peasant uprisings in the Middle Ages and serf emancipation in the eighteenth century were taken up by later urban intellectuals and turned into cultural rather than sociopolitical events.

'That's why Prešeren was so important to us,' Jelko tells me over dessert, a stunning concoction of fresh, wild fruit. 'He encouraged people to see themselves as Slovenian, even though there was no such place at that time. He used our language instead of the imperial language, German, and he wrote about love and the beauties of our country. He was a great European Romantic poet.'

In his attempts to raise national consciousness, Prešeren was up against more than just the German language. Slovenia was always a team player. In the nineteenth century, it was keen to remain in the Austrian part of the Hapsburg Empire, wanting only the unification of Slovenian-speaking regions in return. It didn't get it. In the twentieth century, between 1987 and 1990, Slovenia tried to find new ways to improve Yugoslav federal unity while the larger republics flag-waved and demonstrated increasingly xenophobic tendencies. Slovenian opinion was ignored once again, and when confronted by confederates who were not team players, the game collapsed.

'No-one knows where Slovenia is,' Jelko says as we stroll back towards the river by a different route; after only a few hours, it's clear that Ljubljana is a place where it would be hard to get lost. He's serious as we part, a man on a mission, punks and poetry forgotten.

'Because we are a new country and small, with a small population, we are always being confused with somewhere else . . . Slovakia, Slavonia. People think we're one of those countries in the middle of Eastern Europe that no-one visits, a place with a national debt the size of Africa and a problem with reason. You'll tell them differently.'

The subject of independence from Yugoslavia is one that still occupies Slovenes. The following morning I meet a student named Simon in an Internet bar under Slovenska cesta, Ljubljana's main road. He's eager to talk about his country and what happened, though he can't have been much more than thirteen at the time.

'I don't remember it myself, but everyone says that the first signs of Yugoslav trouble started in Kosovo in 1987 because Milošević was stirring national tensions there between the Serbs and Albanians. So then our government had to look at this new threat, not only to Yugoslavia, but to us. I remember my mother, who's a lawyer, talking about a charter of constitutional amendments which the opposition parties wrote and presented to President Kučan in 1989. I don't remember exactly what it said, though we had to learn about it later in school.' He smiles and drinks the rest of his coffee in one gulp. 'Something about wanting Yugoslavia to respect the sovereignty, rights to self-determination and equality of all the nationalities and minorities.'

'What happened with this charter?'

'Our government accepted it, but of course the Yugoslav Central Committee in Belgrade was pretty mad! So Kučan went to Belgrade to explain the amendments in the "charter", why he thought it was a good idea. The whole of Slovenia watched him on television.'

Simon is obviously moved by his memory of that day. 'What we saw was us, little Slovenia, standing up to the centralists, to the bullying Serbs! We were proud of our leaders, proud to be Slovenian. But that was the difference, you know, between us and the other republics. We were proud of what we'd *achieved*, not of what we *were* or who we *are* . . . all that means nothing, that's just nationalism.'

He orders another coffee for both of us and continues talking.

'I wasn't old enough to vote for independence in 1990, but I was really excited when it happened. Everyone was, because we all knew that something big was happening. Eighty-eight per cent of Slovenes voted for independence, and six months later, on 26 June 1991 . . .' he smiles as he says this, repeating it like something learnt in the classroom, but proud too, 'we celebrated as Slovenia declared itself a nation with its own flag. We were all in the square, my parents and my older sister.' He leans forward, his youthful face and slender hands mobile with memory. 'Thousands and thousands of people were there and we had flags that day. Someone put a flag in Prešeren's arms – you've seen his statue? – that was the best bit. I thought Prešeren would have been happy to see us celebrating, drunk and happy. The president said we should dream, that it was OK to dream on that day, that tomorrow would be a new day. He was right; the next day the Yugoslav army attacked us.'

The war lasted ten days and cost sixty-six lives. The success of the Slovenian government in a situation that many thought suicidal stemmed from the fact that while Kučan and his ministers talked federalism, they'd been preparing for independence for years. And, of course, the Yugoslav Army was still federal, drawn from every region, including Slovenia. There was no real will among the soldiers on the ground to attack their former confederates, and Belgrade misjudged Slovenian preparedness and resolution. Most importantly, there were no major territorial claims or minority issues between the Slovenes and the rest of Yugoslavia, and on 7 July the European Community set up a truce.

'The soldiers were all gone by the next autumn. Then the European Community recognised us as a nation in 1992.'

'Are you a history student?' I ask.

Simon laughs aloud. 'No, I'm studying to be a teacher of mathematics. But we all know these things. I think you remember history differently if it happens to you.'

One of the Internet bar's two computers becomes free and I say goodbye. An hour later I try to pay for my coffees, only to find that Simon has paid and disappeared.

In a clothing shop on Slovenska cesta the elderly owner wraps my socks and looks worried when I seem pleased at the price.

'Cheap, yes?'

'Cheaper than London,' I smile, trying to convey that price and quality are not related in this instance.

The anxious look remains in her faded blue eyes. 'People already shop in Austria, in Italy . . . things are cheaper and better quality than here. We know that, but what can we do?'

'You are worried that people won't buy from you any more?'

'Why should they, when they can buy nicer things in another country? If Slovenia joins with Europe, what will happen to shops like this?'

I explain that my new socks would have cost 60 per cent more in London, but she's not listening.

'I have food, clothes, a warm house. What more do I need? People don't realise the trouble that will come if we join this EU . . .' She almost spits the letters out, which is surprising, as she looks a mild person. 'We will be at the bottom of the pile, the poorest.'

Another customer needs to be served and I make my escape. Later, sitting in a pleasant tea-house in the Old Town, I don't feel I'm in an impoverished country. Slovenia is the most successful former-Communist state in Europe, and by regional standards it's wealthy. It's that word 'regional' and all it implies that causes the anxiety.

Ljubljana has a *feel* to it. All cities have a feel, but most are so big or overwhelming that the specificity is lost; here, there's space and time to look. In so small a city things happen side by side, there are few divisions. Ljubljana's feel is post-Communist and Western; rural and upbeat; Catholic and Protestant. It's not all architecture and trees.

In the concrete underground of a mostly empty shopping mall, Skriti Kot, a café somewhere between a school canteen and 'greasy spoon', serves up vast portions of food to businessmen, labourers and women with shopping bags. Chicken in rust-coloured gravy. Whole fish on mounds of rice. Strangers line up at the steel counter, trays at the ready. Real food and lots of it for about US$3. The tables are covered with white cloths over blue, each with a tiny vase of plastic flowers and a bottle of pale-pink vinegar. On the walls, original works of rustic art are displayed for sale. Outside in the dingy mall, posters advertise *The Blue Room* by David Hare, *Hysteria* by Terry Johnson and something untranslatable by Dario Fo.

The city's contrasts are most evident on the streets. Men and women wait dutifully at red lights on thoroughfares empty of vehicles, only to narrowly avoid being run down by a cyclist on the pavement. There are cycles everywhere, but the illegal pavement is the most popular place to ride. After two days I'm convinced that the majority of heart attacks suffered in Ljubljana must occur on the pavements as a result of cycle terrorism.

Modern fountains dot the pedestrian shopping areas of the city centre, each sparklingly unembarrassed by dirt or coins. This isn't a surprise. After a few days acquaintance, Slovenes appear neither superstitious nor profligate. Catholic by tradition, Ljubljana strikes me as having a very precise, rather Calvinist feel to it, almost as though the Counter-Reformation, which decimated the Protestant population of Slovenia in the sixteenth century, never happened.

There are a surprising number of shoe shops. Having noticed over the years that shoe shops abound in countries experiencing change, I wonder, as I stare through windows just like the ones next door, whether footwear is intrinsically related to transition, to going places. Nearby, philately shops display multi-coloured stamps from around the world in semi-opaque and carefully labelled bags. I peer through the windows at tiny images of birds of paradise, orchids, tropical fish, beaches and aviators, and wonder at the attraction of collecting them; until it strikes me that each small square of paper is a passport to anywhere.

On Wednesdays Prešeren Trg is busy. It's a beautiful day, the sky cloudless above the salmon-pink Franciscan Church that dominates the square. On the bridges, books are being sold. Men and women cross the square from the nearby market carrying beeswax candles, boxes of blackberries and pale-orange mushrooms, jars of honey and cobs of sweet corn. In the upmarket outdoor cafés, waiters, each taller and more slender than the last, swish around calico chairs, arms laden with coffee and fruit and ice-cream sundaes. The square seems full of life, yet it's barely a third full. It's like watching a stage, waiting for the entire cast to appear, but this is as busy as it gets.

Only metres from my table, the dark surface of the Ljubljanica, unmarred by ripple or splash, reflects the perfect white of the Plečnik Colonnade and the trees along the bank. Now that I've spent a few days in Ljubljana, Jože Plečnik's Three Bridges seem neither cluttered nor affected. The central, original bridge carries vehicles; the ones on either side, pedestrians. How wonderful that in a European capital city the pedestrian still has an advantage.

The humane designs of Plečnik, who restored Prague Castle and worked in Vienna and many other major European cities during the first half of the twentieth century, pervade his home-town. While he lived, his eclectic blending of classical, Islamic, Byzantine and Egyptian themes was considered too individual for the mainstream of modern architecture; more recently, he's been acknowledged as an early master of post-modernism. To the visitor at least, modern Ljubljana *is* Plečnik. His bridges, walkways, churches, libraries, markets, cemeteries, steps and gardens, many with his trademark columns and columnar lights, create a unique beauty. Ljubljana has its own blend of Art Deco, Baroque and Renaissance architecture – central Ljubljana lures the eye in all directions – but most vistas lead back to Plečnik and Prešeren Trg.

This square is a gentle feast for the senses. Cobbles underfoot; smells from cafés and nearby markets; river sounds almost lost in traffic and humanity; the green of willow and birch tree hanging limp with heat over the poet's statue, shading the young people sitting at his feet.

'Can you see the head on that building over there?' From our table overlooking the river, writer Andrej Blatnik points to the bust of a young woman, her head and shoulders twisting out of the wall of a house across the square. 'Julija Primic . . . Prešeren is supposed to be looking at her.'

'Didn't he look at pretty much anything?'

Andrej smiles. 'Pretty much.'

A coffee arrives with a whiff of aftershave and starched apron.

'You have very elegant waiters here in Ljubljana.'

'Elegant? Surely you mean pretentious?'

I grin. Taking a closer look at Prešeren's gaze it's clear that he's not looking at the young woman after all, but past her, towards the river. At a time when it was fashionable in the 'right' circles to be a poet, lecher and drunkard, Prešeren was all of these things and yet managed to be a social outcast. Cast in bronze, he's still looking beyond the frame.

Andrej Blatnik, a writer of novels and short stories not at all in the Prešeren tradition, explains about his great forebear.

'He's considered Slovenia's greatest poet, the man who raised Slovenian into a language capable of challenging German, which was what intellectuals and the educated mostly used at the time. He wrote our national anthem, "Zdravljica!", which means "Cheers!" It's a drinking song. He was an articled clerk for most of his working life, probably quite bored a lot of the time.'

A colourful group sits at the poet's feet, the young women as scantily dressed and the young men as seriously fashionable as anywhere. If Prešeren's reputation is anywhere near true, he would have loved modern Ljubljana.

After the biggest fruit salad I've ever seen is placed in front of me, I ask Andrej how Slovenian has changed in recent years.

'It's a very rule-bound language these days, and some people are concerned about the introduction of Anglo-Saxon words. For example, the "language law" says that we should write a foreign word in its original spelling if it's not "domesticated" enough, not part of everyday Slovenian use. The problem is that there's no rule to say when it *is* domesticated enough. A small example is the word "whisky". For some people, whisky is like a pet and so is spelt *"viski"*; for other people it's an invader. The same goes for rock'n'roll, *rokenrol*, and pizza, *pica*.'

He pauses, while I spoon giant blueberries into my mouth.

'I'm surprised you find this grammar stuff interesting.'

'It's not so much grammar as the way language reflects national developments.'

He nods. 'Slovenia is in an unusual position. We're on the fringe of the Balkans and the West, and so belong to both and neither. In many ways we're isolationists, and always have been. We've no foreigners in positions of influence in any academic or artistic institution, as other countries do. We're still not certain who we are as a nation, and until that changes we'll remain inward looking in many things, language being the most obvious. This inwardness can be a problem, especially for writers, because there's a very narrow criteria of what's "good" in a literary sense. Anything remotely popular can't be "good". My wife Nataša and I know a woman who wrote a really great book about Burkina-Faso which sold extremely well here in Slovenia – at least two thousand copies, and with a population like ours that's massive sales. But good sales mean it must be badly written. Great literature requires great pain and suffering you see, for the writer and the reader. If a reader doesn't have to read each page at least three times in order to understand it, the book's not worthy of being called literary.'

'Is it possible to live just by writing here in Slovenia?'

'Not really. There are subsidies of course . . . a leftover from Communism which we're glad of. I also work as an editor for a publishing house. With this and the writing, it's possible to have a reasonable income now, but it wasn't always so easy. We've just moved, with our son Brin, to a new apartment. It seems very large. Before that we lived for years in one room. Strangely enough, it seems to me I'm one of the more fortunate writers of my generation.'

My fruit salad finally finished, we walk along the embankment past ochre-roofed houses, their walls painted white and yellow, their many balconies laden with flowers. We pass through a small glass door into the building where Andrej works. From the outside, it looks much like all the other old buildings that line the river, but inside all is new. The building is modern and efficient, yet at the same time perfectly in keeping with its surroundings.

'Come around to our house tomorrow, if you're not busy. Nataša would like to meet you too.'

'That would be great,' I say. 'Thanks.'

I leave Andrej to wrestle with grammar, and stroll along the embankment past Plečnik's Steps and over his Shoemaker Bridge into the Old Town. The buildings are slightly dilapidated here; grass pushes up between the cobbles and grows in waving tufts amid the roof tiles. Away from Plečnik's influence, the sense of being at a cultural crossroads is more acute, the Hungarian, Italian and Austrian influences more evident. The ripples of a Chopin étude, played by someone who knows the keyboard, drift out through the open windows of a large, tattered house. From the other side of the building, a violin cuts across the piano, playing something fast and wild. A worn plaque beside the entrance says, 'The Academy of Music'.

In the medieval streets that wind below the castle mound, potters and ceramists display their work in shop fronts that have changed little in six hundred years. Among this Central European architecture, the effect of 'Hemmingway', a shoe shop filled with the latest American boots and sport footwear, is close to surreal.

Inside, Jim Morrison is singing 'Light My Fire', and between the door and the window someone has graffitied a small sailing boat, with the caption 'The Old Man and the Sea'.

Ljubljana is a city where people are at home when you telephone in the middle of the day. At home, available, and willing to talk. Andrej Košak arrives at the steps of Prešeren's statue, late, flustered and, with his sombre clothes and flowing hair, looking rather like the poet himself, or at least like his statue.

We sit on the square, in another café with yet more tall waiters, and talk about film, mutual friends in Bosnia, and Slovenian culture.

'I was a punk you know, in the eighties . . . we all were, it was the thing to do.'

I feel I need to get to the bottom of this 'Slovenian punk' thing.

'Did you have safety pins in your face?'

'No!'

'Did you have a mohican haircut?'

'No.'

'Swear, spit a lot?'

'Of course not!'

'So what *did* you do?'

'We just liked the music, you know, and the attitude.'

Film is not what Slovenia is best known for, and its output is one of the smallest in Europe. Košak's film *Outsider*, released in 1997, was a rare success.

'It's not easy to raise money. Some of it comes from European sources, which you apply for like everyone else.' He waves at a folder resting on the table under his mobile phone. 'I'm just about to apply for funding from Rotterdam for a new film, as it happens. The rest, around 80 per cent, you have to raise here, from the Slovenian Film Fund, and that's the hardest. Usually they want to give cash to boring projects, you know . . . costume dramas about serious historical struggles. Every film-maker here wants to be Bergman. Why? No-one watches films like that any more! Here's an example,' he points at the bronze figure under the birch tree and the raised arm of the Muse. 'Prešeren, they're making a film about him right now. The Slovenian Film Fund put millions into it because of the subject, because it's an epic-type film, and it's *Slovenian*, of course!' He snorts. 'It'll be rubbish, and if they use the actor I think they will, it'll be worse. He doesn't have the range to play a character like Prešeren. It will be a cardboard film, all long dresses and long sighs! That's where the money goes for film in this country. There's nothing for directors like me who want to make new things.'

'Have things changed much in film since the end of the war?'

'In some ways. A lot of Serbian actors are leaving Belgrade and moving here to Slovenia and to the West. That's not just because of the war and Kosovo and the lack of money . . . a lot of really good actors are leaving because *everything* is bad in Belgrade now. I tell you, the only cultural experience the Serbian Minister of Culture ever had was as a singer in a kitsch restaurant! Who could work in such a situation! Can you imagine it?'

Strangely enough I can. 'What about American and European films . . . are they popular?'

'Of course, look at what's on in the cinemas here. And that's a problem too. The Film Fund is afraid of everything becoming Anglo-Saxon, another reason why they give money to projects like *Prešeren*.'

'What about Croatia, do they make good films?'

'They used to make more than we did, but I don't know if they were better. Now they have the same problems as us with funding. Anything they do now must be about Croatia, of course, about how great it is and how wonderful its leaders are.'

He sweeps an arm towards the square. 'Do you see many flags here?'

'No.'

'When you go to Croatia you'll see flags . . . flags everywhere!

It's a Fascist state, everything's in trouble, the film industry, everything. Soon it will all collapse. It's like Berlin in the thirties.'

I point out that in thirties Berlin, things were on the up.

'Yes, well, you know what I mean . . . decadent, artificial.'

He looks sheepish for a moment, then opens the folder and places a dozen sheets of close-typed A4 paper on the table in front of me. 'This funding application, it's got a proposal with it, an outline. In English. Would you look at it for me, just to check the English?'

Eight hours and several bottles of wine later, we emerge from Andrej's pleasant family home accompanied by an actress, a dramaturge and an engineer. The plot of *Headline*, Andrej's putative new film, rattles around my brain . . . every word, every character. I'm stiff and square-eyed, but the moment is not without satisfaction. I may have just made a very minor contribution to Slovenian culture.

Nataša meets me at the door to their apartment, Andrej Blatnik grinning behind her. In the kitchen of their bright, white home, we eat macadamia nuts from Zimbabwe and drink Slovenian wine.

'We just came back from Africa,' Nataša tells me. 'I was attending a conference in Harare on African women's writing . . . it's what I'm writing my PhD on.'

A young blond boy comes in holding a book from which he barely raises his head. 'This is Brin, our son. He's always reading.' Brin shows neither shyness nor interest in the foreign visitor; at seven years old, he's already seen enough of the world to be blasé about everything but books. And there are books everywhere here, or so it seems. One wall of the large sitting room is covered in bookshelves and CDs acquired from around the world.

'How do you find Slovenia?' Nataša asks.

'I like it very much,' I answer truthfully. 'Slovenes seem cool and efficient but with Mediterranean warmth – a great combination.'

Nataša and Andrej both laugh at this image of themselves.

'And your project? Andrej tells me you're going to Croatia and Bosnia . . . will you be going to Serbia and Montenegro too?'

'No, but only because I didn't go there in 1978 and this journey's about rediscovery.'

I explain about 1978 and my present plans. 'There are so many things I see and don't understand,' I say. 'Like the underlying feeling towards neighbouring countries, Croatia especially.'

'Partly it's because there are still so many matters unresolved from the Yugoslav era,' Andrej explains.

'Like the matter of the embassies,' Nataša says. 'When the old Yugoslavia collapsed, the embassies went to whoever was ambassador at the time. So if the ambassador was Serb, and many of them were, then the embassy automatically became Serb. The same was true for money and any property across the world.'

'My father owns a house in Croatia,' Andrej explains, 'just south of Portorož. He built it himself, many years ago. Then our government decided that foreigners couldn't own property here – isolationism again! – and the Croats, of course, reciprocated. My father is allowed to keep the house but not to sell it to another Slovene, though I can inherit it. These small issues keep coming up because they're never resolved. They're visible bits of problems which are large and mostly invisible, like the embassies and international finance.'

'And the Serbs? How do Slovenes feel about them?'

'The Serbs are "over there" now we don't have a border with them,' Andrej says. 'There are relatively few Serbs living in Slovenia today and those that are here mostly consider themselves Slovenian. We've never had many mixed marriages either, though Tito, of course, was a Slovene-Croat. All part of our historical isolationism.'

'Serbs are usually more fun than Croats though,' Nataša says, 'more charismatic and charming.'

Andrej grimaces.

'You don't agree?'

'I just dislike national stereotypes, that's all.'

Later, I remember that he failed to grimace at my comments on Slovenian coolness and efficiency.

Unchastened, Nataša says, 'The Serbs I know *are* more fun than Croats.'

The wine flows as we're joined by Eva Marn, a lawyer who until recently worked drafting international treaties of human rights in Sarajevo and Strasbourg. To help me get a feel for the range of Slovenian culture, Andrej plays a CD of Slovenian nationalist songs from the 1940s, which he says are available through the Catholic Church. The words are mostly a blur, but the sprightly, stamping rhythm reminds me of the 'Horst Wessell'.

'What happened to these people after the war?' I ask.

'Some went to Argentina, probably with the help of the Church, which hated Communism. Many of them were killed at the end of the war, accused of collaborating with the Nazis, and though some of them undoubtedly did, I think it's now becoming clear that a great many were just anti-Communist.'

With independence, many of Slovenia's long-buried secrets are coming to light. The matter of the Domobranci, the Slovene home guard which was set up by the Germans to maintain order and fight Communism, remains a source of contention. During the Communist era, the Domobranci were seen simply as Fascists who supported the Nazi invaders. A decade of more-open historical debate suggests that the majority of officers were Slovene nationalists opposed to both Hitler and Communism; squeezed between the two, for many the war ended tragically. Believing that the victorious Communist Partisans were more interested in national domination than liberation, and that they'd stand no chance in defeat, the Domobranci fled into southern Austria in 1945. Most were compelled by the British army to return to Slovenia and Tito's justice. After receiving brief military 'trials', over ten thousand were executed, alongside returned Croatian Ustašis, and buried in an unknown number of mass graves around the country.

'Argentina must have seemed a really good place to be in 1945 if you weren't a Communist,' I say.

'Which is why so many people went. There's a big Slovene community in Argentina that never really integrated. They had their own schools, churches. After 1991, when we became independent, many wanted to come back to Slovenia and they probably have every right to.'

'Some of our leading politicians since independence have been from Domobranci families,' Eva says. 'It used to be considered an embarrassing heritage, even shameful, but not any more.'

I ask Eva about her work in Sarajevo.

She shrugs. 'I was working in Strasbourg for the European Commission on Human Rights for a couple of years. When they created a similar institution in Bosnia, I went to Sarajevo to work as an advisor to Bosnian lawyers who were examining human rights violations. It wasn't easy, partly because lawyers had to draw up every document in three different languages – Bosnian, Serb and Croat. Of course, there's almost no distinction between these languages within Bosnia, and the lawyers would ask me, "How can we make them different?" The same language, spoken in the same country, is being forced into shapes it never had. Mad!'

'And how was it for you, personally?'

She looks at me for a moment before replying. 'I had nightmares a lot of the time, about drowning and trying to come up for air. When I arrived I was optimistic about what could be done to change things, but that feeling didn't last long. We've been lucky here in this country.'

'But there's a long way to go too,' Nataša adds. 'Slovenia *seems* to have come out of Yugoslavia smelling good, but there's high unemployment and political cronyism right through government.'

Eva nods. 'I know that if I wanted to advance my career in Slovenia I'd have to choose a political party, but I'm not interested in being part of that Communist legacy. The same goes for religion. The Catholic Church is getting more and more political power, just like in Croatia. Taking sides is becoming very important here but people rarely speak about it openly. Still,' she says, getting up and looking for her jacket, 'we *are* very lucky. When you see how things are in Bosnia and Kosovo, you realise just how lucky.'

2   *Westward*

T HE FIRST real rainfall of the season hits the dry brown earth and disappears down into Notranjska's karstic underworld. It's late August, and already the crowding forest is turning into a kaleidoscope of rain-drenched colour. Rain falls so fast it's almost impossible to see the road ahead of the bus, though the windscreen wiper cuts through the water like a keel.

Notranjska, which touches on Ljubljana, is the most verdant and remote province in Slovenia, one of the world's most forested countries. Deep in the dark, wet heart of this wood, wolf, boar, bear and lynx still thrive. This is true mixed forest, where oak, birch, pine and fir jostle for space; it's nothing like the sad, man-made rows which pass for forest in most of Europe nowadays.

Trees, more trees, and karst. A geological phenomenon caused by the dissolution of limestone by water, karst was first noted and named in Slovenia in the nineteenth century. Almost half the country is karstic limestone, making the land underfoot a maze of caves and gorges, riddled with periodic lakes, plains of stalactites, the largest underground canyon in the world and entire subterranean river systems.

The bus driver struggles with the elements as mournful traditional music plays on the radio. Through curtains of water, small villages surrounded by fields of maize and cabbages appear and disappear, their names gone before I can read the signposts. Our road runs parallel with the railway line on which I travelled in 1978 to reach the Postojnska Jama, the Postojna Caves. Not long away from the mild Welsh hills, I found the scale of the caverns astounding. As the bus passes a large, legible, signpost to Postojna, I recall vast galleries and halls filled with stalactites and stalagmites of every shape and size. There were footbridges and strings of fairy lights, and the natural beauty of the place was enhanced by coloured spotlights playing across sparkling limestone veils and columns. I'd never seen anything like it. Postojna has been a tourist attraction since the early seventeenth century, when enterprising locals, quick to grasp the touristic significance of their landscape, began charging entry to the caves. Today I'll be stopping at Postojna town, but not to visit the caves.

The unique and unusual is almost commonplace in Notranjska. In what feels like the middle of nowhere we pass a tiny train station, its garden filled with flowers and vegetables, and in one corner an old steam engine, lovingly restored. The emptiness of the platform reminds me that apart from the occasional passing vehicle I haven't seen another person since leaving the outskirts of Ljubljana. There's almost no other traffic on the road, and after a few hours the rain and the trees begin to cause a vague feeling of claustrophobia, of isolation. Sunny Ljubljana seems very far away, though it's less than fifty kilometres. On the radio a female choir is singing a slow, eerie song in a minor key, apposite to the dark light that hangs above the tree line. Across the aisle, a woman with black painted fingernails and a great deal of black eye make-up lies across both seats and talks into a mobile phone.

A man leaves the bus and sets off into the forest through horizontal rain. Watching him go, collar turned up under a broad-brimmed hat, I wonder what lies behind the trees. This is a region rife with legend and folk fears. The Church pursued witches here later than anywhere else in Slovenia, and as the passenger fades into the forest, Notranjska appears much like a combined film set of *The Seventh Seal*, *Dracula* and *Deliverance*. The black-nailed woman across the aisle laughs suddenly into her mobile as the rain continues to beat down on the trees, on the hills, slowly washing away the land.

The true stuff of Gothic nightmare, of Fuseli's monsters and laudanum dreams, can be found at Predjama – the Castle Before the Cave. Predjama isn't the easiest place to reach by public transport, but luckily for me, Tatjana, a friend of a friend in London, is visiting her parents and has offered to show me the castle and another local attraction, the Disappearing Lake at Cerknica. As we drive through narrow winding roads, under surprisingly clear skies, Tatjana tells me her parents own a small logging mill and that as a result she has a particular relationship with trees.

'Trees pay for my studies and my clothes, I'm very grateful to them,' she says, grinning. 'We have so many here in Slovenia and it's important that we keep it like that – and I don't just mean for my sake!'

The castle's bleached and grey-roofed form squats in the mouth of a large cave, emerging out of the natural rock like an elegant fungus. As I cross the footbridge leading into the castle, I glance into the ravine below and meet the bright eyes of a young fox.

'She likes people,' a guide tells the crowd of visitors who quickly gather to stare.

'Pretty puppy! *Pretty puppy!*' a small American girl screeches as her father prevents her from hurling herself over the wall to where the vixen clings precariously to the side of the drop. Tatjana finds the foreigners' amazement at a fox hilarious. She's still cackling as we enter the building.

Most of the dramatic, four-storey castle is sixteenth century, and walking through its stone halls and passageways we step almost literally back through time. Beyond the Renaissance rooms with their arrangements of furniture and mannequins, the building delves into the twelfth century, into the rock itself and the earliest inhabited area. High above the later structure is a cave, hidden and virtually inaccessible, where men and women lived and worked almost a thousand years ago. From this dark eyrie, a natural aperture in the rock opens like the rose window of a cathedral onto a view of the Vipava valley, far below and unnaturally bright in the sunshine.

'Do you like it?' Tatjana asks me.

'It's amazing,' I say, 'like being in a house with an outer skin.'

'Do you know the story of Erazem Lueger?' she asks as we walk down steeply cut steps and towards the present day.

I shake my head.

She smiles. 'He was a famous thief who came to a sticky end just near where we're standing now!'

Predjama's most famous inhabitant was a fifteenth-century robber knight, who in true Robin Hood style looted trade passing through the forest around the castle and gave the proceeds to the poor. As in the Robin Hood story, there was a political side to Lueger's feats; supporting King Matthias Corvinus of Hungary made him an enemy of the ill-reputed Austrian king, Frederick III. Like England's 'bad' King John, Frederick was furious that Lueger seemed uncatchable, and in 1483 the Austrian army made an assault on the castle. Nothing worked; its position seemed impregnable. A secret passageway out of the castle allowed Lueger's men to easily replenish supplies, and they taunted the Austrians by throwing fresh food down to them. Unlike Robin Hood, a rather clean-cut type of hero, Lueger over-reached himself and came to an abrupt and, as Tatjana points out, sticky end. A traitor in the castle marked the position of the privy for the Austrian catapulters, then signalled them when Lueger went to that place to which 'even the Turkish Sultan must go alone', as the seventeenth-century Slovene scientist and man of letters Janez Vajkard Valvasor wrote in his famous history of Slovenia, *The Glory of the Duchy of Carniola*. Lueger ended his life in the lavatory, crushed by a stone cannon ball while answering nature's call. His secret passageway was later walled up because robbers were using it to break into the castle.

South-east of Predjama and Postojna the karst makes a dramatic surface expression at Cerknica, where there's a lake – from time to time. Youngsters skate on Cerknisko Jezero's ice in winter and farmers cut hay on its bed in summer.

When we park beside a rutted track the sun is high, the ground hard and dry; the earlier heavy downpour evidently didn't reach here. Tatjana explains that the lake water has been disappearing since spring, sucked down into the sinkholes beneath the karst field. It's very much larger than I expected, the lake bed an enormous area of cultivated fields and flattened reed beds, interspersed with areas of dried mud and muddy holes. We find a series of sinkholes, the hard mud surrounding them dried into ruts and ropes; it can't have rained here in months. Long slender reeds lie horizontally around one large, perfectly round hole half-full of brown water which bubbles at the centre. Spheres of air from deep below the surface burst into the light with a soft *plop, plopping* of mud.

Tatjana stares down. 'Sometimes I try to imagine what it must look like under the ground, all those caves and rivers linking up in a vast subterranean system of which this hole is a tiny, tiny part. I try, but I can't do it,' she grins, showing small, sharp teeth, 'the thought is too big for me!'

The first-century Greek chronicler Strabo visited Cerknica on his travels and named it Lacus Lugeus, the Lake of Mourning. The name is apt; even under a bright sun, there's a mysterious remoteness to the place which is only partly to do with the enigma of what lies beneath. Why the lake came and went remained a mystery until Janez Vajkard Valvasor discovered that it was part of the vast under and over-ground system of the Ljubljanica River – that same quiet-looking stream I'd gazed at the previous day from a café in central Ljubljana. Valvasor's investigations caused such interest internationally that in 1697 he was elected a member of the seventeenth-century's leading scientific association, the Royal Society of London.

'Have you ever seen an olm?' Tatjana asks as we leave the lake.

'What's an olm?'

'The "human fish", an amphibious salamander. It lives only in the karst caves.'

The ubiquitous Valvasor didn't restrict his investigations to history and inorganic matter; he was the first to describe the karst's most unusual inhabitant, the olm, or *Proteus anguinus*. But it wasn't until the eighteenth century that the creature's uniqueness was realised. Measuring about thirty centimetres long, the olm can live for over a hundred years and doesn't reproduce until its late teens. It's related to no other known species, is almost blind and lives in utter darkness, often going without food for long periods of time.

'People were frightened when they first saw it,' Tatjana giggles, 'because it was pink and you could see the blood inside. It was the right shape and colour you see, for a man's . . . thing.'

'Thing?'

'You know, his penis.' She laughs a great belly laugh and the car swerves dangerously across the road. 'It's just like a penis, only of course much bigger!'

No wonder the locals were scared.

I'm sorry to part with Tatjana, but the bus is leaving for Portorož and I must be on it. She waves, grinning widely as she drives away without looking at the road. Less than an hour later I'm in another world. The brakes squeal in protest as the bus winds its way down steeply curving roads to the base of a limestone cliff over a hundred metres high. Topped with slender pines which stand alone, like sentinels, the edge of the karst is clear and sharp as a wall. Notranjska is behind us; this is the province of Primorska, and forest is already giving way to low scrubland, to cypresses and vines.

There's a sudden plethora of vehicles, their various international number plates the first hint that we're heading for a tourist destination. The buildings are different too; rough, stone affairs surrounded by small vineyards and the ever-present maize. Clumps of what looks like bamboo divide orchards of figs and olives. As we come to the end of a long straight tunnel of gnarled trees, we burst suddenly into light and a world of petrol stations and road signs with the word 'Trieste' and 'Trst' on them. Trieste, Trst. The same place, but a different name for different people. Under the Austro-Hungarian Empire, Trieste was a predominantly Slavic city and Slovenian its main language. Now Trieste's Slovenes live in the poorer suburbs and speak Italian during the day.

I leave the bus at Portorož, expecting to find a polite equivalent of Blackpool or Bondi, but the sweeping seafront, the Obala, looks pleasant and only moderately tourist-infested. From the bus station I walk through the gardens of the disused Palace Hotel which border the seafront, and sit for a while at the edge of a lily pond. Although the Palace is empty, its gardens are well kept. Under the lily leaves, huge goldfish swim in the cool darkness, oblivious to the passing foreigners and their cars; freshwater snails chew their way through the pond's detritus. The hotel's arches and balconies are home to darting swallows; their nests line the building between every architrave and under every eve. I wonder what the Palace Hotel looked like when it was built in 1912. Even now, covered in swallow shit and with battered shutters, it still dominates the front despite the high-rise hotels on every side.

A seafaring town from the thirteenth century, Portorož only became well known as a resort in the declining years of the Austro-Hungarian Empire, when imperial officers travelled here from Vienna to have their arthritis, war wounds and gout treated with salt mud. The Palace Hotel was built in expectation of a visit from the Emperor Franz Josef, but he never made it. As I stoop to pick up my bag, I notice the gardener for the first time. Stripped to his slender waist and holding a rake, he's chatting with another handsome young man in the shadow of a Scots pine.

Overlooking the Palace is the Grand Hotel Palace, a seventies tower block. Compared with the dingy room by the Ljubljana railway station which has been home for the past few days, my fifth-floor suite is perfect luxury, further enhanced by complimentary local wine and yellow roses. Evidently the staff imagine I'm a journalist.

One of my reasons for visiting Portorož is to experience the *terme,* the spa conveniently located under my hotel. Spas are an important feature of Central European life; the rich and famous 'watered' at places like Baden Baden for centuries, while the middle and lower classes visited locations with less conspicuous names. Anglo-Saxon culture, with its anxiety about even the most innocent and health-giving physical pleasure, has generally found matters of the body a source of anal humour. British spas never got much beyond the sipping of sulphur water and listening to damp orchestras.

Slovenia's spas are predominantly about health, beauty being perceived as a side effect of health. For those Austrians, Germans, Italians and Slovenes who use the Portorož spa, two weeks here is an essential, like an annual vehicle check-up, not a luxury holiday. There are people of means staying here, in the hotel's suites and penthouse apartments, but most of the rooms I glimpse on my way to meet the doctor in the spa's clinic are basic. The various lifts play an accordion version of 'Old MacDonald Had a Farm', and nobody looks rich.

A business-like nurse appears in the corridor. 'The lady doctor will see you now.'

A treatment regime awaits me when I enter the room. Having perhaps envisaged a travel writer as someone hale and hearty, the realisation that though hearty this one's not very hale seems to come as something of a blow.

'You have medical problems!'

I smile lugubriously. 'Don't worry, I'll try anything you suggest, treatment-wise. Anything.'

Relieved, she takes my blood pressure and says, 'Good, then this is what I suggest. A sauna immediately, followed by the multi-jet magnesium bath and a massage. Tomorrow morning at eight-thirty, inhalation of brine and essential oil to clear all the bronchial tubings. Afternoon, the Fango Plus . . . fango is our special brine mud, you understand, it is unique to this *terme*. Evening, head massage, followed by the whirlpool. I also recommend a Thalasso Shiatsu, which is a speciality of this *terme* devised by Sergej, our head masseur. Finally, a massage of the face and décolletage. Your blood pressure is low,' she says, putting the equipment away. 'Drink more red wine.'

Business over she relaxes, and despite a growing queue of patients and nurses needing advice, settles in for a real chat.

'Are you planning to visit the Soča valley?' she asks. 'It's a fascinating place, very beautiful and not spoilt. There was a great battle there during World War I, the Italians against the Austrians and Hungarians. Many men died, many Italians – later, Mussolini built a place for their bones, how do you say . . . ?'

'An ossuary?'

'That's right. The Italians lost the war and then built a great big monument. How typical of them – the bigger the defeat, the bigger the monument! Ha ha! Just like Slavs.'

'You are Slovene?'

'Of course a Slovene – a Slav! We are strange people . . . but the Italians! *No-one* suffers from *nervosismo* like the Italians! They arrive here in a very bad way . . . they wait five minutes for an appointment then start to shout and tell you they have waited five hours. After they are here two weeks the *nervosismo* usually improves.'

'Until they go home again?' I venture.

'Exactly! Until they go home again.'

A nurse appears, looking anxious, but the doctor continues unabated. Perhaps there's some justice in the Italians' complaints.

'Have you been to our casino here in Portorož? It's very good. There are shows, dinner-dances . . . you'd like it.'

Actually, I can't think of anything I'd like less, but I say, 'Really? Do tell me more about Slovenia, if you have time, of course.'

'There's a wonderful story which you should include in your book. When God was creating the world, he had an enormous apron and in it were all the things of the world – trees, mountains, rivers, flowers, animals. At the end of the day, God had been all over the world throwing things from his apron onto the land and he was very tired, but there were lots of things still in the apron, so when he reached Slovenia he just threw everything out, which is why we have so many wonderful natural beauties in our small country.

'Now, I must attend to my patients.' She stands up. 'Enjoy your treatments and your stay here. Don't forget to have the sauna and magnesium treatment now.'

The magnesium knocks me out and a massage by the compassionate yet mildly sadistic Sergej leaves me with bruises for days. Dazed, I sit at the wrong table at dinner, a nutritious but regimented affair, and am told off by a waitress in no uncertain terms. Next morning, I escape the inhalations and head for Piran.

Slovenia's coastline is only forty-seven kilometres long, but within that short distance is one of the most fascinating sites on the Adriatic. Piran, a small but perfectly formed Venetian Gothic town on a peninsula jutting into the Gulf of Trieste, has remained untouched by time. The site was settled by Celts, Romans and Byzantines. The Venetians governed Piran from the late thirteenth to the eighteenth century and their hand is visible everywhere. Every twist and turn of the streets and alleyways produces some new sight: a Gothic monastery, a Renaissance house, a Baroque square. The buildings are warmed by the sun and the smell of the sea washes over everything. In the narrow passageways between houses unchanged for five hundred years, it's almost possible to imagine the voices of salt merchants and sailmakers, of fishermen bringing home their catch. But Piran's preservation was bought at great cost to its inhabitants, past and present. Lack of change meant the town stagnated from the nineteenth century until the 1950s, when tourism began in earnest. Even today, Piran's inhabitants can choose to live with little in the way of modern facilities, in dark, cramped medieval homes that the law forbids them to alter, or they can leave and live elsewhere. Many leave.

As I head uphill towards the Church of St George, which dominates the town and overlooks the sea, I'm pursued by a wedding party led by the bride and groom. A quartet playing accordion and guitar accompany them, singing traditional wedding songs. The bride is beautiful in a fashionably simple white dress, the groom handsome, the guests elegant in bright silks and buttonholes. Everyone lines up and photos are taken with the town as backdrop, then the sea, then the church. It's all very spontaneous and casual, yet polished too. There are two worlds visible from this promontory: an ancient one of russet and ochre roofs, and invisible streets; and a peninsula skirted by rock and concrete 'beach' where local children play, tourists sunbathe and everyone eats pizza and ice cream.

In the evening I sit with the locals on one of the stone benches around Tartinijev Trg and watch a group of small children playing tag around the bronze statue of violinist and composer Guiseppe Tartini, an eighteenth-century scion of Piran. Elegant streetlamps light several centuries of architecture, their glow reflected in the pale marble paving of the square. An elderly man sits beside me and mumbles something in German. Everyone here speaks to me in German; for the first time, I have some insight into how it must be for non-English speakers obliged to speak English when they travel.

'Tartini.' He points and makes sawing motions with one hand. I nod.

'*Sind Sie Deutsche?*' he asks.

'No.'

He continues undeterred. From the ensuing monologue, I pick up that Piran has many tourists, and that this is both good and bad. Many better-off people from Ljubljana buy property in Piran. I ask, in pidgin German, if this is a bad thing. He looks at me out of flecked green eyes set among deep wrinkles and gives a heated and unintelligible answer. After a few minutes he gets bored with me and leaves.

I ask the same question of Jadran Rusjan, a botanist and local historian who accompanies me next day to Lipica, original home of the world-famous Lipizzaner horses. The route to Lipica lies between the Italian border and the karst cliff I descended on the bus from Postojna. The traffic is light, but Jadran, a far better conversationalist than he is a driver, is uncomfortable behind the wheel and flinches at every oncoming vehicle bigger than a motorbike. He has no problem telling me what he thinks of incomers.

'No, I don't like people from Ljubljana coming here and buying places they visit only during holidays. The heart of a town has to beat all year round, not just for a few weeks.'

Jadran isn't keen on Ljubljančani in general; he has that vague dislike country people around the world often feel for visiting metropolites. Italians and Croats are on his list too, but the feeling seems to be without malice, reflecting perhaps the polite distrust of a small country for its larger, more assertive neighbours, whom Jadran is quite happy to discuss.

'Most Slovenes don't have a problem with the Serbs,' he says, momentarily taking his eyes off the road to stare at a field of crops. 'They aren't our neighbours and we don't have to deal with them at all unless we choose to. We have jokes of course, like the one about Milošević going to hell. Do you know that one?'

I shake my head.

'Milošević dies and goes to hell. After a few days there's a terrible banging on the gates of heaven, so St Peter sticks his head out to see who's making this terrible noise and finds all the demons of hell crying and screaming to be let in. "What's happening?" St Peter asks. "It's that man Milošević," the demons shout, "he's ethnically cleansing us. You have to let us in!" '

This first taste of regional humour is an eye-opener; jokes in the Former Yugoslavia evidently don't need to be funny in order to be a joke.

'We have jokes about Tudjman and Croatia too, of course,' Jadran continues, 'but it's different with Croats. Our joint border is long and there are still many unresolved disputes over territory, like the Sečovlje salt flats south of Portorož.' He grimaces and the car swerves slightly. 'They've got so much coast, and salt pans of their own, but they want ours too.'

'Why do they want yours if they have so many?'

'Because they want everything.' He pauses. 'But it's older than that. During World War II, Croatia was a Fascist country. You have heard of Ante Pavelič?'

I nod.

'He was an evil man. He did things to Slovenes that are hard to forget.'

The kind of things Jadran is referring to were recorded by aesthete and man-about-Europe Curzio Malaparte in his description of a visit to Pavelič, then military governor of Croatia, in the early 1940s:

> *I gazed at a wicker basket . . . The lid was raised and the basket seemed to be filled with mussels, or shelled oysters – as they are occasionally displayed in the windows of Fortnum and Mason in Piccadilly in London . . .*
>
> *'Are they Dalmatian oysters?' I asked the Poglavnik.*
>
> *Ante Pavelič removed the lid from the basket and revealed the mussels, that slimy jelly-like mass, and he said smiling, with that tired, good-natured smile of his, 'It is a present from my loyal ustashis. Forty pounds of human eyes.'*[*]

* Bruce Chatwin, *The Anatomy of Restlessness* (Picador, 1997), p. 168.

'There was a concentration camp in Croatia,' Jadran says, 'on the island of Rab. Thousands of Slovenes were taken there, and many died. Jews died there too, and Croats who would not agree with the Fascists.'

'And do you think the Domobranci here in Slovenia were Fascists too?'

'Perhaps, but not like the ones in Croatia.' Jadran looks thoughtful. 'Another problem is that Slovenia was always the most prosperous republic in Yugoslavia. Other republics were always being told, "Look at Slovenia, be more like Slovenia." That makes people angry, particularly if they have a lot of national pride like the Croats.'

'And the Bosnians?' I ask. 'I've noticed everyone here talks about them very politely. Do you think there's guilt about what happened in Bosnia after Slovenia got out of Yugoslavia?'

'Who knows. It's not easy to do the best thing for yourself and know it isn't the best for everyone. Some Slovenes have mixed feelings about Bosnia. Older people used to look down on Bosnians because they came here to do all the dirty, heavy work . . . Slovenes don't like to get their hands dirty. Perhaps now these people feel sorry about what happened.'

Jadran knows a great many interesting things about plants. He points to the mistletoe which clusters on many more varieties of trees than in Britain, and tells me its various medicinal uses. I ask him to show me an elm tree, as all the British elms died in the early 1960s, killed by disease. One of his previous jobs was designing herbal teas for a local company. The best known, he says, was called One Thousand Flowers.

At the side of a road, men and women are selling local produce, their stalls covered in boxes of figs and plums, jars of different coloured honeys and bottles of blueberry liqueur, mead and organic wines. I buy a box of soft green figs and some plums. Jadran introduces me to the man selling mead. Thirty kilometres from home he knows people at the side of the road! I don't know the people two houses away from me in London.

'Don't eat the plums and figs together,' he warns as we drive on, 'and don't drink water with the figs.'

The figs are orgasmic, sweet and unbelievably soft; hungry and thirsty, I ignore his advice.

Lipica is a beautiful village set among open grassy pasturelands and ancient trees. With a population of only one hundred and twenty-five, the village revolves around the stud which began breeding the white horses famous throughout the world for show and dressage in 1580. The animals' bloodlines are carefully preserved and recorded, and through generations have been bred for muscle and gentleness, with a long life span and high resistance to disease. Today, the main European studs are at Lipica and Vienna, a bone of contention between Austria and applicant EU member, Slovenia. Vienna claims to be *the* stud, but Lipica, though lacking money and recent investment, is the breed's original home. Lipizzaners have had a hard time over the years, fleeing from Napoleon into Hungary in 1796, seized by Italians during World War I and by Germans in World War II.

Despite my initial concerns about performing animals, I find the horses quite wonderful. They're proud and noble, bred from generations of equines who pranced on their back legs to the strains of Strauss, their dignity intact. The show is a display of skill where riders and horses create perfect geometrical patterns in the sand of the arena with hooves and carriage wheels. It's said that the Spanish Riding School in Vienna puts on a bigger and better performance, but I like the unpretentiousness of this event and knowing that the riders, grooms and stable-hands are locals who have grown up with the horses, loving them.

We avoid the stud and lineage tour and find a paddock beside the early-eighteenth-century stable where the horses are resting and playing. To my surprise, all the youngsters are grey, or even dark brown or black. The perfect 'imperial white' coat develops at between five and ten years of age, and there are whispers that the more unscrupulous among international breeders bleach those unfortunate creatures who fail to turn white with age.

The foals take milk, run, kick and fight their way around the paddock, then race to meet visitors in the hope of treats. The adult horses just stand, motionless; some of them look gaga, but I'm too embarrassed by my ignorance to ask Jadran if horses sleep standing up. Even motionless, they're exquisite. Having never been a 'horse' person, I'm surprised to be moved by the beauty and gentleness of these lovely creatures.*

South of Lipica is a remote village which refers to itself as 'Mediterranean'. This must be wishful thinking, because hard-to-find Hrastovlje is one of the least Mediterranean places imaginable. As we descend into the Rižana River valley, a seemingly endless wall of karst known as the Kraški Rob fills the horizon, creating a dramatic backdrop to the heavily fortified walls of the Church of the Holy Trinity, for which the village of Hrastovlje is famous. It's a remarkable landscape of rock, small vineyards and orchards, in which the Romanesque church squats on its hill looking, in the words of its information leaflet, 'like a shepherd amid the flock of sheep, a role it really played five hundred years ago when the Turcs [*sic*] besieged our country'.

'Can you see?' Jadran points to the distant wall of limestone. 'There and there – villages.'

High above the valley floor I can just make out small clusters of yellow-grey buildings clinging to the karst wall.

'That church up there – its tower leans, like Pisa!' He smiles. Apart from the lean, there's no resemblance between the Tower

---

* Some months after this visit I read in an article that Lipizzaner horses bred in Bosnia had been killed for meat during the war and were still being killed. The story ended happily, however, with a number of British army officers, serving with SFOR, setting up a fund to protect the survivors.

of Pisa and the tiny stone chapel which seems to hang hundreds of metres above the valley floor, and Jadran knows it.

'Are those villages inhabited?'

'One or two may still be, I'm not sure. That one there, Zanagrad, is empty now. The last inhabitant left last year aged ninety-eight. It was too difficult to go on living in such a place, with no real road or facilities. You wouldn't think it was a famous place, but every year the local people took their horses up on St Stephen's Day to be baptised in the church. It's a very old tradition, no-one knows how old.'

'Will it continue, now the village is empty?'

He shakes his head. 'I don't know.'

The near invisibility of these cliff villages was deliberate; their inaccessibility a deterrent. From the outside, Hrastovlje's church is forbidding, a fortified place. Built between the twelfth and fourteenth centuries, the walls fortified in the later sixteenth century, the church was always intended as a haven against the Ottomans; the space between the outer walls and the walls of the church itself is big enough to hold a few thousand people.

Across Slovenia and the entire north-west of the Former Yugoslavia – across whole regions of Central and Eastern Europe from the fourteenth to the seventeenth centuries – churches were built on hilltops or fortified, because of 'the Turk'. Looking at these dense, towered walls I realise how hard it must be for those whose ancestors were born west of Vienna to grasp the extent of the siege mentality that affected so much of European thinking at that time. But it wasn't all bad. In Slovenia, Ottoman raids served to strengthen and politicise the local peasantry who were obliged to pay for their own defences while still paying taxes to feudal overlords. There were more than a hundred peasant uprisings in Slovenia between the mid-fourteenth and mid-nineteenth centuries, but most took place between 1478, the peak of Ottoman expansion, and 1573, the high point of the Protestant Reformation. Protestantism gave Slovenia its first printed vernacular which helped to raise the level of literacy while confirming the status of the Slovenian language. With curious synergy,

Ottomans and Protestants created a climate in which the seeds of Slovenian culture could grow.

Stepping into the cool church, we move from a brutal reminder of what late-medieval life was like in this part of the world to a remarkable example of the medieval world view. The Church of the Holy Trinity contains some of the most exquisite and well-preserved late-medieval frescoes in Europe, including a *Danse Macabre*, the Dance of Death. At a time when few, if any, villagers could read, the biblical scenes painted by the fifteenth-century Istrian artist Janez iz Kastva must have been readily understandable, with their images of the calendar months and the seasonal duties of hunting, planting, harvesting and wine-making. The sacred and profane march comfortably together along the walls; saints and prophets gaze on a still life of bread and cheese.

The preservation is remarkable, the colours relatively unfaded in the dark interior. Every surface in the church presents an insight into a medieval world that imagined it knew and understood the meanings and mysteries of life under God, even the final mystery described in the 'Dance of Death'. Of all the frescoes in this remarkable place, surely this was the most reassuring to the hard-working, probably poor, inhabitants of Hrastovlje, showing as it does the levelling effect of Death as he draws kings and queens, monks, merchants, one-legged beggars, soldiers and infants towards the grave.

In the late afternoon we walk off the Portorož–Koper road under large, striped umbrellas and cross over a small bridge onto the salt flats of Strunjan. South across the bay, Piran's church and campanile appear to float above the sea in a mirage of mist and rain. The light is slowly fading, hastened by low cloud. Oddly, it's perfect weather, the greyness a foil to the water that reflects the pyramids of white salt, heaped like nesting birds beside the dykes and footbridges. Low, tree-covered hills press in on two sides of the sea. Small rowing boats are tied to rotting wooden jetties, but there are no people in this eerily deserted landscape.

'Salt has been made here for over seven hundred years,' Jadran says. 'In the old days, the salt-making families lived in Piran or nearby villages from October to March. In the summer they came here and worked without stopping. Salt was vital for preserving and for health, and they made enough money in six months to live well all the year. Most had houses and vineyards which they tended through the winter and spring: people used to say the salt-makers sat in two chairs because they had two livings – one from the land and one from the sea.'

'Those piles of salt, won't they dissolve in the rain?'

'Of course. And the wind can blow them away too. It's not an easy way to live, that's probably why most families stopped working here in the 1950s. What you see now is nothing to how it would have been a century ago . . . or seven centuries.'

The rain falls more heavily as we drive the short distance to Portorož, which is neither deserted nor beautiful but has the determined energy of the holidaymaker and the gambler. From my balcony I can see the lights of the casino sò praised by the doctor and recall that during the day we passed several casinos, including one in tiny Lipica. Cautious and reticent, the Slovenes don't strike me as being big gamblers. Perhaps on holiday they turn, Jekyll and Hyde-like, into different people.

In the spa I prepare for my final treatment. All the masseurs who've treated me have been highly skilled, and there's no doubt that after three days I feel decidedly fresher and healthier than when I arrived. Now, on this last evening in Portorož, the time has come for my Thalasso Shiatsu. I have no idea what to expect.

In the treatment area I'm met by Goran, an attractive young therapist wearing only his swimming trunks. This is disconcerting, but I follow, sheep-like, into the churning brine of the jacuzzi and sit upright on a ledge, the strong-smelling water up to my chin. Just as I'm wondering how not to float, my thighs are clasped in the strong grip of another's thighs and powerful hands descend on my shoulders. Goran is right behind me, anchoring my body under the water with his legs. Happily, he can't see the expression on my face.

After an hour I'm barely able to drag myself out of the pool. I've been prodded in places I didn't know existed, told that my liver's in a terrible condition and advised that it would take at least a month of concentrated treatment to sort me out. But I don't care. As I float on the surface of the water, my neck and head massaged and stroked by Goran's infinitely capable hands, all negative thoughts disappear. In fact, all thoughts disappear. This, without doubt, is heaven.

3   The Soča Valley

Your waters are lively and playful
As a girl walking from the mountain;
Clear as Alpine air,
Yet raucous as a hearty song;
Oh daughter of the mountain,
You are magnificent and glorious!

To the Soča, Simon Gregorčič

The next day, a Monday, Jadran and I leave Portorož early. It's rain-
ing again. The Obala is deserted; the weekend tourists have returned
to work in Ljubljana. It's also the end of the August holiday, and
Italian visitors to the *terme* have returned to Trieste, Monfalcone and
Venice, pummelled, pampered and less *'nervoso'*. In the garden of the
Palace Hotel, the ivory heads of pampas grass hang, heavy with water.

The landscape changes quickly in Slovenia, and once the Istrian
Peninsula is behind us, the character of houses, churches and farms
alters almost immediately: the buildings are of pale limestone;
churches have round towers that owe little to Mediterranean style;
vineyards are larger and more ordered. I ask Jadran, who seems to
know everything, about farming and food production in Primorska.

'It's the region of food staples,' he replies. 'Oil from olives,
salt from the sea and wine from grapes. Only Primorska has all
these things.'

I look around at the flourishing agriculture, and wonder how Slovenia will fare when it jumps into the shark-infested waters of the EU. The better-quality food served here is some of the best I've ever eaten – all fresh, much of it wild or at least organic – all the things that the English-speaking West has lost and seems to want back again. I wonder how the big European wine producers will feel about being undercut by good, cheap Slovenian wine.

Jadran grins. 'It's not all food and wine here, Primorska has a tradition of literature and art as well. Many artists and sculptors live in this region. Most aren't known outside Slovenia and find it hard to make a living from creative work, so they're also doctors or farmers. One of our most famous poets, Simon Gregorčič, was born in Primorska.'

'Does he live near here?'

Jadran's eyes flicker off the road momentarily, and we swerve dangerously close to a ditch.

'He died a hundred years ago.'

Summer is almost over, and the Vipava valley south of Nova Gorica is ripe and heavy with produce. Beyond the orchards of peach, pear and apple, vineyards stretch to the edge of deciduous woodland. In winter the wind can blow through here at over a hundred kilometres an hour, and the Vipava has a water temperature permanently many degrees lower than nearby rivers. As we drive through the narrow valley I look east towards Ajdovščina, where almost two millennia ago the Romans built Castra ad Fluvium Frigidum, the Fort on the Freezing River, linking Emona (Ljubljana) with Aquilea on the Friulian Plain.

The young Ernest Hemingway drove through here in 1918 while working as an ambulance driver with the Italian/Allied forces based near Gorizia. In 1929 he published a fictional account of the experience in his novel *A Farewell to Arms*, using

Italian place-names for what is now Slovenian territory and was then the western edge of the Austro-Hungarian Empire. When I first read the book, years ago, I thought Kobarid, Hemingway's Caporetto, was in Italy, and for a time it was. Rarely have borders been more fluid than those dividing the former Austro-Hungarian Empire and Italy. Nova Gorica didn't exist when Hemingway described his approach to Gorizia:

> *Now in the fall the trees were all bare and the roads were muddy. I rode to Gorizia from Udine on a camion . . . the mulberry trees were bare and the fields were brown.* *

The trees are mostly still in leaf when we visit, and Hemingway wouldn't recognise the town he knew and the place where he was wounded while driving an Italian ambulance. Gorizia, Austro-Hungarian Gorica, remains Italian, but is part of a sprawling, semi-industrial conurbation divided by an international border. The other half, Nova Gorica, is Slovenian. Here, according to local tourist information, 'the Latin and Slavic worlds shake hands', though there seems little evidence of cross-border co-operation as we drive through the town. Gorica, originally a Slovenian town in the Austro-Hungarian empire, was awarded to Italy by the Treaty of Paris in 1947. Not to be outdone, the new Communist government of Yugoslavia decided to build an equally new, bold town on their side of the border, which they called Nova Gorica and separated from Gorizia with a chain.

Built on functionalist principles, Nova Gorica has a frontier feel. The industrial sites on the town's outskirts lead to leafy tree-lined streets with multi-coloured high-rise buildings in odd settings which seem to me both ugly and fascinating. Posters advertising a tour by the traditional Irish band the Dubliners are everywhere, which makes me think they must be the most exciting thing to hit the place in a while. Nova Gorica

* Ernest Hemingway, *A Farewell to Arms* (Penguin, 1979), p. 127.

is almost Wild West, a gambler's dream, or nightmare, with vast, neon-lit gaming halls on every corner, like jam pots set to draw unwary flies. Gambling, it turns out, is what makes these Latins and Slavs shake hands.

'Why are there so many casinos here?' I ask.

'For the Italians,' Jadran replies. 'Where there are Italians, there are casinos. The whole border's a line of casinos. Didn't you notice?'

'Yes, I wondered about it.'

'Italians love to gamble, who knows why.' He points to a shiny, twenty-four hour, mega-casino called the Perla. 'See that casino there, it's the most profitable in Slovenia. This town depends on the success of these places now.'

Do the Italians come because there are casinos, or are there casinos because Italians come here? The former, according to Jadran, because the regulations on gambling are very much stricter in Italy. My guess about the Slovenes not being gamblers was right, but they're happy to watch other people spend, spend, spend.

In the whitewashed crypt of Nova Gorica's Kostanjevica monastery lie the bodies of Charles X of France, his wife and grandson. Exiled from France after the July Revolution of 1830, Charles Bourbon died in Gorica in 1836. The monastery's cold and eerie crypt has become something of an attraction for foreigners. About ten of us shuffle along the long narrow passage to the tombs in a hesitant crocodile, chivvied by our guide, a fleshy man who sweats despite the subterranean chill. There's a strangely ominous feeling in here which the whitewashed walls only amplify.

Adorned with dead wreathes and faded symbols of grandeur, the royal coffins are squeezed together in a very cramped space; a few of the other visitors are claustrophobia-pale by the time the guide pulls out a French magazine, opening it at a well-thumbed place. He points to an interview with an elegant, smooth-faced young man, head of the House of Bourbon, who requests that his ancestors' remains be returned to France.

'But the last will and testament of King Charles X of France,' the guide says with evident satisfaction, 'was that his body should remain here, in this monastery, in perpetuity.'

The fact that Gorica was then Austrian, and Charles had probably never even heard of 'Slovenia', doesn't dent the guide's satisfaction; nor does the knowledge, which he keeps to himself, that Charles died horribly within weeks of arriving in the town. Whether the ex-king intended to stay here or not, in the end he had no choice. On the subject of the Bourbons, the monastery's small leaflet recalls that brilliant spoof history of England, *1066 and All That*.

> *Charles X. Philipp (1757–1836) became king of France in 1824 and being autocratic he caused the revolution of July 1830. Then he had to abdicate and live in exile: first in the Edinburgh then in Prague and at last as a guest of the Count Coronini in Gorica, but after 17 days he died from cholera.*

Luckily, by the time I read this we've left the monastery.

Just north of Nova Gorica I have my first sight of the Soča, one of Europe's most dramatic rivers; Jadran feels the moment important enough to stop the car. We walk to the rocky bank and I stare, amazed that something so apparently artificial could be natural: the yellow-green of trees clashes horribly with the intense, opaque turquoise of the river in a way I've never seen in nature before.

'The colour can seem denser here than near the source,' Jadran points out, 'because there's a limestone quarry just north of here and the waste sometimes makes the water seem more opaque than it really is. The green comes from the white limestone gravel and a kind of algae that lives on it. Further north you'll see the water is the same colour but very clear.'

Near Sveta Gora we pass close to the vast tunnels and turbines of a hydro-electric dam, and soon after reach the small sleepy town of Kanal. From the high bridge spanning the river, the water is so limpid that at forty metres every pebble and every marking on the golden fish hugging its bank is absolutely clear.

'Marble trout,' Jadran says, 'biggest trout in Europe. It was almost extinct until recently, now there are many again.'

'They're beautiful,' I say. 'Do they taste good?'

He grins. 'The best!'

The small café on the town square is full of sullen, anxious men, who look awkward, almost guilty, for sitting in a café instead of working.

'There's no work here,' Jadran says bluntly. 'That's what it's like since we left the Yugoslav Federation. Before, there was always work. You didn't earn so much, but things cost almost nothing so everyone felt rich. Now, as you see, unemployment is very high. In areas like this, where there's only a little farming and some small industry, it's very difficult.'

I glance around at this charming, yet troubled town, and the feeling of apathy and underlying anger is almost palpable. I wonder what, if anything, membership of the EU will mean here. Slovenes *like* to work, and enforced idleness evidently sits badly on the men in Kanal's cafés. I hope that the future brings money to this part of the country where employment and opportunity are so limited by topography.

Approaching the town of Kobarid, the Soča valley broadens into a flat plain dominated by the Krn mountain range. We pass Alpine-style houses and elaborate hayracks and barns along a road that was the only main route into Italy through the Soča Front. Hemingway probably never visited Kobarid, the Caporetto of his semi-autobiographical *A Farewell to Arms*, though the novel suggests that he did.

> *'The cars are all away. There are six up north at*
> *Caporetto. You know Caporetto?'*
>   *'Yes,' I said. I remembered it as a little white town*
> *with a campanile in a valley. It was a clean little*
> *town and there was a fine fountain in the square.**

He may have heard descriptions of the fountain and campanile from Italian soldiers who'd been stationed there. The campanile still exists and its bell still rings – all night – but the fountain is gone, to make room for traffic. Instead there's a statue of the local poet-priest, Simon Gregorčič. With his round face and round spectacles, Gregorčič looks benign and forgiving; a very different man from that other poet, the tempestuous Prešeren.

Jadran and I have a last coffee together; then he's gone, and his wonderful flow of information with him. I feel slightly bereft, but this is a charmed land and the best hotel in Kobarid, its restaurant reputedly the finest in Slovenia, seems to be expecting me. I console myself for the loss of Jadran with a lunch of Soča trout and wild blueberries.

Few people in the Western world are entirely unaware of the events that took place between 1914 and 1918 in France and

* Hemingway, ibid., p. 128.

Belgium. The horror of war, the loss to many nations of a generation of young men, has been recorded in poetry, novels and film. But relatively few people have heard of the Soča Front. For over two years, the greatest mountain conflict in history took place along the Italian–Austrian border which paralleled the Soča, as the Austro-Hungarian and Italian forces fought for control of the Krn mountain region. The result was stalemate.

In the early afternoon I take the north road out of Kobarid, the road to the mountains, and pass the town's museum, a handsome eighteenth-century building dedicated to the events of World War I on the Soča Front. This small building in a remote mountain town houses a collection envied by many of Slovenia's bigger national museums and praised across Europe for its compassion and ingenuity. Dedicated primarily to the events of the 'Battle by Kobarid' in October 1917, it gives those who took part in this titanic struggle their place in history.

In the museum's entrance hall I realise that, with the exception of Hemingway's fiction, I know nothing at all of Kobarid's war. When the director offers to show me around the museum after it closes for the day, I accept immediately.

'But take this map of the Kobarid Historical Walk with you now,' he says, smiling and holding out a leaflet. 'So you don't get lost up there.'

Back on the trail, I pass a young woman pushing a child in a buggy near the Napoleon Bridge. She smiles at me as she walks by, and I hear her repeating, with something like pride or excitement in her voice, 'Soča, Soča,' and pointing to the rushing river so the child will know its name.

The view from this copy of a nineteenth-century French-built bridge is breathtaking. Green water reflects off the white rock beneath, frothing and tumbling between narrow cliffs down into limestone holes and basins. Perfume drifts by from tiny white flowers hidden under the green and white of cyclamen and orchids. River. Plants. Everything here is white and green. It should be peaceful but you could drown in the water's noise.

Following the Historical Walk's carefully laid tracks, I find it hard to imagine that this area was one of the most fiercely fought over in the world. There must be hundreds of thousands of bits of shell and bones lying around under all the beauty. How any army got its equipment onto these high and painfully jagged mountaintops is a miracle. But they did; despite the snow, wind, rain and fog. Survivors of this battle reported that fighting in the fog was one of the most terrifying things they faced; I can see it now, hanging over the peaks like a formless ghost.

After an hour I realise I've gone the wrong way, despite the map. Looking for the Kozjak Brook, a waterfall surrounded by stalactites, I find instead an Italian trench, part of the Third Line of Defence. Cyclamen and baby oaks grow at the entrance to the bunker, and small harebells push up between the restored concrete floor, trembling under the fine rain that's starting to fall. What must it have been like in here with shells falling from the sky?

Mussolini's ossuary is somewhere on this Historical Walk, but I've gone too far the wrong way now, and the rain has set in. Walking across a suspension bridge, which the map tells me is exactly like the original World War I version, I meet two Slovene women who nod politely as I stop to let them pass. One of the women has a small hairy dog in a tartan bag which she holds in front of her. She looks like a Scottish kangaroo.

Alone on the edge of woodland, the view is sobering, despite the drizzle. The Krn rises to needle points overhead and a long, white track stretches before me into the distance. I imagine animal carts and ambulances, lines of soldiers and temporary shelters filling the track; and all the time the deafening thud of shells. Deep among the trees is a shell hole about 4.5 metres wide and two metres deep; it's half-full of moss-covered stones with hart's-tongue ferns growing in between. Large loose stones lie flung about as if by a giant hand; round and white, they emerge out of the soil looking like the tops of skulls. I touch them, to make sure they're stone.

The light is going and it's raining harder as I walk back into town past old wooden houses, their doors and windows filled with boxes of red, pink and white oleanders. The scent is pure and sweet, but oleanders are poisonous, so Jadran told me.

There are seventeen flags in the museum's entrance hall, representing the seventeen nations that took part in the conflict; most were states within the former Austro-Hungarian Empire, but among them are the flags of the United States, Britain, the Soviet Union and France. The walls are hung with photographs of young men and women who served on this battle front, and with the crosses from their graves. It's 6 p.m., and I'm the museum's only visitor.

'I've got a meeting of the Museum Trust at eight,' the director says, glancing at his watch, 'but I'm free until then. Let's go up.'

Joze Šerbec is a tall, spare man with the energy of a fanatic; when he talks about the war, the history of Kobarid and the museum, his eyes dance with barely contained excitement. We walk up the broad stairs to the first floor as he explains the town's history.

'Kobarid has been in ten different hands in the last hundred years, mostly back and forth between Austria and Italy. There was a Kobarid Republic from September to November 1943 until the Germans came, and after the war the Slovene Partisans took over. From 1947 the area was under the Americans before it was handed to Tito. Now this is Slovenia.' As we walk through the first-floor rooms, he points to this and that and asks, 'Did you see the Italian Charnel House on Gradič Hill?'

'You mean the ossuary? No, I got lost.'

He smiles. 'Mussolini had a good eye for history, or thought he did. That monument was built on the site of a Roman town, most of which was destroyed during the construction. If you had more time you could visit Tonocov Grad, which is unique in Europe – it was occupied from the middle Stone Age, through Antiquity and into the Middle Ages. Very unusual.'

From 1915 to 1917, Tonocov Grad was occupied once again. Photographs show trenches and shelters all around the old hill fort. Mr Šerbec points to a set of dumbbells assembled from an iron bar with concrete lumps on each end, made by an Italian gunner entrenched on Mount Debeljak. I imagine a short, dark, muscular man swinging it on a mist-shrouded hilltop, determined to stay fit and good-looking despite the enemy, despite the cold. Lying there in its glass case, it appears almost like a magic charm devised to keep the gunner's fears at bay.

On the second floor landing there's a small Hemingway exhibition. It includes part of the original manuscript of *A Farewell to Arms*, a first edition, copies of the book in several different languages and photos of a very young Ernest Hemingway taken during the war, in which he looks like a fleshier version of Tom Cruise.

'This year is the hundredth anniversary of Hemingway's birth, so we set this up as a commemoration and borrowed the manuscript and book from America. I think we are the only place in Europe that has such an exhibition.'

'Do you think Hemingway was here in Kobarid during the war?'

'In the book it appears he took part in the fighting here, but that was impossible. He didn't join the war until 1918 and the Front had already been pushed west towards Italy by then.'

We pause briefly to look at the many national and international awards the museum has received, photos of the director with the great and the good. He shows such things diffidently, and says, 'We've had success here, and some of the bigger museums in Slovenia are unhappy that we receive more visitors than they. There's jealousy, even in this business.' His features try to express humility about Kobarid's success, but can only manage delight.

The museum's White Room conveys the feeling of how it was to fight in winter at high altitude, the cold, freezing fog, frostbite and inevitable gangrene merely a different kind of death from that offered by the guns and gas of the enemy. In the Black Room are pictures of the dead – Italians, Slovenes, Austrians, Hungarians. Their frozen, decomposing faces have lost their features but they look more frighteningly human for that. Bodies swollen and blackened lie in rows, in heaps, in pits; without boots, without clothing, without dignity. Corpses hang on barbed wire; in snow, in mud. But worst of all are the photos of the living: legless, arm-less, surprised.

'Look at these here . . .' the director points to close-ups of facial wounds. 'We know they died of malnutrition.'

Two men stare into the lens, the intensity of their clear gaze contrasting with the absence below. From their eyes to the back of their throats is nothing at all.

On the top floor of the museum the director leaps into action, taking me around a remarkable panoramic model of the entire Front. The various battle lines are shown in such a way that the least military-minded person can grasp the scale of what hap-pened in October 1917. 'History', it has been said, 'is the science of what happens once', and the director intends to prove the truth of this statement.

'The Austrians, here,' he points with a long thin stick at a curve of mountain, 'had been trying to push the Italians back for years. The Austrians weren't good soldiers – the Italians were better but they had fewer men – but Austria had its Empire to con-script from and they used *anyone*. Men were just bodies to stop shells and bullets. They took peasants from the plains of Hungary, from places as completely flat as a bubble in a measuring stick, men who got vertigo bending to tie their shoelaces – and they put them up there!' He points to the Krn. 'Imagine how it was for them . . . the mist, the shelling, the ice, the sheer drops.' He moves on again, with me in his wake. 'So, the Austrians know they can't win alone and they're desperate.'

'Why were the Italians fighting here?' I ask innocently. 'Did they want Slovenia?'

'They always wanted parts of the coast, like Trieste, that's true, but why were they fighting here then?' He laughs. 'That was you British, of course! The Allied powers persuaded the Italians to join them and create another front to help relieve pressure on France and Belgium. They promised them other peoples' land after the war was won. Sergeant Mussolini fought here too . . . he was sent home before the final push of 1917 with massive shrapnel wounds. He was lucky.'

A favourite saying of one of my elderly female relatives comes to mind. 'God always leaves the ones he doesn't want.'

'So, to continue . . .'

Joze Šerbec is like Scheherazade, except that his stories are not told to save his own life, but to revivify men long dead. Given a water pipe and a glass of sherbet, I could listen indefinitely.

'Accepting at last that they can't win alone, the Austrians reluctantly ask the Germans for help and between 23 and 25 October their combined forces finally push the Italians right off the heights. The next day is even more successful for the Germans, who use gas to push the Italians west and down into the valley. That day was the first major success of Rommel's career – you know Rommel?'

I nod.

'He helped to alter the whole Soča Front almost overnight, driving his soldiers here,' he points to the south of Kobarid, 'up the valley under the cover of darkness and bad weather. This was something the Austrians would never have done and the Italians were completely unprepared. They fled; many surrendered, and the rest were pushed back into Italy. It was the most successful breakthrough operation of World War I.' He points to a large photo of the victorious Germans sitting in sunlight after the Italian defeat. A very young and very handsome Lt Irwin Rommel lounges on a grassy hilltop, smiling confidently. He's just spent fifty-two hours fighting in appalling conditions, captured two of the Krn's main peaks and taken over nine thousand prisoners for the loss of six Germans. No wonder he looks pleased with life.

'I'll tell you a very interesting thing,' the director says as we leave the panorama room. 'The day of Rommel's success on the Soča, 24 October, was exactly the same date as his great defeat at El Alamein.' He points me towards the projection room. 'It's time for my meeting now. I'll be downstairs. Take as long as you like to look at the film show and don't worry about turning off the lights when you finish up here, everything's automatic.'

Half an hour later as I'm about to leave, the director steps out of his meeting and suggests I take a look at the temporary Hungarian exhibition in the basement.

'You were OK upstairs?' he says. 'Not nervous?'

'Not at all.'

'Oh,' he says airily, 'some people are.'

The basement is very different from the spacious, well-lit rooms above and, suddenly aware that this building is several hundred years old and full of horrors, I talk into my tape recorder for company.

> *There are brilliant photos here of invalid Hungarian soldiers working as basket-makers, locksmiths, shoe-makers. Soldiers sitting outside Budapest's main station after demob. A picture of a youth with a mechanical arm, hoeing. Pictures of young men with arms, feet, legs missing, most look astonished. Lots of maps and drawings. The Hungarians seem to have had a very scientific approach to war – eighteenth-century science. But the attention to detail is remarkable.*
>
> *A report of Lt Colonel Barnabalogh, 'Four dead fell down, eight wounded'. (Barnabalogh? An Irish-Hungarian?)*
>
> *Brilliant charcoal portraits by Ferenc Marton of Corporal Mihaly Kiss, Lance-Corporal Janos Kosmer, Lt Andor Szuts. Grinning, looking askance, smoking . . . the sitter's panache is clear in every line. Drawings by Istvan Zador of men cutting wire, throwing grenades, artillery, flame throwers . . . amazing colours, red and yellows. Telephonists covered in medals.*
>
> *In the tiniest room with images of dead Hungarians . . . hobnailed boots sticking out of the*

*back of carts, people stripping the dead. Photos
entitled 'Soldiers on their last earthly journey'.
Grave crosses made of lumpy concrete are set into
the floor and surrounded by little piles of stones.*

The lights don't switch off automatically down here so I turn
them off and am suddenly in a profound darkness that makes my
skin crawl. I turn them back on and leave them on, not wanting to
stumble into gravestones after the things I've just seen. An hour
ago it wouldn't have occurred to me to be nervous . . . not until
the director asked if I was.

Kobarid in the dusk has an Alpine feel, despite the palms and
Mediterranean flowers. Wood smoke drifts on the cool air. Bright
light passes through the stained glass of the church, spilling
colour onto the dark pavement outside. Inside, the church is surprisingly full, mostly with women. I step out again quietly.

The evening meal at the hotel is spectacular. Game and local
raspberries; sparkling wine and blueberry liqueur. After dinner
the owner invites me to continue drinking with him, but already
far from sober I regretfully say no to the array of home-made
liqueurs and *šnops*.

'You like the town?' he asks.

'Very much. There's such a lot to see and do for a small place.
Has it changed much? Is it very different now from how it was
twenty years ago?'

'Oh!' he grins. 'So different! Then we were all prosperous, no-
one felt left out. Now it's not like that. There's another hotel here
in the town, but it's not easy for them. There's just not enough
business for everyone. That means fewer jobs. So there *is* prosperity, but it's not evenly spread around and there's even less for
people at the bottom.'

His cheerfulness as I say goodnight suggests he's nowhere near that bottom himself. Weaving my way to bed, it strikes me that I never have a hangover here.

Soon after dawn the next morning I stand beside Simon Gregorčič and wait for the Cerkno bus. The light is very low, the mountains concealed by dense mist, and there's a quietness over everything. Local women wait for the bus in silence which is broken only by the commotion of young postal workers in grey and red uniforms arriving to start their day. Girls and boys, arms draped around each others' shoulders, giggle and joke as if still on their way to school.

Leaving Kobarid, the road and river parallel each other so closely that the gravel of the shallow riverbed is clearly visible, though the fog swallows everything else. At Most na Soči we head south-east, and without warning, the Soča is gone, replaced immediately by the Idrijca. Primorska is a promiscuous land; as one river turns aside, another take its place. More mature than its predecessor, slower and wider, the Idrijca is the same glowing, unnatural green.

The bus driver coolly negotiates the narrow winding roads, exuding confidence and mint chewing gum as convoys of lorries laden with tree trunks require him to back up round blind corners. This gorge is so deep in places that the sky is invisible from the window of the bus. A black-green wall meets the eye as tree-covered slopes push up, sheer to the cloud.

The history of what was Yugoslavia has always been intimately connected to its topography, its deep river valleys a cause of isolation and potential xenophobia. Rivers have always been an obvious route of travel – easy to move up or down, but not away from. Beyond the walls of rock that close around a village or town are more peaks and other people, probably less friendly, certainly less known. But this corner of north-west Slovenia is a surprisingly beautiful place, and with few houses and fewer inns to tempt the passing motorist it's not at all tourist-orientated. It's a mix of old and new. New houses are under construction across the river on the narrow strip of land between the forest and the water, linked to this road and the rest of humanity by small wooden bridges. It's also a Gothic place, with roadside shrines and trickling waterfalls that crash across the road in winter and spring. The inhabitants of this valley must like the oozing damp and surfaces that run with water. Even today the locals must see the sun only a few hours a day, even in the height of summer. Old houses appear in unexpected places, emerging like mushrooms from under dark, overhanging rock, or almost hidden by trees; houses at the bottom of ravines, in crevasses without view or vista. What must it have been like here before telephones, cars and computers? As the bus roars past, a large bird of prey lifts into the air, a small animal in its talons.

During our chat, the doctor at the spa in Portorož asked me if I intended to visit the Franja Hospital Museum near Cerkno.

'Would you recommend it?'

'Oh yes! It's a most *wonderful* place,' she'd replied. 'Very beautiful and so interesting to think of all the things that happened there in the war. It's a museum now but made exactly as it was in 1943 when it was a secret hospital. One of my own patients is a doctor who worked at Franja. She's more than eighty-five years old now, but strong. I'm very proud to be her doctor.'

The bus arrives at the small town of Cerkno at 8.30 a.m., and by nine I'm on my way to the Franja Hospital. Without charge or question, the receptionists at the local hotel/tourist office tell the handyman to drop everything and drive me to the start of the Pasice Gorge in the hotel van.

'This man will take you, and when you wish to leave Franja the boy selling tickets will telephone us and he'll come and drive you back again.'

Astonished, I get into the van. It's not just my letter of introduction from the Slovenian Tourist Board; countless ordinary people here have gone out of their way to help me because I'm an apparently helpless foreigner.

After the bright early-morning sun, the forested ravine seems dark, and it's hard to see the path ahead. Sunlight filters through the birch and oak, and the ground slopes gently, then steeply upwards as the gorge narrows and the Pasice hurtles noisily towards its meeting with the Idrijca. After ten minutes the path becomes stone steps that wind around jutting rock and hang above foaming waterfalls. Looking back, all that's visible is a line of green leaves and grey, moss-covered limestone, with no sign of a path. Up and up through the closing walls of the gorge until they part unexpectedly to reveal a gravelled space where a small fountain plays between camouflaged huts. The young man in the kiosk looks up from reading the fattest novel, takes my money and says he'll be happy to telephone the hotel when I leave. He gives me two leaflets about the hospital museum and returns to his book.

One leaflet explains that 'Franja', the best known of the Partisan military hospitals, was set up after German attacks on Central Primorska in 1943 made it clear that the Partisans needed a medical centre so protected it would be safe from any assault. This remote gorge a few kilometres from Cerkno was chosen and named after its head physician, Dr Franja Bojc.

Alone in the sun, I listen to the trickle of the fountain which is almost drowned by the Pasice. The second leaflet describes the everyday working of the hospital. Its camouflage-painted huts acted as kitchens, operating theatres, wards for the wounded, nurses' quarters, doctors' offices. The huts, over a dozen by 1945, stretch up the gorge to its narrowest point where the stream no longer flows but falls; many sit astride the water, staggered from lack of space and linked by little bridges. Some huts are filled with double bunk beds made from rough planking. The examination rooms contain what look like gynaecological couches with foot stirrups, and tables covered with medical instruments and old enamel bowls. All that's missing are the smells and screams.

Over the door between two rooms hangs a photograph of Franja Bojc taken at the war's end. She is, quite simply, stunningly beautiful, with the gaze of Marie Curie and the features of a Hollywood siren. Pictures of doctors, patients and nurses hang on the brown wrapping paper that lines the walls, their stories scribbled next to them; a drawing of Tito hangs above a bleakly humorous sketch of Death wielding a scythe. In the operating theatre is an x-ray machine. An *x-ray machine*, at the bottom of a crevasse, in the middle of nowhere, in 1944.

In the early days of the hospital, local women and girls prepared food which they lowered down the sides of the gorge. Nurses sang folk songs and played guitar to their patients in the long evenings. A Ward Journal was issued at least eleven times, and the hospital had a commissar responsible for cultural and educational activities, including the distribution and supply of books, newspapers and political information.

At Christmas-time 1943 some two thousand parcels of food and letters of support were sent to Franja and the Partisans protecting it. Between then and the end of the war, over five hundred wounded were treated here, and despite attacks and even betrayals, no wounded were ever captured. The mortality rate of about 10 per cent was far lower than in comparable British or German hospitals. Men who recovered but were unable to continue fighting stayed on and worked to build new huts and better defences, among them a German soldier who became the hospital's shoemaker. Stores of food and medicines taken from enemy sources were handed over to the hospital as a matter of course. From 1944 the Allies supplied the hospital by air, but penicillin was unknown at Franja and amputation remained a first course of action. High above the huts, where the gorge is narrowest, I find the small, sad spot where amputated limbs were buried. The cemetery had to be hidden and graves unmarked; the names and details of the dead were put into small bottles and placed under the head of each corpse. Some of these strips of paper, carefully typed and signed, hang on the hut walls, a reminder of the limits of medicine.

As the sun rises above the edge of the gorge it lights the grey striped huts and the concealing trees. It's so very quiet here, apart from the constant sound of water. More than half a century ago the hospital inhabitants lay in their bunks and listened to that same sound. This strange, hidden place has moved me beyond anything I could have expected. Stories of courage and sacrifice merge with the ordinary and mundane, making Franja much more than just a museum or a group of buildings in a breathtakingly beautiful setting. Those involved with the hospital were aware of its ideological significance even at the time; when the war ended in 1945, photo reconstructions documented and recorded the hospital's life and work. Sitting here in peace, I think how Franja is a testament to bravery and human ingenuity that goes far beyond war, or the causes of war; its most remarkable and lasting achievement the value it placed on human life at a time when most of the world was trying to reduce that to nothing.

My reverie is broken when the man from the hotel draws up, obviously delighted by my reaction to the place. He offers to take me to the town museum to see the oldest musical instrument in the world, a Stone Age flute made from the femur of a bear. But the museum is closed for restoration, and I'm not sorry; I want to hold on to Franja for as long as possible, without distraction.

4   Castles in the Air

T HE TRAIN between Ljubljana and Zidani Most is elderly and
socialist, its carriages spartan. I practise the name of my destination, Ptuj – *'p'twee'*, *'puhtui'* – and gaze through clean glass
at the white peaks of the Julian Alps shrinking into the west.

The suburbs of Ljubljana are mostly made up of small farms
and orchards, red-roofed houses with corn cobs hanging on garden hayracks. There are no smoking chimneys, no industrial
estates stretching into a murky distance. As in much of the
Western world, the majority of Slovenia's income is generated
almost invisibly by service industries. Suburbia quickly gives
way to fertile farmland that feeds a capital. The Sava, Slovenia's
largest river, flows east beyond Ljubljana, and with practical
logic the train lines and provincial borders of Dolenjska and Štajerska follow its course. In a land of hills and water, what else
makes sense?

This journey to Ptuj near the Hungarian border is uncharted
land for me, heading in the opposite direction to my route of
1978. Smaller numbers of tourists come this way; the attractions
are fewer and more widely spread than in the west of the country.
For some, Slovenia's north-east is its heartland, home of the
medieval Counts of Celje, the industrial city of Maribor and the
Roman town of Poetovio, modern-day Ptuj.

Just north of here is the Tezen Forest, where a mass grave containing almost two thousand Croat and Slovene nationalists was

discovered a few months earlier. 'Is Slovenia full of <u>Katyn Forests</u>?' one Croat newspaper asked, referring to the massacre and secret burial of Polish officers by Soviet authorities in 1940. Travelling through this pleasant, rural countryside it's strange to think that the landscape may hold secrets half a century old. Some investigators believe there are as many as one hundred and ten mass grave sites across Slovenia, from Celje in the north-east to Kočevski Rog in the south. Mines, monasteries and former tank trenches allegedly contain the bodies of upwards of three hundred thousand Croats and Slovenes who fought for Hitler and/or opposed Tito. As the countryside is disturbed with highway construction and expanding urbanisation, more graves are being discovered.

From Litija to Celje, the Sava valley is a contrast of small industry and rustic charm. At Zidani Most, a tiny station but one of Slovenia's most important junctions, the train pauses to discharge its northbound passengers. The average Slovenian train stop is thirty seconds; so all of us, young and old, race across the tracks and climb smartly onto the Ptuj train, which is new and shiny and has rose-scented toilets. The old, socialist engine chugs away, following the Sava south towards the Croatian border and Zagreb only sixty kilometres away.

At Celje, a large number of trendy youngsters pile on board, giggling and shouting at each other. Two girls disappear into the toilet and emerge after a long time with a secret smirk on their faces. A couple of young, overweight Englishmen sit across the aisle from me, talking loudly about things back home. They appear surprised and vaguely disquieted on discovering I'm British.

'Do you like it here?' I ask.

'Yeah, it's great. Bit quiet maybe, bit like Austria only less boring.' They laugh as though at a private joke.

'Have you met other British people here?'

'No, thank God!'

'We always try and avoid them, you know. I mean, what's the point of going somewhere and just talking to other British people?'

At the next station two attractive girls get on and sit beside them, giggling. The men fall silent, glancing nervously at each other and out of the window. One starts polishing his glasses and doesn't stop until he leaves the train an hour later.

Between Celje and Pragersko the land changes again. The occasional houses and gardens are as well kept as before, but the general impression is of a less prosperous land, of moving away from comfort. Štajerska province has the largest farms in Slovenia, with hops, potatoes, grapes and wheat the primary crops; but for kilometres alongside the railway line there's little more than grass and the inevitable fields of maize. It's a flat, wet land of overgrown canals, pools and ditches that reflect the clouds. Beyond the railway line the Drava flows slow and wide, its bank lined with poplars that shiver in the hot sun.

In the few minutes it takes to use the rose-smelling toilet everything changes, like a shift in the time–space continuum. Dense forest clusters almost to the track which is edged, kilometre after kilometre, with the hot yellow of goldenrod. Smallholdings nestle under fir and pine, and dark goats graze nearby. The suddenness of the change is almost disorientating, and as I'm adjusting, the train pulls into Ptuj.

Ptuj is a strange town with the potential, when wet, to be more than dreary.

'One night is free; more than one night you pay full price.' The hotel manager has sharp features and an unpleasant voice that makes the offer sound like a threat.

Through the windows of a large, echoing room I watch the rain run down three-hundred-and-fifty-year-old roof tiles and splash off chimney guards designed to prevent storks nesting. Water falls in a fine continuous curtain, soundless and chill, and the late-morning light is grey. Below, the wide cobbled street is lined with ancient houses, modern shops sporting striped awnings, and an occasional pavement café – all empty. I wonder why I'm here.

To snap out of the moral dampness that threatens to descend, I head to the information office in the centre of the old town.

'No, this isn't Information. Information is at the castle.'

'You mean, information about the town is at the castle?'

'Yes.'

'And this office is . . . ?'

She smiles at me blankly.

'What about the Roman temples and archaeology? Where will I find them?'

The young woman shrugs and smiles, and hands me a map of the town which informs me that the Information Office is right under my feet.

I'm here because Ptuj ranks with Ljubljana as the most historically significant urban settlement in Slovenia, with a history dating back to Roman times. Poetovio/Ptuj was a significant Roman town, the sort of place Tacitus wrote about in his *Histories*. Just at this moment, however, I don't really care. The rain continues in a steady drizzle, the kind that soaks through quickly and dries slowly. As I look around for somewhere to eat there appears to be only pizza places and an ice-cream shop.

Set like most Slovenian castles on a high point above a river, the Ptuj Castle Museum cheers me up somewhat. The castle information office is very helpful, and the views of the Drava River and surrounding countryside are good, despite the weather. My arrival coincides with that of a party of Slovene-Americans from the Midwest.

'Visiting the old place,' an elderly man says to me as we all squeeze together through grand doors draped with thick felt curtain.

'Enjoying yourself?' I ask.

'I guess,' he says, 'but looking forward to getting home.'

On the ground floor we gather around a remarkable collection of musical instruments, including a 1694 lute, and a keyboard thought to have been played by Mozart himself. Each instrument's sound is re-created, and at each glass case the visitors stand patiently, many with expressions of bewilderment. The woman beside me nods as the sound of a harp dies away.

'Mmm, nice. Purdy . . . yeah, kinda purdy.'

As they move from room to room, the women cling to each others' hands or shirt tails, the men moving determinedly ahead as if to face the enemy. But bewilderment soon turns to ridicule. At the sight of a dragon chandelier made of wrought metal, a younger, bolder woman giggles: 'Oh my! Looks just like he's had his curlers in all night!'

By the time we reach the second floor and the stunning collection of seventeenth-century Turkerie portraits, I'm hanging back. In the room displaying local carnival costumes, the others are just a tinkle of sound. By the time I reach the gallery of Gothic martyrdoms they've disappeared entirely.

Later, in the ground-floor courtyard, I notice an elderly American visitor bending forward, blue hands on knees, wheezing sadly to the Austrian bus driver about the number of stairs in the castle and the fact that he's missing out on all the fun and games. The driver, a beefy, blond man, nods unsympathetically and gazes across the other's head at the grey line of the distant Drava.

The Church of St George stands in the Old Town square beside the *faux* information office and the Orpheus Monument, an elegant column commemorating Marcus Verus, mayor of Poetovio in the second century AD. Inside the church, a treasure house of Gothic art, someone is quietly practising the organ. Music and beauty, all under one roof and for free. The fifteenth century is everywhere here, with a triptych in the south aisle, a statue of St George in the north and choir stalls carved with wonderfully life-like animals which must have entertained many generations of bored choirboys. The chancel's floor tiles shape a black and white rose, the cross at its heart reflecting the late-afternoon light that filters through the stained glass above the altar.

In the nave, four workmen seem to be setting up an exhibition space with boards and long lines of wiring; but nothing much is happening, so engrossed are they in arguing about how the work should be done. As I move around the church the acoustics change, the angry voices echoing more and more loudly off the vaulted roof. One man waves a spanner to emphasise his point; another picks up a hammer to make his.

Like a dragon suddenly waking, the organ crashes a minor chord and the organist launches into a number that makes the floor vibrate. I slip unnoticed behind a door that says 'No Entry' and climb towards the sound. Halfway up the steps I come across a fresco older than anything in the church below; its colours are faded and nothing seems to be protecting it from the likes of me blundering past. I wipe a finger on my trousers and very gently touch the face of a blond, bearded saint in monk's habit. Eyes downcast, one finger sternly upraised, his spiritual message, though flaking, is still clear. 'Up or down . . . the choice is yours.'

Ptuj is not a poor town, or a small one. There's the usual plethora of shoe shops; a supermarket, better stocked than many in London, and stores filled with bland clothes that no-one seems to be wearing. But of restaurants or a social life beyond bars and ice cream there seems little evidence. I buy food in the supermarket, and picnic on my bed while watching CNN.

By the time I've eaten and watched the same news two or three times, it's only seven o'clock and still light outside. Lighter in fact than it's been all day, since the clouds have cleared and the sky's visible and surprisingly blue. I decide to go out somewhere. Anywhere.

Down in reception, an older, well-heeled Australian couple are checking in with an interpreter, a tall and exceptionally handsome young man with the widest shoulders and narrowest waist. Their business concluded, the couple disappear up the stairs, the woman's gaze lingering longingly on the young man below.

'The manager asks if you too would like a guide?' The young man is polite, his English tinged with California.

'No, but thanks.' I nod up the staircase. 'Are you with them?'

He grins. 'Yeah, I'm their sort of guide and driver – I'm a guide to Slovenia, not a local guide. My father owns a tour company in Ljubljana, I work for him.'

'Nice?'

'Sometimes.'

We sit on the hard sofas in the lobby. He tells me he knows Ptuj quite well because he spent three months here doing military service.

'It's a boring place,' he says. 'Three months was too much, really too much when you're eighteen and it's your first time away from home.'

'How old are you now?'

'Nineteen.' He smiles, asks what I'm doing here, then suggests I meet a friend of his, someone he knew when he was a soldier. 'He helped me not be so bored.' He grins. 'Showed all us young guys the places to go. Maybe he'll show you too.'

'You mean there *are* places to go here?'

'One or two . . . just for smoking, that kind of thing. There's a bar down in the town that does strip dancing – it's very funny, not at all sexy!' He laughs, his teeth white and even behind a long, full mouth. 'Oh, and there's the best fish restaurant in Slovenia!'

He reaches into a trendy backpack and takes out pen and paper.

'Here's Rudi's address. He lives not far. Tell him Janez told you. He won't remember me, he was always too stoned!' He laughs, running his tongue over his lower lip and a hand the size of my face through his cropped hair.

'Thanks,' I say, 'thanks,' and step outside for some fresh air.

Behind the Renaissance façades of Ptuj, with their Baroque double doors and Franz Josef door-knockers, Gothic courtyards, some six hundred years old, crumble gently in the damp. Almost everything in this town is a reminder of a time when Ptuj was altogether more significant than it is now; when it was part of the Roman Empire, part of the Hungarian and then the Austro-Hungarian Empire and later, part of a country called Yugoslavia. Now Ptuj is a small town sulking in the rustic hinterland of a small country.

In a courtyard once alive with dogs, horses and servants, broken cobbles roll underfoot and damp grass pushes up between steps and paving. A chained dog barks, pulling on the leash until it chokes itself into silence. A man appears on the first landing under a pointed arch.

'What do you want?'

'I'm looking for Rudi.'

'American?'

'No, British.'

He hesitates. Maybe I should have said American.

'Come up,' he says.

As the heavy wooden front door closes behind us, he turns to get a good look at me. 'Where did you get my address?'

'From Janez . . . tall guy, used to be in the army here. Said you helped him.'

He shakes his head; his face is round and flushed. I guess he must be about thirty-five. Dark hair and eyes remind me of the drawings of Hungarian soldiers in the Kobarid Museum.

'Don't remember.'

'He said you wouldn't.'

I tell him why I'm in Ptuj, that Janez thought he'd be a good person to talk to, and hold out a bottle of wine like a peace offering.

Two hours later the bottle is empty and more with it. Three young men are playing cards in a corner of the large room which is decorated in a dark-red mixture of the last and last-but-one *fin de siècle*. A fourth is rolling a spliff and watching *Pinky and the*

Brain on the Cartoon Network. After a few minutes I notice that he's mouthing the words, practising the diction of a mad American mouse.

'Does the army do blood tests?' I ask.

'For smoke? No. Maybe other places, but not here. The army knows what young people do. If they make you go in the army when you don't want to, what's the point of testing for drugs? They find smoke in your blood, they throw you out, and then you're happy! So they know, and don't test. It's better for them – better for everyone.'

He passes me a fourth shot of *sadjevec*, three fingers of liquid that looks as innocent as water. I tell myself it's only fruit juice but the far corners of the room are already shimmering.

'You think this is a boring town? Compared to London?'

I shake my head politely.

'Lots of things happen here.' He sounds almost boastful. 'Did you ever see the film *Deliverance*?'

'Ptuj is like that?' I must sound incredulous because he looks offended.

'Sometimes. Things happen here that you wouldn't believe . . . stranger even than in London.'

Clearly, I'm supposed to ask what things.

'All sorts. Out in the country, so far from anywhere, anything can happen. People disappear. Animals disappear. Families not speaking . . .'

That's not exciting, I know lots of families who don't speak; but being polite I ask, 'Why don't they speak?'

'Their tongues don't work.' He slugs at the *šnops* and refills his glass, glancing at mine still untouched. 'In the farms, the men work hard and drink; they beat the women and the women beat them back. Everyone beats the children.'

'Not everyone, surely?'

He giggles suddenly. 'No, not everyone.'

One of the young men playing cards suddenly speaks to Rudi and the others laugh.

'He says I should tell you about some people in a village

twenty kilometres up . . .' he waves north. 'This man and woman, every day they see only farm animals, but they are very . . . what's the word?'

'Jealous,' the young man in fatigues says sniggering, 'they are jealous.'

'Yes, jealous. Every day when the woman goes out to the animals the man weighs her tits like so . . .' He makes juggling motions with his hands. In the corner the three are giggling fit to burst. 'He thinks she makes love with the goats – they milk *her* maybe – ha ha ha! And when the husband works with the sheep, the wife weighs his balls when he goes and when he comes back, like so . . .' He grabs at his crotch.

One of the conscripts has fallen off his stool and the other two are laughing at him, the story already forgotten. I stare in what I hope looks like diplomatic amazement and after an appropriate lapse of time ask, 'Have you ever been to London?'

It's late when I get back to the hotel. The receptionist lifts his head from the sofa where he's fallen asleep watching MTV with the sound turned down. He looks, nods and falls asleep again.

The next morning it's raining but at least I don't have a hangover. There's a train at midday, the manager tells me, plenty of time to visit the Roman remains before then.

The taxi driver doesn't speak English and though my Slovenian is severely limited, I *can* tell the difference between a Roman temple and a railway station. When I point this out, the driver swings out of the station, hands over the radio intercom and shows me how to use it. I don't know how to say 'roger, roger' in Slovenian but the controller roughly translates and we end up on a small track near the village of Zgornji Breg, a few kilometres from Ptuj.

'*Mitra,*' the driver says, pointing at a small stone building standing forlornly under dripping trees.

Excited at the prospect of seeing a real Mithraic temple, one of five in the area and among the largest and best preserved outside Italy, I set off through long, wet grass. Mithraism, a male mystery cult derived from Persian Mazdaism, was popular among the Roman legions, partly because it hinted at immortality but mostly because it was a kind of ancient 'masonic' brotherhood, an aid to upward mobility and career success in the military.

The door is, of course, locked. Standing on tiptoe, the large square plaque at the far end of the building is just visible. It depicts the young god-man Mithras, in his soft Persian cap, as he kills the bull whose blood will grant fertility and immortality to the world. The bull's blood was believed to turn to wine and its marrow to bread, a ceremonial meal which was at the heart of Mithraic ritual. Early Christians complained that Mithraism parodied their ceremonies, but it's far more likely to have been the other way round, since Mithraism pre-dated Christianity.

The taxi driver shrugs politely at the locked doors and drives me back to the hotel, just in time to leave for the railway station.

Within a few hours, Ptuj and its ways seem positively quaint and entertaining. Celje, a much larger and more diverse town, has a closed and stifling atmosphere, not helped by the rain which now falls in solid walls of water.

If Ptuj seems saddened by the fading of past glories, Celje is positively bitter. My letter of introduction, coming as it does from 'the capital', produces nothing more than hostile glances. The owner of the Turkish Cat Hotel shows me to a small, narrow and expensive room. At the local museum I'm refused admittance half an hour before closing time.

'But you're open for another half an hour!'
'Too late. No time to see everything.'

'I don't want to see everything, I'd just like to see *something*. The Celje Family exhibition maybe?'

Several staff stand around jingling keys in their hands. There's a strong smell of alcohol in the air and one woman in particular looks as though my presence is a personal affront; but I don't move. It's now twenty minutes to closing time.

'I'll show you the exhibition of the Celje lords,' a woman appears from a back office. 'Go on home,' she says to the others, who stand around now looking shifty. 'I'll lock up. Come,' she says to me.

Some Slovenes envisage the Celje counts as a Slavic dynasty, carving a Slovenian proto-state against the Hapsburg odds. The line began with Geberhard of Saun, who died in 1144, and ended with the murder of Ulrich II in 1456. Brutal, fascinating and typical of the period in which they lived, Geberhard's descendants married into most of the ruling houses of Central and Eastern Europe, producing poets, soldiers, bishops, female alchemists, economists, assassins and Holy Roman Emperors. There's continuing debate over whether the Celje lords were German or Slav, but as the museum information puts it: 'They were simply their own people and could be found wherever there was a possibility of advancement. Wherever something glistened or tinkled. This is why they were reviled in many lands . . .'

It's quite an experience coming face to face with this family which would make any modern soap opera seem tame. Vivid pencil portraits of Frederick I and II and the murdered Ulrich show fur-clad, bearded men with intent eyes and battle-scarred faces.

'Are these imaginary likenesses?' I ask.

'No,' the curator waves at me. 'Come.'

We pass through a door and suddenly everything goes black. For a moment I think I've left the building and it's already dark outside, but that's impossible. The second, more paranoid thought is that, bored with showing me around, the curator has shoved me in a cupboard for the night. Then I can see again, and startled, I laugh aloud. The only light emanates from the Counts of Celje, or rather, from their remains. The room is full of tall, coffin-shaped boxes, each with a skull set at head height. One box is shorter and contains the small skull of a child.

'We found the family remains in a local church. They'd been moved at some time and only the skulls remained. We've done DNA testing, they are all related and all male. The portraits you saw are made from reconstructions of these skulls, so it's really how they looked.'

How odd to be standing face to face with men whose lives you've just discovered for the first time. The machinations, plots and sub-plots that reached across Europe emanated from these curves of bone; empty now as the eye sockets.

'This is Ulrich II, the last Celje lord . . . his head's not so good . . . you see the great split here? You've heard of the Hungarian King Matthias Corvinus, the Crow King?'

I nod.

'Ulrich was murdered by Laszlo Hunyadi, Matthias's brother. Maybe it was this blow to the head that killed him.' She moves on to the other skulls. 'We know who most of them are from their facial wounds, or from the age of the bones.'

I notice a large Celje family tree as I leave the room. Unlike most family trees, which start at the top and work down, this starts at the roots and branches up, spreading into Poland, Hungary and Bohemia, Serbia, Bosnia, Liechtenstein, Luxembourg, Germany, Italy and Bavaria. I look back at the skulls. Then the curator presses a switch and all is darkness again.

Youngsters hang around a McDonald's, one or two sucking on milkshakes. I'm reminded of the provincial towns where I grew up, where there was also nothing much to do and excitement meant ogling the local boys over a cup of tea in a grubby café.

But on a street corner near the Turkish Cat, something's happening. Grateful for any distraction, I follow a group of people through a door and enter a different world: a white world where portraits line the walls and fine, white textiles hang from the roof and upper gallery. Wine, figs and grapes are offered by young men and women who are happy to speak English.

'It's Mojca's degree exhibition,' they say, 'she'll talk to you about it if you ask her. Here she comes.' They all turn with bright eyes to their friend in her moment of achievement.

Mojca Janzeli is young, happy and polite. 'You'd like to know about my work?'

'Please.'

She points to a single framed image. 'I found this pictogram in a skip and reproduced it in different ways. Then for this show I made these photo-portraits of my friends . . . some of them you see are here, tonight.' She points to young men and women drinking and chatting beneath their own black and white faces. 'I used the pictogram in different ways to represent my feelings for each of the friends I photographed, so everyone has their own individual pattern. The patterns are also here and here . . . in the muslin and chiffon. These fabrics are also my feelings for friends.'

She smiles and the idea suddenly seems brilliant to me. She poses among the portraits and hanging fabrics as I photograph her – images of the image-maker. She knows from practice how to stand, how to look, yet underneath is a youthful self-consciousness that sees feeling in a skip and turns it into art.

An attractive blonde girl comes up to talk to me, a college friend of Mojca's.

'You are from Celje?' I ask.

'Oh no!' She laughs as though the question amuses her. 'We're all at college together in Ljubljana. Most of us are from Ljubljana.'

'Why have the exhibition here?'

She shrugs. 'I don't know really, I told her she should hold it in Piran. But this is a well-known gallery and a good space, don't you think?'

'Very good indeed.'

'We're glad you came.'

'And I'm very glad I came.'

Hundreds of metres above the town, the ruins and reconstructed buildings of Celje Castle look strange jumbled together, like Lego on a bombsite. I trudge up and down the castle's grassy banks in the rain while the young man who runs the ticket kiosk makes us coffee.

'The key will come soon,' he says.

'Key to what?'

'To inside.'

'What's inside?'

'Nothing much.'

This is an understatement. Hollow, stone rooms would have been fine, but when the key finally arrives, escorted by half a dozen workmen who eye me suspiciously, the unlocked doors reveal a bizarre past. Inside the restored tower, modern rooms reveal mounds of rubbish, empty beer bottles and men's clothing scattered across the floors. It looks like someone's been squatting here recently.

'This used to be a restaurant,' the young man from the kiosk says. 'Look . . . kitchen, table, window.'

Why is he showing me these things? What have I said or done to make him think I want to see them? Maybe he's just practising his English?

'That was ten years ago, the restaurant . . . before we were independent.'

He leads me into a half-moon room filled with broken plaster-work and large picture windows.

'I come from that village over there,' he says pointing to a distant clump of trees and houses.

We stand in silence and peer through wet glass across the river, across the town and its industry, to the distant hills. A perfect view of enemies, friends and subjects. I try to imagine Frederick or Ulrich of Celje standing here, but the castle's reconstructions and Communist restaurant clutter the imagination.

Ljubljana seems sunny and welcoming until I get back to my lodgings near the railway station. The landlady, an elderly woman who in a more southerly country would be wearing full black, is obsessed by locks and counts aloud the number of times I turn the key behind me on entering the house. I loathe being locked in, and having to wear someone else's house-shoes on my feet, and not being able to leave my towel in the bathroom, and not being allowed to wash my clothes. There are bars across the window of my dingy basement room and the whole place smells of age and bitterness. There is a phone, but it's got a lock on it like a chastity belt which offers of money won't induce my landlady to undo. Escape is the only option.

I phone Andrej and Nataša from a call box.

'We're going to the countryside this afternoon – why don't you come with us?' Andrej's voice is warm and friendly at the other end of the phone.

'And bring a bathing suit,' Nataša calls in the background.

Twenty minutes later I walk though the doors of my friends' warm, bright home and the dampness of Slovenia's north-east falls away.

'Are we ready?' Andrej's pale trousers and jacket remind me of former BBC reporter Martin Bell, who was shot in Bosnia, and I wonder if this is going to be an expedition requiring fortitude.

'Where are we going?' I ask.

'To Bled and Bohinj, and maybe the Savica waterfall if there's time.'

Bled and Bohinj, jewels of the Triglav National Park, are Slovenia's best-known destinations. On my last day in Slovenia, luck is with me after all.

Our route takes us north-west, past the airport and the maize fields, following the Sava into the heart of Gorenjska province. Ahead, the limestone of high mountain peaks is dazzlingly white in the afternoon sun. The Julian Alps fill the western horizon and the Kamnik-Savinja range marks the border of Slovenia and Austria to the north.

We pass through the provincial capital of Kranj, and at Radovljica I notice the confluence of two small rivers.

'Is one of them the Sava?' I ask.

Nataša leans forward from the back seat; Brin, who's reading with his head in her lap, mumbles complaint. 'Both are. The Sava has two sources which meet here – one comes from Lake Bohinj and the other from further north near Kranjska Gora, right on the border with Italy and Austria.'

'Doesn't Brin get carsick reading like that?' I ask.

Nataša repeats the question to Brin, who replies, without raising his eyes from an illustrated version of Homer, that reading could never make him sick.

Soon after we reach Bled, and eat a late lunch at Andrej and Nataša's favourite place, a climbers' inn in the heart of town, just below the castle. The waitress brings vast bowls of wild mushroom soup on which dollops of thick cream float like lilies, and plates piled with bread and fries and salads; far more than we can eat.

'Would you like to visit Bled Castle?' Andrej asks me.

'You've been there?'

'Many times, but we don't mind going again if you'd like to.'

I shake my head. 'Thanks, but three castles in three days would be overkill. I'd rather see more countryside if that's OK.'

We drive around the southern edge of the lake, which is smaller and more beautiful than I expected. Although the bright sun of earlier is partly hidden by mountain cloud, the lake's blue-green waters sparkle and the red roof and white walls of the church on Blejski Otok, the tiny island at the lake's heart, seem to demand that the stranger get into a boat or swim to its shores. The setting of Slovenia's only true island among mountains and rocky castles is the breathtaking stuff of brochures; but Bled and its lake are much more than that. Despite many years as a European tourist destination, it remains unspoiled; nature still predominates here.

It's not hard to understand why Bled was always such a draw for tourists and locals alike. Bypassed by the Romans, it was an original Slavic settlement with unique animal myths and legends of goddesses and their mortal lovers. Best remembered is the tale of the golden-horned chamois, Zlatorog, whose image sells Slovenia's most popular beer. The wonders of Bled and its thermal springs were first mentioned in Janez Vajkard Valvasor's *Glory of the Duchy of Carniola,* which introduced the town to early health-conscious tourists. Until World War II, Bled was the summer home of the King of Yugoslavia and his family, and Tito continued the patronage.

We pass the Hotel Vila Bled, which has a slightly faded 'Agatha Christie' look, as though the British aristocracy of another era might suddenly reappear to perform dark deeds within its walls.

'Tito used to entertain there,' Andrej says.

'Imagine all those huge, political dinners!' Nataša laughs in the back of the car. Brin has seen it all before and finds the *Odyssey* preferable to scenery.

We leave the car at Savica to walk upwards over rock and through dense trees. It's soon clear that Nataša's a serious walker, and Brin too charges ahead, his slender limbs flailing with excitement as books are momentarily forgotten. Andrej and I bring up the rear, talking a little breathlessly about publishing in Slovenia.

'Have you read *Landscape Painted with Tea* by the Serb writer Milorad Pavić?' Andrej asks.

'I'm sadly ignorant of modern European literature,' I reply. 'Is it good?'

'Very, and there's a particularly great story in there. You remember we talked about black humour and Yugoslav jokes? Well, afterwards I remembered this . . . it's almost an extended joke. Would you like to hear a précis of it?'

'Of course.'

'It's set in the Soviet Union and there's this physicist who works as a nuclear scientist. One day he learns that he's about to be indicted for something, so he escapes to Siberia where he thinks no-one will look for him. When he arrives he hasn't eaten for three days, and he's cold and starving and has no money. So he goes to the authorities and asks, "What jobs do you have here?" They tell him that the only jobs are sweeping the roads, so he takes the job of road-sweeper and does this for a while and is very good at it. Unfortunately, people notice that he's very good and after a while they start to comment and say, "Fjodor Aleksejević, you're such a brilliant road-sweeper, wouldn't you like to join the Communist Party?" He doesn't want to of course, so to wriggle out of it he says, "But I'm just an ignorant man who understands nothing." "No problem!" they say. "We'll send you to school where you can learn everything to become a good Party member." So off he goes to night school, where there are lots of other workers all learning to read and write and do arithmetic. One day the teacher is doing sums on the black-board and she writes 1+1=2. Suddenly it's all too much for him, and he leaps up shouting, "No it isn't! No it isn't!" "Of course it is . . . everyone knows that one plus one equals two," says the teacher, at which Fjodor Aleksejević goes to the blackboard, snatches up the chalk and starts writing complex maths all over it. The teacher's mouth hangs open in amazement. But at the end of the equation Fjodor Aleksejević suddenly realises he's lost it, he can't remember how the theorem of 1+1 not being 2 should work out. As he stands there feeling desperate he suddenly hears many voices from the class behind him, urgently whispering, "Planck! Planck! You've forgotten Planck's Theorem!" '

I laugh out loud at Pavić's mix of humour and tragedy. 'That's a great story,' I say, 'maybe I should read a lot more Slav litera-ture!'

We're interrupted as the ground slopes suddenly down-wards and the Savica waterfall is below us. Now at the end of summer, the water is more trickle than cascade, but it's still powerful enough to drown conversation and soak the unwary. White foam tumbles over a high ledge, falls sixty metres into a shallow basin and miraculously turns a dark turquoise green. The great Romantic, Prešeren, made the waterfall and surroundings famous in his poem *Baptism at Savica*, a retelling of the ancient Slav story of the priestess Bogomila and her lover Črtomir. We take photos of each other, though down in this green place the light is poor and only Nataša's bright hair, Andrej's suit and Brin's laughing face stand out against the backdrop of pool and water.

The light is already fading when we reach Lake Bohinj. Nataša puts on her bathing suit beside an old stone bridge, and she and Brin wade into the water and start to swim.

'Come in!' she laughs. 'It's not too cold.'

But Bohinj is a glacial lake and I can see from her face that it's bloody freezing.

While they brave the water, Andrej and I walk to the nearby Church of St John the Baptist. The tiny church is closed but some of the frescoes are just visible through the windows. I can just make out John the Baptist's head being presented to a pair of smirking ladies in fifteenth-century court dress, while his headless corpse pumps blood over the floor. Not far away, Cain and Abel take their places near a row of vampiric angels. The rest is in shadow and we content ourselves with gazing at the stars painted on the roof of the wooden portico.

Dusk falls quickly in the mountains. Lights come on along the lakeside, and the bridge fades into the landscape. Only the white shapes of Brin and Nataša are still bright in the evening light.

5   Zagreb Days

DESPITE the sun, Zagreb seems stark after Ljubljana. From the back of a taxi I search for a point of recognition, some corner or street remembered from before; but there's just grime-dark buildings, citizens in mourning colours and the trams roaring down the main thoroughfares on lines cut deep into the cobbles. I'm momentarily stunned by the change, and must appear vacant because the taxi driver overcharges by the price of a hotel room. Shrugging at my protest, he refuses to give change and pockets his 'tip'.

My hotel is expensive, the rooms like flimsy shoe boxes. The receptionist – the owner's daughter, a round, pink-cheeked young woman – speaks English brilliantly and is eager to discuss anything and everything within moments of taking my passport, from the tackiness of the rooms to her father's mistresses.

'My name's Elena. This is your first visit to Croatia? You were here twenty years ago! I was two years old! I will talk to you, tell you everything about Croatia, about Zagreb – everything. You would like some tea? It's on the house.'

A notice beside the fax machine makes it clear that credit cards are not welcome, but that cash, preferably dollars, is. A first glimpse of what Croats call 'the grey economy'.

'You will like Croatia. This is a good country for foreigners – so many things to see.' Her face changes. 'But for us, it's not so good.'

'In what way?'

'No money . . . and our government's the worst, our politicians are crooks and thieves. They all have money, but ordinary people don't. I'm a student, but you see me here. I must work because how can I study without money? Here's your tea.'

Her whirlwind conversation rushes on, so I take the mug she hands me and sit down on my bag.

'I don't want to stay here in Croatia. No young people want to stay – there's nothing for us here. You work and work, you have two or three jobs, and you never have money.'

'And when you were younger?'

'Oh, that was completely different. We always had money. Even though I was a kid, I could always buy music or jeans. It was good then.'

'Do people wish this was still the old Yugoslavia then?'

She pauses, considering, then shakes her head. 'No. I don't think anyone wants that now. That's the past.'

She shows me to a room beside the reception area that fits a bed and a TV, with one corner converted to a bathroom. Every sound and word is clear through the papery walls, and using the toilet is almost embarrassing.

Things seem different in the dark; the city centre is livelier, and full of men and women drinking beer at open-air cafés. People are dressed as if for a party, the dark clothes of the day replaced by shiny purples and golds. In the main square, Ban Josip Jelačić, the nineteenth-century hero of Croatian independence, sits astride his horse, sword raised, watching the endless trams and trickle of cars.

The trams are fewer and the laughing people more scattered as I head up towards Kaptol, the low hill where Zagreb was born. Much of the city's earliest history is unknown, but Kaptol and its twin hill, Gradec, were the first Slav settlements in the region; by the late eighth century each probably had forts or churches on their low slopes. The road sweeps round an upward-curving bend, and abruptly I'm in a world that seems closer to the English cathedral green than the strident city only a few streets away. Lit by sodium and moonlight, the spires of the Cathedral of the Assumption loom over a square of low, red-roofed houses; at its heart, a column topped with a golden Virgin.

The name Croatia was first used in official documents in AD 852. At that time, the northern part of the country was under Frankish rule and Dalmatia was nominally controlled by Byzantium. Croatia emerged as a coherent entity in the 920s, when the great unifier King Tomislav merged Pannonia and Dalmatia, creating a powerful, independent state to which many Croats in the intervening years have looked back with longing. After the death of its last king in 1102, Croatia entered a union with Hungary which would affect its destiny for almost a thousand years. A Hungarian king built a church and created a diocese on Kaptol in 1094, making it the ecclesiastical heart of the future city of Zagreb. But when the Mongols swept through a hundred and fifty years later, tradition says they stabled their horses in his cathedral.

Outsiders were not the only source of conflict for Kaptol. When the Mongols departed, leaving devastation in their wake, King Bela of Hungary gave neighbouring Gradec a royal charter as an incentive to reconstruction. He freed Gradec from financial obligations and ordered that walls be built for future protection. Kaptol remained a diocesan town under church law, and the distinctions between the two – though only a few hundred metres apart – created envy and financial rivalry which lasted many hundreds of years. When Kaptol excommunicated Gradec, Gradec looted and burnt Kaptol; only commercial incentives such as the big annual fairs could induce the two to get along briefly and conduct their mutual purse and throat-slitting quietly. Not until the early seventeenth century, when most of Croatia was under Ottoman control and the Turks posed a greater threat than each other, did the rivals slowly merge, to become Zagreb. It would be another two centuries before the twin towns would become a real city, with an expanding population, a developed economic and cultural life, and the railway that would link it to Vienna, the Austrian Empire and a new reality.

The next day is a round of meetings and visits. My reception at the Croatia Promotion Centre isn't quite as warm as I'd hoped for. Waiting in the corridor of a tall office block just off the main square I watch tall, slender young women in high heels and skirts like belts make tea and conversation. They eye me dubiously and the air of vague suspicion would have been confusing if the Croatian PR office in England hadn't explained things months earlier.

'They're a bit anxious about writers these days. They used to be very welcoming, but since the war a few visitors have written dreadful things about the country, about it still being like a war zone etc. I'm sure you understand their position.'

The promotion officer looks slightly harassed when we finally meet. 'You were here twenty-one years ago?'

I nod.

'Things were very different then. Our tourist industry was starting to take off, and we were becoming a great country for visitors.' She opens a report filled with coloured bar charts and columns of statistics. Leaning across her desk, she shows me the gradual rise in visitor numbers to the country from the mid-1970s to 1985–86, when numbers peaked.

'Many people came here. Yugoslavia was rich – everyone had what they needed. Then we had the war and it was all over. Last year was the first time the numbers of foreign tourists to Croatia improved, and we were happy because things looked good. Then there was Kosovo and this summer the numbers fell right back down again. People think everywhere is a war zone, they don't know anything about geography. Kosovo is two countries away.'

She looks tired and depressed as she says this, and I wonder if she'll add, 'You will tell them differently,' but she doesn't. Instead, she hands me a pass for the coastal ferries, a Croatian copy of my Slovenian letter of introduction and a fat, photocopied list of contacts.

The streets leading to the British Embassy are lined with shops. Expensively trendy 'boutiques' sit beside stores redolent of the seventies and Communism, their windows dotted with batteries, nuts, bolts and the elements for boilers and heating systems. The distance is greater than the map suggests, so I board a tram and hope it's heading the right way. Despite the brightness of the sun, the feeling of grimness remains. Looking around the carriage, I wonder whether this has more to do with the citizens than the city. These seem hard people, who don't trust easily. Women's conversations have an edge to them; the laughter of a couple of elderly men seems forced. I wonder briefly if it's me, if I came here with subconscious preconceptions. But the dour doggedness that resists the veneer of smart clothes and Italian shoes is no more a figment of my imagination than the frowns on the young-sters' faces. Thinking back on my conversations with Elena at the hotel I wonder if it really is all about money, if the frowns reflect economic hardship and overwork. Here in the heart of the city, it's impossible to distinguish rich from poor. I wonder who patro-nises the Baroque antique shops and buys the heavy gold in the jewellers' windows. There's money here, but its scent is elusive and distant.

David Austin, the Deputy Head of Mission at the embassy, is expecting me. Over tea in his office he talks about the Former Yugoslavia, about Dayton, Milošević and Croatian football.

'When President Tudjman changed the name of Dinamo Zagreb to NK Croatia, the fans were furious. The club president is one of Tudjman's henchmen, so it's politically interesting too.'

'What was wrong with Dinamo?'

'Too Communist, too much like Dynamo Kiev and that sort of thing.'

'What was the general feeling here about Kosovo and the NATO bombing?'

'I wasn't here at the time, but after what the JNA and Serb paramilitaries did in 1991–92, it would be surprising if most people didn't feel glad that the Serbs got a taste of their own medicine at last. I must say I rather liked the Serbs I knew personally when I worked in Belgrade, most of whom opposed the Milošević regime. They were always very welcoming and helpful.'

'You met Milošević?'

'Many times. During the summer of 1995, when I was political advisor to Carl Bildt, I spent many hours over many days at Milošević's villa at Dobanovci, near Belgrade. Bildt had taken over from Lord Owen as negotiator for a Bosnian cease-fire. We sometimes sat in the garden, rarely more than four of us – Bildt and myself, Milošević and his *chef de cabinet*. What struck me at the time was that during those marathon sessions he spoke to no-one, even by phone, except his wife. Sitting there, watching it all, it seemed strange that a president could be away from contact with world or national events for so long. But it was typical of the man. He's intellectually arrogant, believes he can achieve everything alone – or at least, with only the help of his wife.'

He drinks his tea, still thinking about Milošević. 'He often asked me about my family. He knew that we'd recently had a baby – he mentioned her within seconds of our first meeting. It was quite unnerving actually. On the surface he was being courteous, but then you always think, "What's he really saying here? What does he know?"'

'And Tudjman?'

He laughs. 'What a pair! Paranoid autocrats, dictatorships with the trappings of democracy. One a nationalist; the other prepared to use nationalism for his own political ends. Tudjman's a hypocrite and a bigot, pursuing deeply unpleasant policies. Not as astute politically as Milošević, but clever enough to surround himself with plausible talent.'

'So what will happen when Tudjman dies?'

'That's when the big choice will have to be made: will Croatia look to the West, or will it choose continued isolation? If it decides to join the West, to apply for EU membership and all that, it'll have to give up its ambition to destroy the Bosnian state . . . Tudjman's interference in Bosnia is a real problem. The hardliners in Tudjman's administration want to help their Croat 'brothers' across the border in ways destructive to the Dayton Accord. In other words, they want to incorporate Hercegovina into Croatia, even though they've tried that once and failed. Then there are the liberal politicians who want to turn their backs on interference and forge new relationships with their neighbours and the West. They see the Croat leaders in Hercegovina as backwoods criminals who are keeping Croatia impoverished and isolated. Most Croatians feel like that.'

Biscuits arrive, brought by an unsmiling young man in a dark suit.

'Tell me about Bosnia during the war.'

'I hated it. Being shot at was very frightening. But Sarajevo is really reviving now I'm told. I haven't been back there since 1996. There was a summit there recently on the regional Stability Pact; it was about closer ties to the EU and NATO, democratisation, human rights and security, all the things the war just flattened.'

'It's hard for outsiders to understand what the Serbs want, since the Western media has so demonised them.'

'As I said, I like them and enjoyed living and working in Belgrade, and now I've got many Serbian friends . . . they say of themselves that they make bad enemies but the best friends. Unfortunately, some of their political leaders perpetuate the idea that wherever there are Serbs, or even Serbian graves, is Serbia – the logical extension of that being that they own the whole world.' He gives a short laugh. 'It's a tremendously arrogant position. Have you read *Balkan Express* by Slavenka Drakulic?'

I shake my head.

'It's a good book and there's a great bit in it where she describes coming through the train station in Vienna and seeing graffiti that reads, "This is Serbia".' A Rich Tea biscuit snaps briskly between his fingers. 'Many Serbs have this powerful sense of injustice, so powerful that they've allowed themselves to become tools for Milošević's ambitions – which is a very great tragedy, not just for them, of course, but for this whole region. It's impossible these days for anyone to write about Croatia or Bosnia without grasping Serbia.'

He looks into his empty teacup. 'It's been hard for Croats I think, seeing the Slovenes win their independence at relatively little cost in 1991, then being outmanoeuvred by the Serbs, who proceeded to cut Croatia in two. So after all the suffering of the war, the Croats didn't get what they hoped for. They got independence, sure, but not the economic freedom or prosperity they thought would come with that. Instead, they got a corrupt, bad government for almost ten years which has left most people surviving on the grey economy.'

As I get ready to leave, he says, 'Have you heard any Balkan jokes yet?'

'One or two. Not exactly hilarious, are they.'

'No, but I think that's the point. Let me tell you the one about the Moon.' He grins. 'A Bosnian Moslem, a Croat and two Serbs land on the Moon. Each has a flag and each tries to plant it and claim the Moon, but they can't decide who got there first. Then one Serb kills the other Serb, buries him, sticks the flag on his grave, and says, "*Now* this is Serbia." '

The open-air market at Britanski Trg sells fragrant, shining fruit and vegetables. There's something wonderful about buying produce in markets, and here, where it's grown in rural gardens and brought daily to the city, the transaction has a timeless quality. The heaps of scarlet peppers, green lettuces, red potatoes, purple grapes and plums, and perfect, half-moon domes of white goat's cheese remind me just how much the English-speaking world has lost. The markets of my Wye Valley childhood are mostly gone now, and standing here, in the heart of Zagreb, surrounded by colour and bustle, I miss them.

Beyond the produce stalls, vibrant floral displays tempt the passer-by, though flowers are only part of the visual feast. Exotic leaves mix with three or four different varieties of berries in red, white and green, all clustering round an artificial peach, apple or pink pineapple. One stall specialises in roses arranged with grasses and ivy; and at the heart of each rose something winks and shines – a gold bead set among the petals. Bending down to get a really close look, I notice that many flowers are hung with fine gold chains, their leaves dusted with sparkling metallic powders. The words 'gilding the lily', or in this case 'chaining the rose', spring to mind, but the overall impression is curious and charming.

'Why are you making photographs? Are they for yourself or for someone else?'

The speaker, a middle-aged woman, looks wary and almost hostile.

'They're for me. Why do you ask?'

'You never know . . . sometimes people make things for bad reasons.'

'Really, it's just for me. But you speak great English.'

'I lived many years in Australia, in Melbourne.'

'Why did you come back to Croatia?'

She blows her cheeks out dismissively. 'I believed all the propaganda, that Yugoslavia was a forward-looking country where everything was possible. The Communists said Yugoslavia needed us. So we came back, thousands of us, from all over the world . . . Australia, South America, England. I wish I'd never seen this country again. It was all a lie. Tito died, then we had the war. In Melbourne I had one job, I had a house, I went to the beach. Here I have three jobs, I never stop working and I have nothing. It was a mistake to come back.'

She looks at me without expectation of a reply, which is good because I don't know what to say.

'I like to speak English again,' she says. 'It reminds me of Melbourne.'

Searching for medication for a stomach virus that struck on arriving in Zagreb, I find what looks like a pharmacy but turns out to be a surgical appliance store. The customers, all pensioners and frail, stare at me, surprised.

'Medicinal charcoal,' the assistant says helpfully as she measures a truss, 'but we don't sell that. There's a pharmacy along the road, not far.'

Before I can ask how far, my hand is seized by a very elderly woman who pulls me out of the store with surprising strength.

'I will show you, no problem at all,' she says in German.

'Danke,' I say, and stand hand in hand on the curb with this woman so bent with age she barely reaches my chest. She must be over eighty. Gazing at the top of her head, with its braid of white hair, I think of what's inside, the stories and the times she's lived through. Trams roar past and she grips me tightly in case I should make the fatal error of stepping off the pavement. We cross eventually and she shows me the pharmacy.

'Danke sehr. Do you speak English?'

She shakes her head, smiling, and says in German, 'But my son is Professor of English at the University of Verona.'

There are a great many elderly people out and about in Zagreb. Often they seem the jolliest passers-by, perhaps because compared with the decades of history they've lived through, the present seems less oppressive. Or maybe, unlike the city's frowning youth, they have the trick of enjoying what there is.

In an outdoor restaurant overlooking the cathedral I eat luke-warm soup and watch three elderly, overdressed locals eat cream puffs. The trio are so decrepit they can barely lift their hands, and instead they drop their mouths towards their forks. Nobody speaks. They eat as if indulging a solitary vice, determined, concentrated. I watch, fascinated, as the man pours salt over his cake. The woman beside him wears canary-yellow silk and chews with the focus of a sumo wrestler. The second woman moves cream and pastry with blurred rapidity from plate to quivering, dewlapped face, until cream hangs in thick strands from her trembling lips. The Austro-Hungarian Empire has much to answer for, not least Central Europe's love affair with cake.

As I leave the restaurant, I look up at central Zagreb's imposing nineteenth-century façades, and imagine the city at the height of Austro-Hungarian power, a peaceful time of cultural diversity and prosperity. But it seems there never was such a time for Croatia. After Napoleon fell in 1815, Austria tightened its grip on Dalmatia, reinstating its Italian élite, while Hungary claimed the rest of the country. In public, Croat intellectuals and the upper-classes spoke German, Hungarian, Italian – the language of the colonisers; the German spoken by my elderly guide, a ghost from that time. Croatian, or 'Illyrian' as it was then called, didn't become an acknowledged, school-taught language until after the revolutions that swept Europe in 1848, and then only in the face of Hungarian opposition.

For a day or so I rest, eat charcoal, and listen to Elena's conversation. She draws diagrams of the Croatian education system which seems Byzantine in its complexity. She tells me about Canjuga, an HDZ politician, one of Tudjman's lot she says, her mouth twisted, who recently used a sanitary towel analogy for one of the minor opposition parties.

'Lots of women's groups didn't like it at all,' she says, and giggles before adding, 'but some women in our media said that things must be looking up politically if Croatian men realise that women have periods at all, and even know what sanitary protection they wear!'

She laughs, bouncing on the balls of her feet with pleasure, and offers me another cup of herbal tea. At that moment the doors fly open and her father arrives.

A tall man, cashmere coat draped over his shoulders despite the heat, he strides up and down the hotel's short hallway, shouting and posturing like a martinet. His girlfriend, a thin, blonde, over-made-up woman, about whom I know everything there is to know, thanks to Elena, stands around smoking and pretending nothing is happening.

I escape and head for the peace of the city centre and a meeting with a man in a Gradec bar.

Ivo Korošić is tall and handsome, with taut energy. I'd wondered what to expect. A grizzled hack? The stereotypical war correspondent? He lights a cigarette as I place a bottle of beer in front of him, and ask how his life has changed since the end of the war.

He smiles at me briefly, and in response to my question about the past says, 'It seems mad now, I know, but we all thought history was behind us in 1996. We breathed out for a while, then 1999 and Kosovo showed us we were wrong.'

He grimaces through the cigarette smoke. 'For me personally? It was much easier, more challenging too of course, being a war correspondent. Things were happening all the time. Now it's over I write political and financial stuff, and sport. I enjoy doing sport. In this country it's never far away from politics, which is all tied up with economics, and that again has its own interest for me. There's a universal language, an understanding of finance across the world, something we can all agree on. War reporting was naturally more exciting, but it seems to me that human interest and greed are no different whatever you write about.'

He stubs the cigarette out. 'You were here twenty years ago?'
I nod.

'The difference is unbelievable. I wouldn't believe it if I hadn't watched it happening. Does this seem the same country to you?'

'No, but then I've not been here long. I've just come from Slovenia and I'm surprised by the difference. Here, everyone tells me how bad things are; there, very few people said anything at all.'

'They haven't had a criminal government for the last decade,' he says abruptly. 'But where we and the Slovenes do coincide is in wanting to be part of the West, but at the same time not wanting that at all.

'You know, people here talk about everything being bad because talk is all they have. No-one trusts the political process any more. Tudjman has played on our anxieties for years now . . . about the West, about how the West will force us into a Yugoslav-type federation again, a new Yugoslavia. Croats loathe this idea, and Tudjman and his kind know that and use it. We *want* to be seen as a separate country, but he's made us look like the Serbs, just two sides of one coin.'

He lights another cigarette and offers me one.

'People believed in Tudjman when they voted for him in 1990. He'd been a Partisan, he'd stood up to Belgrade against centralisation, gone to prison after Tito's death, was anti-Serb. The HDZ talked about the greatness of Croatia, about King Tomislav. In the end, paradoxically, it was Milošević's ambition that forced independence on us, though no-one wants to admit that.'

He gestures at the empty bottles, 'You want another?' and raises a hand to the waiter, who nods and disappears.

'Back in 1991 Tudjman told the Slovenes he wanted independence alongside them, but at the same time he was negotiating with Milošević to cut up Bosnia and take Hercegovina. Milošević told Tudjman, "Noooo my friend! We Serbs have no interest in Croatian territory, don't you worry about anything!" ' He snorts. 'Tudjman was stupid enough to believe him. It was like your Chamberlain with Hitler in 1939 – foolish men believe what they want to because it suits their egos.'

'It seems like Tudjman's been ill for years. What'll happen when he dies?'

'The HDZ has used nationalism and fear of the outside for too long and it's wearing thin. The opposition parties talk about welfare, quality of life. People are starting to care more about those things than about a Greater Croatia.'

'Is that how it is? Tudjman dies, things get better?'

'Perhaps. There are many shades to democracy, especially in the Balkans.'

'So Croatia *is* the Balkans?'

He looks at me with surprise. 'Of course. Who told you different?'

'I just wanted to be absolutely sure.'

He lights another cigarette from the last one. 'The HDZ has a power that has nothing to do with democracy. They control the army, the police, the TV. Even if an opposition party gets elected, the status quo remains. Without Tudjman, maybe their control will weaken . . . but we're talking about greedy men, used to power, who think fraud and deception are normality. Only recently Tudjman wire-tapped journalists. He lies about his assets. His wife had *eleven* secret bank accounts while the average monthly pension here is about US$130 a month. His lawyers said, "Cash is not an asset." Can you believe that?'

I watch him turn the beer bottle round and round in his hands, and wonder what to say.

'I think it must be normal,' he says, 'to feel politically helpless in this part of the world, just like in Eastern Europe. It's our Communist heritage. Nationalism has just made it harder for us. What criteria can we use to decide whether to join with Europe, or remain isolated? How can we make those decisions when our decision-makers are criminals?'

'People seem angry,' I say, 'and depressed. It's hard coming from the West, to grasp what that feels like, that mix of anger and helplessness.'

He looks at me through cigarette smoke. 'I know,' he says. 'I know it is.'

In Jelačića Trg a small crowd has gathered to watch a man playing music on empty green bottles. The sound is piercingly beautiful. Without looking I wouldn't believe the complex melodies being drawn from lines of bottles suspended from a wood frame by bits of string. The musician is small and dark, and might be from anywhere. It seems a brave thing to do, to set up his instrument in the middle of this daunting space.

In a restaurant off the square I eat plain rice and talk to an elderly British couple who tell me about the time they drove from Tanzania to London in the sixties.

'Oh yes, we used to do fun things all the time. On that occasion our children were two and six and we camped all the way.' The woman pauses to suck the large prawn held in her fingers. 'I remember washing our clothes in village fountains in the south of Italy. It was marvellous.'

'Couldn't do that today,' her husband says, 'the world's changed so much in thirty years. Everything's regimented.'

'Wouldn't *want* to do it now!' the woman laughs. 'We're great-grandparents, and a bit of luxury's fine with me!' The mound of prawn heads almost reaches her chin, and she sucks noisily on each fat, pink body with the gusto of someone who has enjoyed life and intends to go on doing so. 'We're driving up to Bled, then down to Dubrovnik. I must say, we're looking forward to it. Makes a change from Berkshire.'

Later, as I walk from the restaurant to a central Internet café, I can still hear the bottle music, its ethereal sound echoing over the pop and club sounds thudding out of the various bars and shops. After some searching, I find the café at the rear of an unlit courtyard, and stumble, cursing, over broken paving, as curtains twitch in the darkness.

Inside, the café is full of computers and helpful young people; lamps, plants and vibrant colours decorate the space. It's cheap, organised and efficient. This is a Croatia whose existence I'd begun to doubt, one that seems unrelated to that other world only metres away.

The trains to Rijeka are slow, and I'm told it's not possible to arrive before evening. Trying to book a room in the city using the promotion office's contact list doesn't help, as the telephone numbers have either changed or are incorrect – the deputy major of Croatia's largest port city isn't at all happy at having his breakfast disturbed. But after a few hours I strike lucky, and somewhere in Rijeka a bed awaits.

Elena shakes my hand and wishes me a good journey. People have been helpful and kind to me here, but this is a disconsolate place. Bitterness coats everything and the tension is palpable. I'm not sorry to be leaving, but grateful that I can.

On the tram with my bag, I find that being so obviously a foreigner makes people more friendly. Advice on where to get off and the times of the train to Rijeka is offered freely. Passing Jelačića Trg for the last time, I see the bottle musician surrounded by half a dozen policemen. The tram turns a bend and I look back to see what's happening, but can only make out a wall of uniforms.

A young, muscular man with a limp lifts my bag down onto the pavement from the tram and smiles as I thank him in Croatian. Entering the station I swerve, just fast enough to avoid the jet stream of spittle produced by an elderly, L-shaped nun.

The unofficial station porter who takes my bag admits that he's unofficial. 'What else can I do? I must feed myself,' he says.

I want to buy bottled water for the journey but the porter and my bag are already disappearing from sight. On the platform I pay what I would pay a London porter. He grimaces, and realising there's no more, asks in a resigned voice whether I want first or second class.

'Second,' I say. 'I don't think there's a first on this train.'

'No first class in Croatia,' he says, 'everything here is second class.'

From Zagreb to Rijeka is about one hundred and twenty kilometres, but for some reason the journey time is five hours and there's no food or water available on board. While still in the station, crowded carriages are being turned into boudoirs. Up and down the train, elderly women remove their cardigans, take off their shoes and draw the window and corridor curtains, before getting down to serious gossip and the sharing of tea and delicious things drawn from grease-proofed paper and plastic boxes.

The last time I travelled this route it was night. The train was about a kilometre long, or so it seemed as I hung out of the windows and looked back along the track at an endless, rattling glowworm. After twenty years, that journey remains with me as a long, stiflingly overcrowded nightmare of screaming infants and vomiting women. There were bodies in the corridors, in the toilets, in the doorways. My carriage was filled with soldiers and sailors who smoked and gambled and spat their way from stop to stop and never slept.

On this comfortable train with padded seats, smoking is forbidden and men and young women stand furtively in corridors blowing smoke through open windows. Today's fellow passengers are low-key. A pleasant-looking man reads a book, and two young women smile at me shyly. An elderly woman, a kind of Croatian bag lady, sits between me and the window clutching a small fertiliser sack held together with wire. It's noon and a very hot day, but the woman wears a maroon overcoat and a headscarf. She checks and re-checks her ticket before replacing it with her money and ID card, in a well-used plastic bag which she drops into a pocket and closes with a large safety pin. Her coat matches the carriage décor exactly; she's close enough to touch but manages to almost disappear into the seating.

As the train moves off, the woman hurriedly puts on a pair of dirty white lace gloves, leaps to her feet and stands at the window, arms outstretched like a crucifixion. She stays like this, rigid and upright, despite the train's jolting. Perhaps she's saying goodbye to Zagreb. Perhaps there's someone she's leaving behind, someone she'll never see again. Or perhaps she's not quite right in the head and does this on every train from every station.

Twenty kilometres later she's still there. What at first seemed eccentric now seems bizarre and bloody-minded. Now I *really* want to be able to see out of the window, and am working up to saying so when she sits down abruptly, pulls the scarf over her face and falls asleep, fertiliser bag clutched on her lap.

We all breathe a communal sigh of relief. But looking at the scarf blowing in and out with her breath, at the safety pin protecting her money and identity, she appears fascinating and mysterious. There are few obvious symptoms of war in Zagreb; the only scars are the frowns of the young, the men who limp, the elderly with hungry eyes and mouths. Is this strange woman a casualty of war, of trauma, or someone the medical world has failed? Or both, perhaps? Thinking back over the past days, it seems to me that Croatians are trapped in unbearable stasis. There can be no going back – everyone agrees on that much – and forward motion has been held back by war and ambition. Croatia is wedged on the sharp edge of past and future, with Zagreb the focus of that conflict, and I'm only surprised not to have seen more trauma, more distress. But the Croats are proud people. 'Don't be fooled by appearances,' the director of the British Council in Zagreb had told me when we'd met. 'A Croat would rather starve than appear in public badly dressed . . . and these days, many do.'

The train chugs slowly westward, through Karlovac and across the Croatian karst. Here, only a few kilometres from the border with Slovenia, the land is very like Dolenjska, with kilometres of goldenrod lining the track, and beyond them, dense forest and emerald flashes from the Kupa River. But it feels different from Slovenia. There's an air of despondency; the patches of arable land are under-used, and many lie empty. The barns and houses are rarely hung with flowers, and the maize and pumpkins seem thin on the ground, as if there aren't enough people to care for them, or perhaps they've forgotten how.

As we descend the last few, thirsty kilometres through the Kvarner region towards the sea, I gaze hopefully at the city that spreads along the curve of coastline. Far below, high-rise blocks of flats and offices crowd the strip of land between hills and sea. There are docks, cranes and large container ships; and little ships that ferry passengers up and down the coast from here to Zadar, to Split and to Dubrovnik. The horizon is filled with islands of another world, an altogether different Croatia, if I remember rightly. And I do remember. I recognise and remember this place, and the feeling's good.

As we pull into the station, the quiet man beside me asks the two young women with whom I've been chatting if I have somewhere to stay.

'Yes,' I say, 'I don't think it's far.'

'He says his wife is meeting him here, they'll take you to your lodging.' They smile apologetically. 'He doesn't speak English, as you see.'

I say there's no need, but the man is politely insistent and the young women advise me to go with him because he wants to be kind.

The man carries my bag until his wife and two small children appear at the station exit, at which he promptly drops it so that he can seize and kiss them. He introduces me, explaining that I'm to be dropped off.

His wife, an attractive young woman, seems to enjoy her husband's eccentricity and we chat in bad German as she drives uphill, away from the sea.

'Is this the right place?' she asks, as we stop outside a block of thirties flats overlooking the city. I glance up from the pavement and see a large, blonde woman standing on a balcony, waving down. I check the address in my hand. 'This is it.'

High above us, the woman is still waving. As the car draws away, taking the kind strangers with it, I look down again on the crowded, crescent moon of Rijeka. The air is unexpectedly soft and warm. Mediterranean air. Holiday air. As I close my eyes and breathe in change, a set of keys crashes onto the pavement at my feet.

6 Rijeka to Rab

FRAU ERCEVEG, a big, blowsy woman with a blonde beehive and tight sixties dress, seems to prefer prisoners to guests. Escape attempts are thwarted with a breakfast of *rakija* and home-made elderflower cordial, designed to loosen the tongue. But without a language in common, the extent of our intercourse is doomed to limitation. Or so I imagine.

As she swallows her blood-pressure pills with strong black coffee chased with *rakija*, Frau Georgia, as she calls herself, lures me into a Croatian–German conversation way beyond my linguistic capacity. But oddly enough, I think we understand each other very well. My first impression, that she would look well in uniform, is not misplaced; her loudly expressed politics are considerably to the right of Tudjman, whom she's evidently torn between supporting for his anti-everyone stance, and condemning for being too soft. She seems surprised when I don't fall into line.

'The Serbs were the aggressors,' she says, 'but we're supposed to live with them now! It all started under Tito . . . Serbs grasping power. Then we have Milošević and all the Croat professionals, the doctors and scientists, begin to leave this country because they are shoved aside by Serbs.'

'Are they really about religion, these differences?' I ask. 'You speak the same language, you have the same . . .' Unfortunately, *'Genetisch'* is the only word I can think of in German.

'No, no, no!' A forefinger wags up and down at me. 'We are

not the same, not at all. We are different people, completely, completely different. We have the same language as those Moslems . . . but language is nothing. *They* are all *mujaheddin*, wanting to spread Mohammed into Croatia again, into Europe.'

I point out that this isn't quite the picture most Europeans have of the war with Bosnia.

'*This* is Europe!' she says, stabbing a long-nailed finger at the table. 'Croatia is the West, it is not the Balkans. We are not like those people, those countries.'

'Do you think Croatia has a European *outlook*?' I ask as best I can.

This is ignored, due perhaps to linguistic incomprehension. 'We have a European culture, European history!' Her voice rises and arms wave; I can see why she has high blood pressure. Between struggling to listen and struggling to respond, I can feel my own starting to rise, and edge towards escape.

The quickest way into town is down several flights of stone steps, through stands of pine, past modern flats, nursery schools and tiny two-stool bars. At the top of one flight I sit and admire the view of sea and shipyards. Replaying our conversation, I realise that Madame Erceveg is the only person I've met in Croatia who hasn't made a complaint against circumstances. Her very real anxiety is all directed outward, away from herself, from the government, from her country. She doesn't seem well-off, though she says she has children and grandchildren who are 'good' to her. With a stranger's naïvete, I wonder if anger and disappointment can truly bring greater comfort than food and fuel. Perhaps that's the sacrifice nationalism demands, that individual need becomes inexpressible.

'Croatia is the West . . .' Here in Rijeka at least, it feels like it. Sitting on pine needles, looking across the harbour to the islands in the <u>Kvarner Gulf</u> and beyond to invisible Italy, I wonder what 'the West' means. Europe, the West, Western Europe. The concept seems as powerful here as 'Serb aggression' or 'the Croat nation', and brings to mind a comment, one of those passing remarks overheard on radio or TV, about the nature of Europe.

'Europe,' the speaker said, 'is only in part a geographical phenomenon. The essence of Europe is the Judaeo-Christian tradition, and more significantly is the experience of a Renaissance, a Reformation and Counter-Reformation. Without these historical–cultural dimensions, a country cannot consider itself European.'

By these criteria, Canada and Israel are European, Russia and Turkey are not. Croatia, divided and fought over for many hundreds of years, is, as Ivo Korošić told me, in the process of deciding which of its different cultural traditions is dominant. Madame Erceveg's head may be in Europe, but her heart and voice seem firmly elsewhere.

Rijeka has relatively few tourists. Croatia's largest port and the main city of the Kvarner region, it's a working city, a transport hub, a place people pass through en route to somewhere else. But it's also an elegant city of squares and fountains, of medieval and Baroque churches, a cemetery to rival Highgate or Père Lachaise – albeit on a smaller scale. In Hrvatske Republike Trg, the girls and boys wear loose pants and skimpy tops; their pierced lips and eyebrows twinkle in the sun. The ambience is much trendier than Zagreb, the influence of nearby Italy and Rijeka's Italian community clearly visible.

Rijeka's Old Town stands on the site of Roman Tarsatica, and there's been a city and an Italian influence here since ancient times. Italy seized Rijeka in 1918 and the city passed in and out of Italian control until liberation by the Partisans in 1942, when it became part of Communist Yugoslavia. Although the buildings in the big squares and wide streets are predominantly Austro-Hungarian, there's an Italian atmosphere of pavement cafés, ice cream and fashion.

Sitting under a bright café awning, watching the world go by, I notice some of the more punchy-looking youngsters being cornered by police and informally questioned. A man several tables away is either very ill or very drunk, or both. He swears and coughs, sweat running down the sides of his face. Each intake of breath sounds like a generator starting up. When a car across the square backfires, he almost throws himself out of his seat. I jump too, but not as high or as fast as the locals, some of whom press themselves against the walls.

'You might not notice it, just passing through, but there are severely traumatised people in this city,' Ken Davies, an American chiropractor, tells me as he thumps my spine back into line. A big man, with long, greying hair, Ken has a manner that says my bones are safe in his hands. In moments he has treated the lumbar twist I gained from lifting my bag onto a luggage rack the day before. I move to get up.

'Lie down, we haven't started yet,' he says, and glad of an English-speaker on the table, he talks and cracks joints with equal gusto.

'I was invited here a while ago . . . promised all sorts of things. Nothing has turned out as I expected . . . or was led to believe. But it's hard to complain, you know, when you see all the suffering around you.' He rolls my neck between his hands then quickly jerks my head with an almighty snapping sound. 'What looks to us like political grumbling and grouching is actually a front for much deeper issues. As I said, these are traumatised people with a lot of personal problems that go unacknowledged because there are no facilities for help within the culture.' He sits me up, and just as I think it's all over, a pair of large, warm hands begin to probe my face from behind.

'Sometimes I go to the outlying villages to do work there. I was appalled when I discovered that people are still being killed and maimed by mines. Pets and domestic animals are blown up every week. How can anyone relax living in the middle of that? Your jaw isn't right . . . let's fix that shall we?' and with a sudden jerk of the wrist he adjusts my face.

'However difficult it is here for me, I can always leave,' he says, pulling on a rubber glove. 'How can Serbs and Croats get on with each other with all that's still going on? It's not even about the past . . . How can you be friendly with someone when your house is cold and you know theirs is warm because they have your heater?'

Blinking away tears of shock, I stare open-mouthed at the rubber glove – which is a mistake, because a large finger suddenly probes the inside hinge of my jaw with agonising effect. Too stunned to bite, I bellow loudly. Torment over, Ken laughs, rips off the glove and gives my limp form a big bear hug, then proceeds to his next patient.

Leaving the building I look at my watch. The whole experience lasted less than twenty-five minutes.

The walk to the nearby Jadrolinija Line office takes me past shop windows filled with lingerie and expensive perfumes. The prices are close to those in London or Paris, and I wonder who buys these things and how; then I remember the grey economy. Most Croatian women under sixty look as if they spend hours on make-up and dress, and many are wonderfully fragrant. Croatian men are often fragrant too, though not quite the same way.

At Jadrolinija I ask for a timetable for the offshore ferries and am given an incomprehensible leaflet.

'Can you tell me how often the boat for Split and Dubrovnik calls at Rab?' I ask. 'I'm going to Rab this afternoon and I need to know when the next southbound boat will leave from there.'

The young woman behind the desk wears so much lipstick her mouth seems unable to move under the weight. I repeat the question, though the problem seems deeper than mere language.

'Thursday,' she mumbles. 'Thursdays.'

'So the boat only calls at Rab once a week?'

'Tuesday, the boat leaves Tuesdays.'

I show the pass given to me by the promotion office in Zagreb. She holds it between thumb and forefinger, almost sniffing at it, before handing it back, saying: 'There are many buses from Rab, it's easy to get a bus.'

As I walk away, I try to remember whether it was this difficult in 1978. My memory is of plain sailing. I want to travel south by boat for no other reason than that's how I did it last time. So many other things have changed here in twenty years, it seems a good idea to try and do at least one thing that hasn't changed at all.

In 1978 I travelled the length of Croatia's coast from Rijeka to Dubrovnik, stopping at all the coastal cities and many of the islands. It was September and warm; I slept on deck with other young travellers from around the world. I'd never seen water so green, so clean and so perfectly transparent. Occasional dolphins swam alongside, and many metres below the surface, shoals of silver-backed fish danced and twined in sea that looked fresh enough to drink. After the grey North Sea and cold Atlantic, the Adriatic seemed miraculous, the ferry boat a charmed vessel.

Today, sitting on the upper deck of the *Liburnia*, I realise that this is very likely the same boat. I imagine I can see the place on the deck where I slept, and wonder why certain memories should be so much clearer than others on this journey. Perhaps it's because in that past, boats and sun and sea were rare and left an indelible memory of happiness. As we swing out of the harbour in a wash of green and white I look back at Rijeka, a city of two hundred thousand people, remembering how vast it once seemed. Twenty-one years later, it's small.

With the mainland still in sight we enter the straits between the islands of Krk and Cres. I buy a coffee and ask an elderly woman peeling plums if I can sit at her table. Her grey hair is pulled back severely from her tanned, deeply lined face. She must have been very handsome in her youth, and now has the air of a woman who prefers the company of women. After a few minutes she tells me her name is Ana and that she's a Slovene from Ljubljana.

'I've made this journey every year for many years,' she says, offering me a plum. 'I stay with my friend in her caravan on Hvar island. Usually we travel together, but this year my brother visited from Pasadena and so I'm late.'

'Did you enjoy your brother's visit?' I ask.

'Oh yes. He came with his wife and son. My nephew's thirty years old and a fireman in Pasadena. It's strange, he looks like my brother but he's so different. He speaks no Slovenian, only Californian.'

I ask how she thinks things have changed in twenty years.

'It's much better in Slovenia now. Before, things were organised from Belgrade and now they're not. But in every situation there's good and bad.' She pats the tartan hold-all that seems bursting with fruit and vegetables. 'I've been married twice you know, but men are no good. The first I divorced, the second I am separated from. Failure is just life, just normal,' she says with a sigh. 'When you reach my age – I'm sixty-nine – everything becomes a failure, even your body is a failure. Last week I had nine teeth removed,' she opens her mouth to show red and empty gums.

She looks older than sixty-nine, more worn, more tired.

'That's awful,' I say. 'Why so many at once?'

'They just crumbled away in preparation for the next world.' She shakes her head. 'To be young is to be happy . . . there is happiness only where there are young people.'

'Surely that's not always true.'

'Perhaps not,' she says. 'But if you aren't happy when you are young, with age it gets worse.'

'Were you happy when you were young?'

'Oh yes, I had a wonderful time. The only bad thing was the war. I was nine years old in 1939, but I had three older brothers. The youngest was seventeen. One day he went to school and never came back. The Fascists murdered all the children in his class. We never found his body. I used to think he was still alive . . .'

She pauses, momentarily lost in that distant, but still vivid past.

'You said it was a wonderful time too.'

'Oh yes, because I had many pen friends all over the world. My mother worked in America when she was young and spoke very good English. Then she returned to Yugoslavia and had children. As we grew up she encouraged us to learn English and be international. She knew many people in America, so we had introductions to many pen friends. Are you visiting a pen friend here?'

'No, I don't have any pen friends.'

She looks at me compassionately. 'I went to America myself in 1955,' she says, 'after I finished university. I went from Split to New York on a cargo ship carrying marble.'

'That must have been amazing, all that way on a cargo boat.'

'It was very exciting. I remember when we crossed the Straits of Messina, the sailors on our boat said we should write our last letters home. They told us to write a postcard and put it in a sealed bottle with a cigarette, then they took the bottles and threw them into the sea in one big bag. I thought it was a joke, so I only wrote the date and "Dear Mum and Dad, I'm sure you won't receive this." ' She smiles, remembering. 'Later my parents told me it arrived three days after it went into the sea.'

'How?'

'Local fisherman picked up the bottles, and the cigarette was payment for the stamp they would stick on the card . . . that's how things were done in the Straits back then. When I got to America I stayed one night in Manhattan. It was unlike anything

I ever imagined: so many people, black and white and all colours, and such tall buildings, and the dirt. Then I went to Boston, to my uncle, and to my pen friend in Kentucky. I thought of staying.'

'Why didn't you?'

'I got the results of my university exams. I'd studied Economics and I did very well so my parents wanted me to come back and make a career.'

'Do you ever wish you'd stayed?'

She shakes her head. 'No. I liked America, but it's better to stay in the country where you were born.' She looks towards the sea, invisible now in the darkness. Overhead, the stars are coming out.

'My brother will be almost home in California by now.'

'Were you sad when he left?'

She thinks about this for a moment. 'No. But I was glad to see him because he's older than me. Maybe we won't meet again.' She stares beyond the lights of the boat, then grins wickedly. 'I've already made my will. Everything is left to my second brother's son. I have nothing, only my pension, my garden and my bed. I'm not divorced you see, only separated from my second husband, but he'll have nothing from me, nothing at all.'

Ahead, the lights of Rab town shine brightly in the clear night air. The three-hour journey has passed in moments thanks to Ana. As I say goodbye, she presses a bag of purple plums into my hand.

'From my garden,' she says, 'in Ljubljana.'

Walking down the gangway in a warm Adriatic breeze, I notice the small crowd on the dock and someone standing apart; a short, bearded man who looks more like a teddy bear the closer I get. As I reach the dock he smiles and walks forward.

'Hello,' the voice is sweet and quiet. 'I am Mladen Travaš from Rab-Tourist, the Rijeka office told me you were coming.'

Mladen takes me to a faceless hotel overlooking the town marina, where I spend two dreary days. The stomach virus has worsened, perhaps due to a surfeit of plums, and I lie up, read Raymond Chandler, and listen to the wind and the German tourists below. When it seems safe to venture out, I wander through the town.

Rab's tourist industry was almost a hundred years old when I visited in 1978, and the islanders were already blasé about foreigners. Like everyone else, I ate ice cream in the square beside the Prince's Palace and walked up through narrow streets to the Venetian churches and ramparts. I met a blond boy with glasses, a student home on Rab for the holidays. We sat on the wall overlooking the sea and talked. He seemed happy, healthy and clever. I wondered how that could be if everything I'd heard about Communism were true. I couldn't see an Iron Curtain and Rab didn't feel like Communism – but then how would I have known?

Italy was what I imagined when I looked at Rab in 1978, though I'd never been there. Closer to Ancona than to Zagreb and almost as close to Venice, Rab's similarity to Italy was more than coincidental. The Croat-Hungarian kings sold the island to Venice in 1409, along with much of Dalmatia. For almost four hundred years, the Italian élite and Croat commoners jostled for space on this small piece of land. The local oil, salt and fish were bought for a song and sold at a premium in Venice. The beautiful churches and decorative stonework are testaments to Italian Renaissance culture, but they were paid for by the virtual slave labour of the island's Slav population.

The buildings look just as I remember them, and the many campaniles are still elegant. The municipal *loggia* and the paved streets retain their shady timelessness, though peering through cracked doors and shutters I notice that many of the oldest houses are derelict inside and filled with rubbish. I rediscover the wonderful carved balcony of the Prince's Palace and the wall overlooking the sea where I sat with the blond student. But somehow none of it's the same, and I feel a vague sense of disappointment.

It's late in the season and there are relatively few foreigners. The T-shirts, key-rings, postcards and other tat on offer in the many shops lining the narrow streets look almost as tired as the shopkeepers. It's the dilemma of tourist resorts around the world, that conflict of needing visitors' money but not wanting the visitors. It's possible that the run-down feel reflects an absence of foreigners, a result of the war and the continuing conflict in Kosovo.

I stop for coffee on Sveti Kristofor Trg. The bartender tells me he's studying to be an engineer in Split, and asks if I'm German.

I shake my head.

'Good,' he says. 'There are too many Germans here.'

I smile, and wonder what he says about the British.

'I watch. Every day, round and round they go. This church, this stone, as if it's a duty to see everything.' He drinks sparkling water, setting the glass down with a smack on the counter.

'Is it bad that foreigners admire your culture?'

'Of course not, where would Rab be without foreigners? It's the Germans, there are so many of them. There's been so many of them for so many years now that Rab people forget that we are not the same. Many try to copy Germans.'

'Imitate German ways?'

'Yes. Old people too, not just young people like me. They see a car, boat, money, and they want these things. It's natural, but they can't have them. So they become disappointed, then angry. But what my friends don't understand is that German people come here to escape from their country for a while.' He shrugs and finishes his water. 'If Rab becomes like Germany then Germans won't come here.'

'What about the British?'

He grins. 'There are not so many of you – and you have less money.'

By the third day of diarrhoea and continuous heavy breeze, it's time for peace and quiet. I'm rescued by Mladen Travaš's wife, Marina, who drives me through semi-urban sprawl to the family home at Barbat, the island's most southerly beach area. Rab reminds me, oddly, of Eire because there, like here, new, characterless houses are built beside the old, which are left to slowly decay. This has always seemed a gross act of ingratitude, a poor repayment for years of shelter, but the new red roofs and white walls of Rab make the place look prosperous enough.

'All these houses were built before the war,' Marina says. 'There was money then. Now there are many problems and people can't pay their debts.'

Barbat is one of the more recent housing explosions on Rab's west coast, which seems to have become a long stretch of identical private jetties and homogenised houses with the word *'Zimmer'* outside. The Travaš home is at the pleasant far end of Barbat, a place where further construction would seem impossible. As we pull up outside the Travaš's modern three-storey guesthouse, a handsome boy appears, leading a toddler by the hand.

'These are two of my sons,' Marina says, lifting the infant into her arms. 'This little one is Neven.'

The older boy shakes my hand. 'I'm Tin,' he says, grinning and tossing a thick, blond ponytail. 'Would you like to go for a ride on my scooter?'

Before I can say yes, Marina says no.

Tin droops.

'He wants you to go because he's twelve years old and not allowed to drive on his own. Can you drive a scooter?'

I shake my head.

'But I drive very well,' Tin says, winking at me. 'I'll teach you!'

'OK,' Marina says resignedly. 'But be careful!'

Tin's right, he's a very good driver. There are not many twelve-year-old boys I'd feel happy to ride with, and fewer still who'd consider the cemetery a point of local interest.

Rab's dead are housed as well as the living. Huge black marble sarcophagi sit in neat rows, most with unflattering portraits of the occupant carved into the stone; some have a living spouse's name and date of birth, with a space waiting for the stonecutter's hand to mark the date of death. I remember the first time I saw this custom in a rural Alabama cemetery, where a friend's grandfather lay under a stone with his own and his living wife's name on it. It was bizarre looking at the grave of the woman you've just had lunch with, but my friend said his grandmother was comforted by knowing this was where she too would lie. I've often wondered since whether the British disregard this custom because the inevitability of death is something they prefer to ignore until the last moment . . . or perhaps an eccentric sanguinity allows them to believe they will somehow be spared, despite overwhelming evidence to the contrary.

'This is my great-grandmother's grave,' Tin says, crossing himself with genuine respect as we stand beside a big marble tomb. 'She died four years ago . . . I remember her.'

Nearby, concrete-lined vaults yawn at the sky and empty shelves wait to be filled. Black-clad crones, twisted with age and arthritis, change water in plastic pots and arrange fresh flowers. Tin leads me to the furthest end of the cemetery and a new grave, invisible under a hill of wreathes.

'He was a friend of my brother Iris,' Tin says. 'Many young people came to his funeral. Hundreds. Everyone brought a wreath, even though they cost a lot of money.'

'How did he die?'

'He was diving without oxygen, but he had a marker in the water. A boat drove over him, they didn't see the marker.'

'Who drove over him?'

'Tourists. Foreigners.' He hesitates. 'Some people say it wasn't an accident. The police came, but no-one was arrested.'

'Do you think someone would do that on purpose?'

'Who knows, maybe they were psychopaths.' He shrugs, but his tone isn't casual.

A single large candle burns in front of the grave, its light almost invisible in the bright sunshine. Two dozen multi-coloured fish candles have burnt down around the grave and a semi-circle of grease darkens the gravel. Observing the trappings of death, Tin's youthful face is momentarily careworn; under that pretty blond hair is a mind that's already learnt to look on life as a very serious business.

'You drive back,' he says as we walk away.

'I don't know how.'

His quick grin returns. 'I'll show you – it's easy!'

But it's not easy and after a few near crashes, he politely suggests that we change places.

Later, we sit on the jetty where Mladen's boat is moored, and Tin tells me he'd like to be a pilot, but not in the airforce; he doesn't like the military.

Suddenly he takes a running jump into the sea and comes up laughing and spluttering. 'Do you know the greatest soldiers who ever lived?' he shouts up from the water.

'There are lots – which ones do you think are the greatest?'

'At school they told us that Alexander the Great, Carlos Magnus and Napoleon are the greatest generals who ever lived.'

'What about Julius Caesar?' I ask as he clambers out and throws back his long wet hair.

'He wasn't so great as the others because he only reconquered bits already conquered.' He pauses, frowning. 'I love playing war games and I've got lots of plastic soldiers but I can't imagine being a soldier myself, having to kill someone.'

'That's good isn't it?'

'Yes, but then *I* might be killed and if I died I'd like to remember this life in my next one.'

'Next one?'

'You know, when you're born again. They say you don't remember what you did before, and that's no fun. I want to remember *everything*!'

Over the next few days I relax on a beach near the Travaš's house. At three o'clock sharp each afternoon a small number of elderly, naked Germans arrive wearing broad-brimmed hats and not a lot else. Glad of sunglasses, my swimsuit and stiff-upper lip stay firmly in place. When I mention the nudists to Mladen he laughs.

'The British are to blame. The first naked bathing in Croatia was started by your Duke of Windsor and his Mrs Simpson.'

I never discover whether this is fact or tourist myth, but it's entertaining to imagine passing Croatian fishermen gazing in horror at the bare bones of the woman who believed one could never be too thin. Clearly, the Duke's upper lip was just as stiff as it needed to be.

Three generations of Travaš's live here in Barbat. There are olives, grapes, lemons, beans and peppers in their garden, and somewhere under or behind the house, Mladen's father has his workshop and distillery. All the guests are German-speaking; some of them have visited Rab every year since 1964, in war and peace. To make me more comfortable some of them talk in English, even among themselves, and offer helpful suggestions for the cure of stomach viruses. In the end the cure, like many discoveries, is accidental. One evening Mladen's father offers me a large glass of his home-made *rakija*. The next day I drink two more. The virus disappears. The moral of this appears to be that to stay healthy in the Balkans, strong alcohol is a daily requirement. And all the while I'd been thinking people drank so much because they liked it.

Luckily for me, Mladen's wife Marina is on leave from her job as a senior nurse at the island's mental hospital. She is a great companion, who knows the island's moods and variations, and shows me a Rab much larger and more diverse than I'd remembered. We start our tour at Mišnjak, the island's barren south-east point. Only a few dry-stone walls mark ownership of the withered, brown land.

'This is where local ferries come from the mainland,' she says. 'When visitors arrive here at Mišnjak they think Rab's a dead island, or like Mars. You can tell they're afraid it will all look like this.'

Most of the eastern side of Rab is a bare, dry landscape, broken only by the green hand of the Lopar Peninsula reaching into the Rapski Channel. As we drive north and west, I see another Rab in the lush, forested regions of Supertarska and Kalifront. At the island's heart, tree-covered hills encircle fields of maize and pumpkins, groves of olives and herds of goats. There's not much of anything, however; the fields are small and couldn't support more than a few families. Without the ferry bringing food from the mainland, Marina tells me, Rab couldn't survive.

We pass the hospital where Marina works. It's a big place, set among pine trees in a large garden, behind a high wire fence. I wonder aloud that there are so many mentally ill people on Rab.

'We have patients from all of west Croatia, not just here,' Marina laughs.

A dozen or so men wearing striped pyjamas wander through the garden. Some of them wave at passing cars or shamble around the trees. Others press their faces against the wire.

'They look mad, don't they,' she says, 'but I tell you, there are more really mad people out there,' she gestures at the world, 'than in that hospital.'

The stripes, the pyjamas . . . for an instant it's Belsen and Bedlam. But as we drive on I think of the mentally ill living cold and hungry on the streets of Britain and other 'developed' countries, and the pine-tree garden seems less horrific.

People wave a lot here; at trains and cars, from boats and buses. In one village, Marina recognises someone waving and she stops and gets out of the car. As she chats, I watch a large man barbecuing a mountain of flesh for a group of men playing a kind of *boules* in sand beside the beach. Seeing me, he holds out a huge meat sandwich and laughs when I shake my head politely. In a nearby pool, several others play water polo.

It's Sunday and there are only men here. As we drive on I ask Marina where the women are, what they're doing.

'With their families,' she says, 'visiting friends, sisters, mothers. Cooking. Eating.'

'But do they play? Like the men . . . games, you know?'

She looks at me sideways. 'Games? When have we time for games? Children play. Men play. Women work.'

Near the village of Kampor, we pass a cluster of tall and elegant trees.

'There was a camp there during World War II,' Marina says. 'A big one. Would you like to look?'

Jadran Rusjan told me about this place on our drive to Lipica, about the Germans and their Ustaše allies who brought Jews, Slovenes, Croat intellectuals and anyone who opposed them here to Kampor. We park in a lane beside two cars with elderly occupants, and enter the empty, silent garden.

Among the trees, a slender monument stands surrounded by row on row of small metal plaques, each with a name or number. Sun filters down through the leaves, reflecting on lines of bricks that Marina says represent how the camp was laid out. Sheltered from the elements by a curving concrete roof, a brightly coloured mosaic sets out the horrors of war like a storyboard. On one level are skeletal men, dead animals, gallows and ruined houses. Below, twin boys feed from a she-wolf amid the *fasces,* the trappings of Fascism, representing Italy's more recent role on this island.

Marina's son Neven toddles off to stare up at the tall, stone monument, watched by the group of elderly men and women who followed us into the monument from the lane. For a few moments they look at the lone child among the name plaques, before disappearing into the depths of the garden, each with a bunch of fresh flowers. Back at the car I notice the vehicles parked beside us have Slovenian number plates.

As we drive home, Neven dozes in his baseball cap and large white sunglasses. He's two years old and has just stopped breast-feeding. Witty, clever and childlike all at once, he's not above wrestling foreign children twice his size into creating a scene, then pirating food or wine when no-one's looking.

'Naughty Neven!' I say with mock severity each evening at dinner, assuming he speaks not a word of English.

'No naughty Neven!' he replies, a steely glint in his eyes.

'What does your eldest son do?' I ask Marina as we drive past a group of young men walking along the beach, arms around each other's shoulders.

'He's at college in Istria, a good college. He wants to be a priest.'

'A priest?' I must sound surprised.

She shrugs. 'It's what he wants. He's a good boy, very clever.' She points to the glove compartment and I pull out a small photo album. Inside is a picture of Marina with all her sons. Iris, a good-looking young man with his father's stocky build and his mother's slender features, cuddles the baby Neven. Seventeen. The same age as Ana's school-boy brother when the Ustaše killed him and his classmates.

'Do you mind if I ask what Mladen did during the war, Marina?'

She shakes her head. 'I don't mind, but he never talks about it. The army took the men away from Rab and up into the mountains inland from Zadar. For months and months I heard nothing. I thought he must be dead.'

'Did he know anything about fighting?' I try to imagine the short, bearded man with the soft voice wielding a gun.

'When it's like that you *have* to know. There's no choice, is there?'

Near Suha Punta, we pass a group of crones all wearing the standard widow's black. I tell Marina, a slender, modern woman, that I've always found the wearing of black in hot countries very odd. Like a badge . . . I sweat, therefore I suffer.

She snorts politely. 'Oh yes, it's for suffering. The suffer-ing of everyone else around them! It's our culture . . . a woman gets to a certain age, relatives die, her husband dies, and suddenly everything changes. Before, she's OK, normal –

then pouf! She's eaten up inside, twisted. Now her job is to make everyone else suffer.'

That evening as I watch the Cartoon Network with Tin and Neven, Mladen suggests something interesting to do on Wednesday. This is odd, as he knows I intend to get the boat to Split next day. When I ask what time the boat leaves, everyone looks uncomfortable. There is no boat; the Jadrolinija ferry leaves only on Thursdays. I'm not surprised. 'Tuesday', 'Thursday' – what are these but sounds in the ether to the woman with immobile lips in Jadrolinija's Rijeka office.

'Stay,' Mladen says. 'What difference is two days?'

'I have to be in Sarajevo quite soon to meet a friend and I was hoping to get to Split and Dubrovnik before going to Bosnia.'

'Then you must take the bus.'

How did I guess it would come to this? But, of course, even the bus isn't straightforward: on Tuesday it only goes north from Rab to Rijeka. For the south and Split, I must go back up the coast to Senj then down again, and wait and change, and maybe change again.

The next day Marina and Neven come to see me off from Mladen's office, which is also the bus stop. Mladen's mother has given me fruit from the garden. We all wave to each other and I feel the familiar sadness that appears, ghost-like, at partings from people whose company you've enjoyed and whom you're unlikely to see again.

7   Split

On the first day of May in the year 305 AD
Diocletian abdicated, put down his crown after all
those years of ruling in exchange for the deep blue
of the sea, for the light breeze that blows from the
sea and the scent of the broom flower in bloom.

Vedran Matošič

The driver of the bus from Senj to Split wears dark shades and a brutal haircut; a toothpick hangs from his lips. The first time he overtakes
a petrol tanker on an uphill bend I yell, 'Fuck!' involuntarily as we
miss a truck heading straight at us by millimetres. My fellow passengers pay no more attention to the expletive than they do to the driving.

On this bus full of uniformed men and old women, the feeling of
isolation is not imaginary. I'm studiously ignored, apart from the
couple of crones who smugly inform the ticket collector that I've yet
to pay my fare. The soldiers at the back of the bus are mainly hard-
looking men in their thirties and forties, and I have the strange feeling of travelling with people who may, in the recent past, have done
'bad' things, 'Un-European' things. The driver's lack of fear borders
on the psychotic; I can see his face reflected in the rear-view mirror,
his eyes straining ahead, anticipating the ultimate hit, that vehicle
coming the other way. After a few more near misses it seems best to
look out of the window and accept what can't be changed.

Rocky cliffs edge the left side of the road; the right borders the sea, and when the road drops to within a few metres of the shoreline, every rounded stone on its bed is visible. Across the water the spine of Pag island lifts out of the waves like a whale's back, paralleling for a time the undulating coast road. With its dry scrub and occasional cypresses, this road could be almost anywhere from the Aegean to the Atlantic, though few places can boast water this limpid and emerald-green. Cesarica, Islam-Latinski; lit by the headlights of passing vehicles, the names of towns and villages flash past revealing Dalmatia's history stamped on its landscape like a map of the past. With few private cars on the road, most of the traffic is buses, trucks and vans. Cars remain beyond most people's reach.

The coastal city of Zadar is less than a hundred and fifty kilometres south of Rab, but by 6 p.m., seven hours after leaving the island, Zadar is still ahead. The conductor turns on the radio for the *futbal* – NK Croatia is playing Manchester United. There are furtive glances in my direction, and though I have little interest in soccer I find myself hoping that United doesn't let the side down. The women passengers don't appear to notice the invasion of cheers and manic commentary. The things that count in this country right now are overtly masculine: the army, the police, football. Regardless of age or professional position, many Croatian women behave towards men with a combination of the maternal and provocative which makes me feel uncomfortable. But the men seem to like it.

We reach Zadar at seven and Šibenik by ten. Illuminated with blue light, Šibenik's Sv. Ana fortress dwarfs everything, its curving walls cold and stark against the night. With its Italianate squares, churches and campaniles, the city is smaller and more attractive than I remember. I glimpse walled gardens and what looks like a marble boulevard along the seafront. This place has its share of unaesthetic buildings but these are softened by trees and an extravagance of ivy-covered balconies and flower-decked shrines. Like most places in this part of the world, Šibenik in the late evening is eerily empty of people.

One of the advantages of being in a country where a great many people smoke is that buses have frequent nicotine stops.

After more than eight hours together on the bus, the remaining passengers have loosened up a bit. As we stretch our legs in Šibenik's almost empty bus station, a few nod at me and one or two men ask me where I'm going. When the electricity fails, plunging us into darkness, even the soldiers grin sheepishly. I don't know whether to be pleased or sorry that United only managed a draw with NK Croatia.

It's after midnight when I finally reach the Hotel Bellevue in Split and fall into a large uncomfortable bed. Next morning I realise exactly where I am. Twenty years ago I walked through Republike Trg, past the elegant arches of the colonnaded square and the lively shops, and noticing the Bellevue, thought how great it would be to stay there rather than the grubby room near the bus station that was all I could afford. Now the shops are mostly closed and graffiti covers their shutters. The Bellevue still nestles among the colonnades, a reminder of Split's better days.

From my hotel window I look over the square to a municipal fountain and the harbour beyond. So what if the sink is cracked, the bath enamel rotted away and the thin mattress several inches too small for the bed – the price and the location are perfect. But within hours of waking on my first morning in Diocletian's city, I learn that few things are what they seem.

'This hotel is owned by the government and we have a saying here in Croatia . . . anything owned by a government is bad, anything owned by the government of Croatia is twice as bad.'

Ivan Blažević, white-haired and in his late fifties, works at the Bellevue, or at least appears to. What he actually does is unclear, though his duties seem to involve gossiping and playing cards with other members of staff. Glad of an opportunity to escape this routine, he decides to introduce me to the Director of Promotion for Split. Having nothing else to do, I go along. Ivan is clearly a fount of information, hinting darkly at hotel secrets and eager to air a stock of political saws and grievances against all governments, from Croatia to Australia.

'We have a joke here that every country has a mafia, but here in Croatia the mafia has the country.' He barely pauses as we stride along under a direct sun. 'Tudjman is a criminal, of course. Things were much better under Tito, *much* better. Tito was a great man and even *he* didn't surround himself with as many military and police as Tudjman does. Tudjman behaves like a pharaoh! We have four and a half million people in this country and a police force of thirty thousand; Germany has a population of eighty million and a police force of only sixty thousand.'

Unable, from lack of information, to agree or dispute, I say nothing. We walk from one side of the city centre to the other along the seafront and I listen in silence to the stream of Ivan's consciousness. On a concrete 'beach' the young and beautiful of Split arrange themselves to best advantage. Now, at the end of summer, all are dark brown and sleek as otters.

Seizing a pause I ask, 'Where did you learn English?' Ivan's vocabulary is wider than most English-speaking people and there's a slight, unplaceable accent.

'I lived in Australia in the late fifties and early sixties,' he says, 'but I didn't like it there . . . too many rules and regulations. I was fined £10 for playing football on a piece of grass! I didn't know it was a *private* piece of grass. Ten pounds was a lot of money but it didn't stop with just a fine. Later, when I tried to get a job, I had no luck because I had a police record for trespass. I told the man who refused me the job that I didn't like Australia anyway, that I wanted to go back to Croatia. "How can you not like Australia?" he said. "Here you can wear a suit and tie. God knows what you'd be wearing back there – robes or something." I was pretty angry at that, let me tell you, so I looked him in the eye and said, "When my grandfather was wearing a suit and tie, your grandfather was wearing chains." '

Ivan has obviously told this story many times before, but his bitterness today is as bright and new as when the incident happened forty years ago.

We finally reach an office at the far end of the harbour, and I shake hands with a large, red-faced man whose stiff grey hair stands up around his head like a brush. His computer looks like it's never been turned on, and apart from a large pad covered in doodles, his desk is empty. As he and Ivan chat, the man never lifts his eyes from the pad, but continues to draw as if compelled. Slowly, my name appears on the paper surrounded by an ornate frame of leaves and flowers. I wonder what else he does all day in this empty office.

Abruptly, he gets to his feet and we all shake hands again.

'What was that all about?' I ask as we retrace our steps.

'He's the Director of Regional Promotion, not City. Anyway, he doesn't speak English, he's no good for you.'

I rather regret agreeing to traipse around the town and suggest giving up; but determined to present me somewhere, Ivan's like a bloodhound.

'No, no. Vrhovec is the man you want, he knows everything there is to know about Split. He's a big man, an academic. I've known him for years.'

It's always worrying when someone says, 'So-and-so is an academic.' It usually means the person is a know-all and a poseur.

After a lot of hand-shaking, Mr Vrhovec waves his arms and asks, 'You like this office?'

I nod. It's large, quiet and right in the centre of town.

'Bah!' He shakes his head at my lack of taste. 'It's too small! Much too small. I'm having a new office built, a beautiful office. It will cost a million dollars.'

Ivan's eyebrows raise.

Mr Vrhovec is a short, dark-skinned man with intensely blue eyes. His shirt is shocking pink, his greying moustache clipped and he smokes a cigarette through a long holder. He looks like a Mameluke sultan deciding how large his next palace will be.

For the next two hours Ivan and Vrhovec argue. It's a remarkable double-act. For every question I ask about Split or Croatia, the pair come up with a contradictory answer. I hold my breath and watch the 'friends' in action. While Vrhovec declaims reams of obscure, forgettable history, Ivan mutters about rotting food tins killing more soldiers than bullets, and about the lack of toilet paper in state hospitals.

Vrhovec is clearly quite affluent by Croatian standards, perhaps from a line of well-to-do professionals. Ivan is clever, well travelled, worldly – and poor. He's aggravated by Vrhovec, yet wants to appease him. Vrhovec, on the other hand, is putting on a show for the foreign woman and is torn between making light of his old friend Ivan and being drawn into an argument he may just lose. From time to time his eyes rest on one of the youths who drift in and out of the office, well-built lads in tight T-shirts whom he sends out for cigarettes and sweets.

Agreement is reached on a few points only.

'The Serbs have aggressed our country since the nineteenth century, since they tried to shake off the Turks in a general paranoia which they imagined gave them the right to treat Croatia and Slovenia like colonies.'

Ivan nods. 'That's true. I agree. And in 1991 the Serbs continued that. Any Croat who had money in Serbia, in what they thought were *Yugoslav* banks, lost everything. Many elderly people and businesses lost everything. Then they tried to carve up Croatia.'

Vrhovec also nods. 'They wanted access to the coast, always that, because they have none. But now . . .' he pauses, taking a long drag on the distant cigarette, 'now I wish them well, I really do. Just not here.'

'I don't,' Ivan growls. 'I don't wish them well anywhere.'

And they start arguing again. Beyond the open windows the day gets hotter. Faint scents from the fish market twine with the sea breeze which stirs the papers on the long table at which we sit. The sound of traffic seems faint and far away compared to the booming of the ships' horns as they enter and leave the harbour. I no longer ask questions; the conversation, conducted in English that verges on the theatrical, has a life of its own and I need only sit and listen.

'I'm bitter and disappointed with this government,' Vrhovec says, 'but optimistic at the same time.'

'It's easy to be optimistic when you don't have to go to hospitals that have no cotton wool, no medicines. How can you be optimistic about criminals?'

Vrhovec shakes his head and tuts gently. 'I don't like to hear you saying these things, my friend.'

'What things? You mean it's not criminal to make people work without paying them?' He turns to me suddenly. 'I will tell you why the things in the hotel are no good, why everything's old and broken. It's because there's no money. I haven't been paid for twenty months. No-one has been paid. The man behind the reception desk has a one-year-old child, a paraplegic. He can't afford treatment for this child. Religious organisations build new churches . . . every week a new church here, there. But do they help people who have nothing? Never!'

'How do people live then?' I ask. 'How do the staff live?'

Ivan looks shrewd and taps his nose. 'You've heard of the grey economy?'

I nod.

Vrhovec interrupts. 'We don't want the lady to think we are all criminals or complainers. We must have some pride.'

'Pride?' Ivan flushes with anger. 'I have pride in my country, I have pride in Croatia. Just don't ask me to have pride in the way my country is run, handing it over to the bloody Church and the mafia.'

'You aren't the only one to suffer for what you believe, Ivan,' Vrhovec interjects quickly, turning to me. 'During the Communist period, when I talked about democracy, people called me Ustaše. They said I was a Nazi, anti-Party. I lost my job, if you remember,' he turns to Ivan, 'and we were on the same side then, we believed the same things.'

Ivan has calmed down slightly, but he still chews his lower lip and wipes at his face with a large handkerchief.

'Even now,' Vrhovec says, 'every time I open a newspaper some journalist writes that I've been sacked and gives the name of my successor. I'm no more popular now than I was in Tito's time. I still say what I think.'

'You're a dreamer,' Ivan says, shaking his head, 'a dreamer, my friend.'

He repeats this as we leave the office and walk back to the hotel. 'That man is a dreamer, but he'll wake up one day.'

For the first time on this journey I've been shown how hard it is even for those on the same side of the political chasm to agree. But looking on, it seemed that class and money divided these men more surely than what they might call politics. As Ivan returns to his card-playing duties, I consider the lesson to be learnt for the rest of my journey. If friends can't agree, what is there for enemies?

Split reminds me of Rome, and not just because of its remarkable antiquities. Like Rome, Split has adapted and integrated over the centuries. Today it's a colourful, modern city that lives and breathes alongside and within its ancient architecture. But despite the many changes to the heart of the Old Town, the hand of Diocletian still hovers over the luxurious palace-fortress he built for his retirement home and tomb.

Born in AD 245 near the town of Salona, modern-day Solin, Gaius Aurelius Valerius Diocletianus was one of five soldiers from the Roman province of Dalmatia to rise through the legions and become emperor. A city of sixty thousand inhabitants, third-century Salona was known as 'Little Rome', and it was this proximity to the regional capital that made Spalatum (Split) such a desirable location when Diocletian chose the site of his new palace. When Salona was destroyed in the seventh century by Slav and Avar invaders, the Romano-Illyrian refugees fled to the remote coastal islands; some later returned to rebuild their lives in abandoned Spalatum. Similar Slav and Avar invasions forced population shifts all along the Croatian littoral; in the south, refugees from the Roman city of Epidaurum fled down the coast and founded the city of Ragusa, modern Dubrovnik.

The Brass Gate, one of the four entrances to Diocletian's city, is hidden among the café parasols and shops of the Obala, the wide, palm-shaded boulevard beside the harbour. Stepping from bright sunlight into the dark basement hall of the palace is a shock to the eyes, but I remember where I'm going and if I get confused there's always the official *Guide through Diocletian's Palace* to 'warn' me that I've 'started along the ROAD TO HISTORY'.

The scale of the hall is astonishing; the souvenir stalls, cafés and artists' displays are dwarfed by the thick columns supporting the barrel-vaulted Roman brickwork overhead. The fungus-green lighting creates an unintentionally mildewed look. From here, Diocletian could access his private study, his baths, his dining room and the *peristyle*, the palace's central square and ceremonial entrance to the imperial quarters and the Temple of Jupiter. The red granite columns that lined the *peristyle* in the emperor's day are still there, holding up nothing. The square itself was set slightly lower than the surrounding buildings, just low enough to make Diocletian seem larger than life when he faced the crowds from the raised platform of the *protiron*.

The emperor lived to be nearly seventy, not bad for a man of blood in a period of turmoil; unlike most of his power-hungry contemporaries, he had the foresight to make a planned retirement in preference to a sword in the back. His mausoleum, the largest of the palace's four temples, is now the Cathedral of Sv. Dujam; an appropriate irony for a ruthless persecutor of Christians. This morning, students and coffee-drinking tourists lounge at the base of columns, spread themselves across the steps to what was the emperor's mausoleum and straddle the black sphinx guarding it.

The palace must have been magnificent in its prime, filled with the flowers and music Diocletian is said to have enjoyed. Now it's all slightly depressing, with its closed-up buildings, piss-stained doorways and litter. The Italian couple walking in front of me kick the locked door to the Temple of Jupiter in frustration, and it occurs to me that a new office is not necessarily the best use of Mr Vrhovec's dollars.

Yet few places have built so harmoniously on the past as Split. Beyond the palace walls, Roman masonry was freely integrated in the construction of the medieval city. Many of the narrow streets are little more than passageways, every turn of a corner brings a fresh surprise: a Venetian square, a jewel-like Gothic palace, a Romanesque church. After Rome fell, Split was ruled by Byzantium but as that empire also declined, the city enjoyed a time of autonomy, during which many of its finest Romanesque structures were built. When Venice took control of southern Dalmatia in 1420, the citizens of Split faced the same cultural upheaval and social decline as those of Rab.

On the corner of an elegant Gothic square, a long line of people queue patiently outside a stationery shop. Inside, parents clamour to buy school books for their children, waving money at the harassed assistants. The previous evening the streets around the Bellevue had been lined with students selling textbooks of psychology, anatomy, advanced chemistry and veterinary science. Under a warm sky, the young people laughed and joked, having perhaps already learnt how to make the best of a bad situation. Since 1991, Croat dignity has helped Split conceal its relative poverty behind the wealth of its inheritance; but the social cracks are visible. On a wall beside the Bellevue's main entrance I notice the 'White Boy' graffiti that's common here, and wonder what it means in a country without black people.

Next morning I leave the hotel early and head for the nearby central fish market. It's already a warm day and the strong scent of fish leads me to an open space in front of the market hall. Under brightly coloured awnings men and women shout the prices and weights of crates of fish. There's no ice to keep the fish cold, and things sell fast. Stallholders smoke cigarettes and talk on mobile phones while dumping snapper, mackerel and flat fish into plastic bags. In the side streets around the market, elderly women sell bundles of herbs and bunches of grapes from worn baskets.

There's a different atmosphere in the market hall. The smell is different too, acrid and heavy. Serious business is done in dark corners where men stand around boxes of exotic-looking fish, bidding quietly and intently. One man displays slices of tuna as wide as a man's waist and red as beef steak. I watch his cleaver thud through what remains of the carcass, sending blood running along the gutter that crosses the floor between the stalls. On a white marble slab, freshwater mussels and large-shelled cockles spread a pool of thin red mud around them. Crabs and lobsters struggle in crates; one or two make a bid for freedom only to be recaptured, their legs waving hopelessly. Slapped down on a weighing scales, an octopus lies in an untidy heap of pink and grey tentacles. The smell becomes oppressive.

This is an Adriatic fish market, like hundreds of others the length of the Croatian, Italian and Slovenian coasts. But in the city's Obala Lazerata market, I find things unique to this region; like the organic lavender of Hvar island. With close to three thousand hours of sunshine a year, Hvar is a leading producer of organic lavender, rosemary and heather. Here in the Lazerata are stalls selling nothing but herbal products. There are bottles of pure oil, bags of flowers, lavender soap, and honey tasting of lavender and hot sun. The elderly, lavender-scented women who capture and sell these wonderful things knit placidly behind their wares.

I buy several bottles of oil as gifts for friends, and walking away still examining my purchases, bump into someone. Without thinking, I apologise in English and meet the cool stare of a large woman wearing many, many beads and a big straw hat.

'You are English?' she looks at me from over the top of her sunglasses.

'Yes. Sorry, I didn't see you.'

'Take your sunglasses off. Let me see your eyes.'

Wondering, I do as she says.

'Good. You have honest eyes.' She smiles. 'My name is Miriana, I'm a professor of English in Zagreb. Do you live in London?'

'I do. Have you been there?'

'I taught in London for seven years. I lived in Kensington and have a friend who lives in Ladbroke Grove. You know these places?'

'Of course. Ladbroke Grove is walking distance from my house.'

She laughs, a large, bracing sound, and says, 'The world is too small for people with a big heart.' Lowering her voice, she whispers theatrically, 'That's a Serbian proverb!'

We walk together into the sun-filled street. 'Split is beautiful, isn't it?'

'Very.'

'I was here during the war with Serbia. It was so sad what happened. It's hard for the West to understand, I know, but I saw that we are too intelligent to be a warlike people.'

She plays with her beads, eyes twinkling under the straw hat. 'Are you married?'

'Not at present.'

'I've never been married, I have no children . . . but I've had many lovers, many opportunities. As you get older, the opportunities get fewer.'

'I know,' I say.

'But you are young! I am sixty-four, but I never stop enjoying life. I am in love with a man in Zagreb, he doesn't know this yet . . . but he'll find out!'

We exchange addresses and part in the street. Watching her colourful figure moving away, I wish there was more time for the things that matter.

In an alleyway beyond the Golden Gate, the north entrance to the palace complex, I find a tiny English-language bookshop and leaf sentimentally through what must be the most expensive copies of Shakespeare and Dickens in the world, two or three times what they would cost at source. Evidently not intended for local customers, and beyond the purse of any sensible traveller, I wonder who buys them.

The shop is also an Internet centre, and after checking my email I chat to the young man who runs the place. He tells me his name is Hrvoje, and he doesn't seem at all concerned at the price of his books.

'But you can't sell many.'

'Sometimes we do, and if we don't . . .' he raises his shoulders.

Two of Hrvoje's friends arrive and the shop is crowded, so he locks the door. One of the newcomers, also called Hrvoje, has brought a bottle of beer which they all share, slowly. My offer to buy everyone a drink produces grins, and while the first Hrvoje and the friend called Sinisa download clips from an obscure European film onto a computer, the second Hrvoje helps me carry beers from a bar across the alley.

As the beer is handed round, the first Hrvoje says, 'We don't like all that Hollywood stuff, which is just as well, because we can't afford to go to the cinema much anyway.

'We've been friends for a while,' he says in answer to a question, 'and we sometimes work together for a voluntary organisation called KUU UZGON – it stands for Cultural Artistic Organisation. It's about making democracy through more communication.'

'This government is only successful because people are ignorant of things,' Sinisa adds, 'ignorant of what really happens in the world, of how the rest of Europe sees us.'

'That's what UZGON is – it also stands for detonic power. Do you know what that is?'

I shake my head.

'It's the opposite to the force of gravity, it's the force that pushes things upwards.'

'Like "detonate"?'

'Yeah . . . and that's what we try to do with our work, bring communication skills like computing and the Internet to young people so they can make decisions about their lives and the world, and use that to move upwards, away from where they are now.'

Although the two Hrvojes are twenty-five and twenty-six years old, and Sinisa twenty-seven, they all say they remember how things were under Tito.

'I was seven when Tito died,' Sinisa says with a gap-toothed grin. 'I remember it very well. I was at a football match with some friends but the game ended early because the news came that Tito had died. I remember there was a big silence all around the ground and then people just started to leave. So I went home and my father asked me why I was so early and I said, "Tito died so we all left." My father thought I was making it up, so he punched me in the head and shouted "Tito will never die!" '

They all laugh at the story and I think of the book Andrej Blatnik gave me in Ljubljana, a collection of short stories called *The Day Tito Died*. Sinisa's story brings home to me what the death of the man who guided their country for nearly forty years meant, and still means, for Former Yugoslavians. Tito's death marked the end of an era, and in different ways everyone seems to have known that. People aged less than two years old in 1980 claim to remember the shock of that day, and not just from hearsay. It's far more than a 'where were you and what were you doing when . . .' matter here.

'My father thought Tito was God,' Hrvoje says, and the others nod. 'I remember everything going very quiet, a big silence went over everything.'

'And what happened after?'

'It was a good time. I always had enough pocket money for ice creams, food, school books, clothes – for everything. And I went on holiday. Now I have two jobs and I haven't eaten in a restaurant for four years.'

'Everything is shit here,' Sinisa says. 'We all want to leave, all young people want to leave Croatia. In a few years time most of the young people here will have left.'

'There's a really big problem with drugs and alcohol,' the second Hrvoje says with a sigh. 'Because Split's a port, its easy for stuff to get in here from anywhere and from here it goes in all directions, even to remote islands. But it's not surprising: if people have nothing else to do, they do drugs. This is a small city but we have the world's second or maybe third-biggest injecting-drug problem. And because no-one can get clean needles there's a big

AIDS problem too, but the government hides this because of the Church and what the Church wants.'

'Alcoholism and Catholicism – that's what Croatia is about now,' Sinisa says, 'even among young people. On Sunday we have all-day religion on TV, which is really bad. This government is brainwashing the people into religion and Fascism so they don't question what's really going on.'

For a moment they all look dejected.

The first Hrvoje breaks the silence. 'I'd like to go to Slovenia. I really liked Slovene people when I worked there and they make good films.'

'So why do you stay here?' I ask.

'Because we feel responsible for all the younger people,' the second Hrvoje explains. 'We really want to leave, but if people like us go then who will help the younger ones? UZGON couldn't work if everyone like us left.'

'There are half a million people in this city,' the first Hrvoje says, 'and four public computers. In Ljubljana there are four *free* Internet cafés. The Slovenian government *tries* to provide the things young people need.'

I mention the books being sold on the streets and the crush in the stationer's.

'That's because so few new books are ever printed now, so books are like gold.'

'And the new ones that are made, I don't understand what they say!' Sinisa grins. 'I looked in my nephew's class book the other day. He's seven and I couldn't understand 30 per cent of the language – the Croatian language! This government is introducing new words all the time and bringing back old words from the past, Ustaše words, Fascist words, to go with all the flags and nationalism!'

'Do people take these changes seriously?'

'No, not ordinary people. We'll always speak the same, no-one can make us change that. But for young kids learning this shit it will be hard. The government is trying to get rid of the "j" spelling of words; so, for example, milk would be *"mlieko"* not *"mlijeko"*.'

'And "sport",' the second Hrvoje says, 'now you must say *"šport"*.' He pronounces the word *'shporrt'*, and giggles. 'It's mad, soon we'll all be speaking like King Tomislav!'

'Would you like to hear a joke about Croatia?' Sinisa asks.

I nod, grinning.

'OK. Clinton, Tudjman and Milošević are all called to heaven. Sveti Petar meets them and tells them that the end of the world is coming and they must go home and prepare their people. So Clinton goes home and makes a TV announcement. "People of America," he says, "I have two pieces of news, one good, one bad. The good news is . . . God exists. The bad news is that we're all going to meet him next week." '

Their grins broaden as they watch for my reaction.

'Milošević goes home and makes an announcement on TV. "People of Yugoslavia," he says, "I have two piece of news, both bad. The first is . . . God exists. The second is that we're all going to meet him next week." '

Despite knowing the punchline they giggle, wriggling on the hard, wooden stools.

'So, Tudjman comes home to Croatia. "People of Croatia," he says, "I have two pieces of news, both good. The first is . . . God exists. The second is . . . I am going to die in office." '

I get the joke about Tudjman's cancer and laugh. Sinisa almost falls off his stool cackling, and the two Hrvojes laugh with him.

When I leave, they give me a copy of their propaganda – a witty, slender and rather male-orientated organ. 'Which would you rather have?' the message runs, comparing images of bosomy blonde girls on the beach with pictures of elderly women crusading outside a church. A photo of young graffiti artists is compared with images of the Austro-Hungarian court; rock musicians with folk dancers; and, coincidentally, a cleaned-up Manchester United team with a topless and fractious-looking NK Croatia crowding around Tudjman's plump and sweaty henchman, Canjuga.

Returning to the Bellevue along the Obala, I call into the British Consulate to keep an appointment with the British Honorary Consul, Alexsij Mekjavič. Made famous by fiction, the title 'Honorary Consul' sounds at once important and vague, and I'm here to find out what it means to be a British 'HC'. Captain Alex, a short, dapper man perhaps in his sixties, is happy to dispel any confusion.

'As you say, the job description can seem vague but the most important part of any Honorary Consul's work is liaison – between government bodies in local situations; between British nationals, in my case, and locals; between British organisations, both civil and military, who have dealings in this part of Croatia. For example, things are very quiet here now, but during the war with Serbia I was busy twenty-four hours a day, flying out to the British ships at least twice daily, liaising between the land and sea forces and local interests.' He smiles, perhaps at the memory of past excitement. 'There were many British and NATO supply ships off the coast here while the fighting was going on; they had to support the troops in Bosnia. We have only one British ship here now.'

'Do you find Split today very different from twenty years ago?'

He gestures with both hands. 'Oh, so much has changed. Then we were an important city in a large country. Being on the coast was a bonus; it attracted people from the West and we had the hinterland of Yugoslavia behind us, a resource and a destination. Now there is nothing behind us: a few kilometres of mountains, then Bosnia, which is another country. Industrial production here is 30 per cent of what it was in 1990. Tourism is down a great deal because of conflicts, and much of the excitement that we once had as a vibrant cultural centre has gone, though I believe it will come back.'

Captain Alex disappears to summon tea, leaving me to wander around the room with its small balcony overlooking sea and palms. The Queen of England gazes down from the wall; it's a particularly pretty picture and must be almost fifty years old. Other members of the royal family appear around the room;

Prince Charles chatting with British General Mike Jackson and Captain Alex; Captain Alex receiving his MBE. The case beside the window is filled with books on royalty and works with titles like *The Spirit of England* and *Nelson*. This is not the office of a mere Anglophile, but of a man with an English soul.

'There's a long history of links between Split and the United Kingdom,' my host says, offering tea in a flowered cup and saucer. I think of the Duke of Windsor and Mrs Simpson naked, and flinch.

'There was Fitzroy Maclean of course, who spent a lot of time in Dalmatia during and after World War II. He was a most interesting man, very charming and colourful.'

'The Fitzroy Maclean Ian Fleming supposedly used as a model for James Bond?'

Captain Alex smiles. 'I think Fleming used many men, though Fitzroy was a great character and there was a lot of James Bond about him.'

The near-legendary Maclean was a diplomat in Paris and Moscow before the war. In 1939 the Diplomatic Service refused his request to join the military so he stood for election as an MP. Having won a seat in the north of England, he persuaded his constituents that it would be good for morale if an MP was seen to join the front line. Following undercover operations in the North African desert with David Stirling, founder of the SAS, Maclean was sent to Yugoslavia with the Special Operations Executive. His personal brief from Churchill was to ascertain which of the various anti-Fascist groups was the most successful and to assist them against the Germans and Ustaše. In 1943, Maclean met the Partisan leaders for the first time: Croat-Slovene Tito, Slovene Eduard Kardelji, Serb Aleksander Ranković and Montenegrin Milovan Djilas. From then until the end of the war, despite initial suspicions on both sides, Maclean supported the Partisans, advising Churchill that regardless of the inevitability of Yugoslavia becoming Communist should Germany be defeated, Tito would be The Man, with or without Allied help. Maclean effectively became British Ambassador to Partisan Yugoslavia. Although no individual guides the destiny of a country, and only James Bond can single-handedly save the world, for a short time circumstance made Fitzroy Maclean pivotal in Balkan history.

Captain Alex hands me a piece of paper from his desk, a cutting from the newspaper *Slobodna Dalmacija*. 'Tito's Englishmen on the Island of Vis', the caption reads, followed by the wording of a plaque recently unveiled at a commemoration ceremony. *In memory of the British Forces who from this island of Vis gave their lives in comradeship, supporting Tito's army of liberation 1943–1945.*

'A group of veterans comes to Vis every year, though each time they come there are fewer. Like me, they're getting old.'

'Surely you were too young to fight in that war yourself.'

He laughs. 'I'll be seventy-eight in two days time.'

'Happy birthday,' I say, trying not to stare at his youthful, energetic face.

'If you don't have time to see Vis, perhaps you'd like to visit the British ship in the North Port? I'll telephone the Captain and see if he's free.'

Ivan Blažević is waiting for me at the Bellevue's reception when I pick up my room key.

'You've had a good day?'

'Great,' I say and sketch my movements.

He sniffs, and just for a moment appears less than pleased that I've managed things without his guidance. He draws me aside.

'I have friends who would like to meet you,' he says conspiratorially. 'And I would like to invite you to my home for lunch tomorrow so that you can see how people here live.'

'That's very kind.'

'Kind? No. It's good for me to be able to show you things. And at my house you can meet my friends. They would like you to go with them to their home in the countryside, to show you what it's like there since the war.'

'Where exactly is their home?'

'They're from the Krajina, near Knin.'

I feel a sudden surge of enthusiasm for the rather forbidding Ivan.

'That sounds great,' I say. 'How will we get there?'

'My friend has a car, he tells me Knin is about two hours drive.'

Croatia's inland infrastructure is less than hospitable, with poor roads, little public transport and less accommodation. Without a vehicle, I'd all but given up on seeing the Krajina. War with the Serbs devastated much of the region and today the only foreigners who get to visit are diplomats or staff of international security organisations like the OSCE.

Ivan pauses, glancing around. 'They don't go there much now, I was surprised they offered to take you; but it will be interesting for me too, I've never been.'

'Why don't they go?'

He drops his voice, and with an expression at once anxious and defiant, whispers, 'Because they are Serbs.'

8 Meeting Serbs

O N THE FIFTH floor of a suburban high-rise, the woman who shares Ivan's home (or maybe he shares hers?) has prepared a lunch of fish soup, rice and meat.

'This is Elena, my housekeeper. She's a Serb.'

Bearing in mind that few things are what they seem here, I look at the tired, grey-haired woman, and wonder what 'housekeeper' means.

Ivan takes off his shirt and sits at the table in his vest, drinking from an unlabelled bottle. The doorbell rings and a slender, spotty boy, well over six foot tall, enters the room.

'Aha!' Ivan says, 'here is the son of my friends. Give him some soup, Elena. Where are your mother and father?'

Unattractive even for a teenager, the boy's manner is worse than his appearance. 'They aren't coming, they're too busy.'

He bends steeply down towards the soup bowl placed on the table before him and in excellent American says, 'Ugh! I hate soup, soup is fattening.'

Ivan and Elena look on indulgently.

'What *do* you like?' I ask conversationally.

'Hamburgers, pizza . . . American things.'

'Pizza and hamburgers are more fattening than soup,' I suggest, 'and anyway, are you worried about being fat?'

'Girls don't like fat boys.' He pauses to spoon more of the despised soup into his mouth. 'At least hamburgers and pizza taste nice. Soup is boring.'

'You have a difficult choice then,' I say, 'between girls and hamburgers.'

'He's fifteen,' Ivan says by way of explanation.

The boy's parents arrive, another tired-looking woman and a precise, neat man with a grey crew-cut.

'This is my friend Borislav – <u>Boris</u> we call him. He's an economist and works in a bank. <u>Svetlana</u>'s a doctor, a surgeon at our biggest hospital.'

We all shake hands and the newcomers are plied with food by Elena, who hovers like a servant at the back of the kitchen.

'They don't really speak English,' Ivan says, pouring another shot of *rakija* for himself. 'I'll translate for you all.'

Sensing a serious discussion coming up, the boy leaves. The couple check me out with wary politeness. I must appear reasonably honest because they start to talk.

'We are from the <u>Krajina region</u>, north-east of here,' Boris says, 'but I have lived in Split since leaving university, and so has my wife.'

Svetlana asks if I'm interested to hear about the war.

'Of course.'

'It was very difficult for us then,' she says, plunging straight in. 'Some of our neighbours told us "What you see on TV is nothing compared to what will happen to you." ' She stops abruptly.

'Why did you stay?' I ask them both.

'We have two sons and they were both at school. We have responsible jobs. This is our country, our families have lived in Croatia for more than four hundred years.'

I consider the last statement. 'So,' I hesitate, not wanting to blunder, 'your family have lived here for more than four hundred years. You are a Slav then, like Ivan, and speak the same language as him?'

Boris and Svetlana both nod.

'You were all born in the same country and had Yugoslav passports for most of your lives. But you and Ivan are in some way not at all the same. Can you explain to me why that is, what it is to be a Serb in Croatia today?'

Ivan translates and a long pause follows. Svetlana and Boris talk back and forth, shaking their heads.

'I don't know,' Svetlana says finally, in English. 'I don't know.'

'No, that's not right,' Boris says, 'we do know. It's religion, that's the difference. We say "Serb" because we are Orthodox.'

'Are you religious?' I ask. 'Do you believe in God?'

Both smile wryly and shake their heads. 'We're atheists,' Boris says.

'Perhaps it seems odd to you,' I say, 'but I really want to understand this if I can. It's hard for outside looking in to grasp what these things mean – just as it's hard for strangers to understand the problems of Northern Ireland.'

They nod, accepting the comparison with Ulster.

'So, if it's not religion, and it's not language and it's not racial origin . . .'

They nod again, agreeing.

'Then what *is* it?' I ask. 'What's *so* strong that after four hundred years you still don't feel part of this country?'

There's a pause, then after a brief exchange Ivan says, 'They ask that if you write about them you change their names – they're afraid that they might have problems if they're identified.' He shakes his head. 'It's very strange, I can't understand why they feel like that.'

'Of course I'll change their names.'

Boris nods and continues. 'To be Serb in Croatia means having your own tradition – the same tradition as Serbs in Bosnia or Serbia or Montenegro. Even if you are an atheist you still follow tradition. In the Krajina, where we are from, tradition was strong for Serbs but we lived very well with everyone – with Croats and Jews. We all had our own ways and that was good. Then the war came and everything ended. My wife and I have lost our family homes, we have only empty stone walls and a roof. That's not a home.'

Ivan translates faithfully, and at the end says in English, so only I can understand, 'But don't forget what they did to *us*, don't forget why the war happened there in the first place, all those Croats murdered and made into refugees when the Serbs set up their <u>Republic of Krajina</u>!'

I nod, surprised.

'What do you think of Milošević?' I ask the Serbs.

Svetlana snorts angrily. 'After the Krajina he should have been hung upside down by his ankles, like Mussolini – he betrayed the Serb people. Now he's just another madman. But Tudjman is to blame too. Honest Serbs who never hurt anyone should be able to return to their homes, their investments . . .' She starts to cry. Boris's face becomes even more stiff and Ivan looks awkward.

'My father is eighty years old,' Boris says, 'he lives in Belgrade but he's a stranger there. Our sons are both very clever but they won't find good work in Split because they're Serbs. People with lower qualifications are promoted over our older son, and he's very unhappy.'

Svetlana looks up from her handkerchief. 'Croatia is my home. The Krajina is home, but I don't go there now. After the war ended I paid for my family house to be fixed, I hoped everything would be as it was before. I was stupid. Each time I return, our old neighbours have taken what they can carry away – roof tiles, floor tiles. Soon the house will be just walls again.' She twists the handkerchief between her fingers. 'When I went to the police about it, they just shrugged and blamed Croat refugees from Bosnia.'

'Remember *why* those refugees are there in the first place,' Ivan says to me. 'Remember why they were pushed out of Bosnia. When they say they hate Milošević now, is it because he failed them in Krajina, or because he's an evil man?'

Boris and Svetlana watch these exchanges between Ivan and myself without understanding. As he continues to drink, Ivan's blend of translation and comment becomes more frequent and I start to feel very uncomfortable. Having invited me to meet his friends so that I can get their version of life and events, he now tries to control what I hear and how I hear it, while giving what I feel sure is an oddly faithful translation.

'I know what you're saying,' I tell Ivan. 'I *know* what happened, you don't need to remind me.'

'Good,' he says pouring himself another glass. 'Good.'

'So who do you hold responsible for what happened in Krajina?' I ask.

'I blame the HDZ,' Svetlana replies, 'but I also blame Milošević for what he did there.'

'Krajina Serbs didn't care about a Greater Serbia in 1991, but they were influenced by puppets of Milošević,' Boris says, animated for the first time. 'He used extremists to whip up the passions of poor and ignorant people. And it was easy. Compared to much of Croatia, the Krajina is socially backward, with high unemployment. Desperate men like to be given hope, even if that means war.'

'If Tudjman had supported the moderate Serb politicians who truly wanted a democratic solution, there wouldn't have been a war in Krajina,' Svetlana says, wiping her eyes. 'But the HDZ didn't want decent Serbs on their side, it would have spoilt their heroic image.'

Ivan tuts and shakes his head as he translates this, adding, 'They're ready to accept that Serbs did bad things to Croats, but not why. They just can't admit *why*.'

Boris turns to Ivan. 'I will tell you something,' he says, 'something I never told anyone outside our family. More than fifteen years ago I wanted to send my sons to school in Belgrade. I knew if they stayed here they would face the same discrimination that I have had to face in my career.'

As he translates this, Ivan's face registers conflicting emotions. Almost spluttering, he finally says to me, 'You see! You see . . . they were never happy here, even when things were good, they always wanted to be in Serbia!'

I wonder why the dispute doesn't become more open, why Ivan doesn't confront the couple about the things with which he disagrees. Instead, he confines his asides to me and the conversation continues, his voice a raven on my shoulder. 'Don't forget why they weren't happy, don't forget what they did, don't forget

Kosovo, Vukovar, Dubrovnik . . .' I don't mention the murder of Serbs by Vukovar Croats less than a month earlier, probably for much the same reasons that Ivan holds back from challenging his Serb friends.

The discussion widens as we discuss the collapse of the Soviet Union, Estonia and Latvia. Boris in particular is very knowledgeable about international affairs, and the role the world has imposed upon him as a Serb clearly rankles.

'The West thinks we are nothing more than a wild tribe waiting to cut our neighbours' throats. It isn't true. What happened here could happen anywhere.'

'So,' Ivan says, getting to his feet with difficulty, 'we are going to the Krajina tomorrow, yes?'

Svetlana looks quickly at me and then at Boris, and says something wry.

Ivan laughs. 'She says she expects him to behave himself.'

'Aren't you coming too?' I ask hopefully.

She shakes her head. 'There are operations to perform tomorrow, there's always work. But I hope that you see what you want and make use of it however you can.'

I make noises of genuine disappointment and smile politely at Boris; he doesn't look the philandering sort, but then the quiet ones are always the worst. Or so they say.

Two messages are waiting for me at the Bellevue. One is from the Bosnian friend who's expecting me in Sarajevo; the other is a note from the Captain of the British ship anchored in the North Port, inviting me for drinks that evening. The thought is surprisingly appealing. A small piece of Britain, floating in water. Britain. Normality.

I run a bath and lie in it for a long time, thinking about what was said and not said over lunch. When I eventually climb out, shrivelled and white, the residue of conflict is still there, clinging to me; such things don't wash away that easily. The prospect of the next day – of witnessing Boris and Ivan together in the

Krajina – isn't a pleasant one. I consider not going, but the lure is too great.

Hanging out of the open window I gaze at the blue-green waters of Split harbour reflecting the low afternoon sun and make a significant if somewhat belated personal discovery: I don't have to understand people to do what needs to be done. I don't even have to like them.

The sea is almost black when I approach the North Port in the early evening, and the grey ship's lights sparkle against the dark blue of the sky like diamonds on an elderly dowager. As ships go she's not large, but still towers over me as I look up from the dock. At reception, a cubbyhole full of wires and gadgets, I'm met by Dave the first officer, a friendly, informative man who offers to show me around the ship before going on to the officers' bar.

On the control deck I fiddle with the gleaming brass wheel, peer at the radar screens and sit in the Captain's seat. It's all rather *Starship Enterprise* and I feel like a kid in a toy shop. Dave looks on indulgently and explains what the ship's doing here.

'At the moment we're functioning as an ammunition dump, helicopter pad and liaison unit between SFOR and the outside world, mostly because Bosnia doesn't have a deep-water port.'

Through the control room's glass screen I look down on the deck with its wheels, cranes and coiled steel ropes. Row on row of SFOR vehicles from Bosnia wait to be shipped home. Across the water, the homes of Split's wealthier inhabitants twinkle among dusk-stained cypresses. It looks idyllic, welcoming.

'That's where a lot of the local mafia live,' Dave says. 'The police quite often come across bodies inside burnt-out cars over there, but they don't do anything much about it. A couple of stray bullets find their way here from time to time – at least, we assume they're strays.'

'How much longer will the ship be here?'

'Until a new ammunition site is built up the road, at least a year. It's not a bad life, but it's not as comfortable as it looks either. People die here. I've seen four send-offs in nine months. They come to us from Bosnia and Kosovo because Split's an international airport. We sent a chap home yesterday . . . twenty-two, just married. He was cut in half by a vehicle with failed brakes. Six hundred soldiers were lined up to see him off at the airport. Can you imagine the sight of hundreds and hundreds of men with tears pouring down their faces?'

Deep in the bowels of the ship, the officers' bar is as anachronistic a piece of England as it's possible to find. The beaten copper fire-hood, the patterned carpet and padded bar stools are uniquely English, as is the Captain, who lies back in his chair, feet on the table.

'Where are you from then?' he says to me, tucking his hands under his belly.

'I'm Welsh.'

'Oh my God!' he bellows. 'A bloody Blodwen!'

'You don't like Celts?' I ask, smiling politely.

'They're alright,' he replies grudgingly. 'I'll have you know my own family has Irish origins, but as Wellington said, "Just because you're born in a stable, doesn't make you a bloody horse." '

I try not to laugh; the humour is that mix of school-boy and barrack-room that will only get worse with encouragement. But the Captain needs no encouragement, and as we talk about Croatia and the world in general he seems bent on trying to charm and horrify.

'These Balkan types don't know how lucky they are having us lot around to stop them slicing each other up. Let's face it, after the coming of Jesus Christ the next best thing to happen to the world was the British Empire. Just look at India, for God's sake. It used to be run like clockwork by two thousand people; now they've got millions of bloody bureaucrats and what a mess!'

'The Captain's politics are a little to the right of Genghis Khan,' Dave whispers, grinning sheepishly.

'He's lucky I'm not a journalist who'll repeat all this stuff.'

'Oh, he doesn't care about that! We had two journalists here the other day, he was even worse with them – he's holding back tonight because you're female.'

Other senior officers join us, smiling at their Captain's 'naughty' humour. 'Bloody East Timor!' he says. 'Bloody Indonesians, why does the world let them get away with that stuff? All it would take would be one or two decent fighting ships to hove into view over that horizon and they'd run for the trees. Problem solved!'

He picks up the folder he's brought with him and produces photographs of tall ships and himself.

'That's me there, up the rigging, third on the left. The rest are all Russians and Krauts. The Russians have the best tall ships these days, them and the Krauts. It's odd, I know, but lots of my friends these days are greasy Krauts.'

The carpet, stools and bar are a version of home, part of 'normality'. That was what I thought I wanted after my afternoon with Ivan and the Serbs. But this is not home and it's far from normal, and somehow the façade of familiarity and the appalling bonhomie make home seem further away than ever.

Speeding back into town with a Croatian customs officer whose car and services Dave commandeers for me, I breathe out with relief. Maybe the Krajina won't be so bad after all.

Like most towns along Croatia's coast, Split inhabits a strip of land between stark, barren mountains and jewel-like waters. The eastbound road rises fast and steep, and far below the city shines in the morning light, its palmy shore gracefully curving to meet the sea. Split is beautiful.

Near the ruins of Solin we pass the aqueduct that carried water to the city in Roman times, each perfect arch a masterpiece of ancient engineering. A few kilometres further and we enter a feat of modern engineering, a shiny new tunnel that emerges from the mountain near the fortress of Kliš. Perched on a jagged crag, cypresses give the only clue that the fort's near-invisible walls are not part of the rock face.

'It was built against the Turk,' Ivan says, 'but they captured it.'

'In 1537,' Boris adds. 'It was the closest the Turks got to Split, but they captured the rest of the coast almost to Dubrovnik.'

Ivan is quite a different person today, sober and restrained. Both he and Boris have brought food in plastic bags as if for a long haul, though Knin is less than eighty kilometres from Split, and our destination, Boris's village, only another fifteen or so beyond.

Earlier in the morning, I'd been surprised to discover that Ivan had only a vague idea where Boris and his family live. As we drive they chat in what for them is still Serbo-Croat. It's clear they aren't 'friends' as I understand the word; 'acquaintance' is probably a closer approximation and even that seems compromised by the layers of history unspoken between them. Ivan frequently refers to Boris and himself as 'civilised' men, apparently unlike the majority of their fellow countrymen. The words 'civilised' and 'civilisation' crop up frequently both in English and Serbo-Croat. Perhaps the relationship is important for both men because it embodies 'civilisation', their ability to co-exist without violence or rancour despite difference.

Away from the coast the land is barren. Here, in the foothills of the Dinaric Alps, the landscape is almost lunar, its dry rockiness broken only by clumps of scrub and tree. The occasional homes look new and prosperous, their green and well-tended gardens anomalous in the midst of infertility. I watch a man push a wheelbarrow filled with giant cabbages past a shed with corn drying on the roof. Two men drive a horse and cart loaded with wood across a maize field. Outside an industrial workshop there's a kennel with the name 'Ajax' scrawled on it. A small, black dog, Ajax hangs his head and paws forlornly.

Near the town of Sinj we turn north and east into the Cetina valley, and rockiness is replaced by orchards and small vineyards, the roads lined with cypresses. There are few people around, few cars and only a handful of trucks, which is good because Boris is a nervous and temperamental driver. Several times in the first hour he strays into the path of oncoming traffic while turning to speak with Ivan. It's good to be sitting in the back seat.

'We are in the Krajina now,' Boris says, as we cross some border visible only to him.

Historically, the Vojna Krajina was not a territory but a military zone. Following the defeat of Hungary by the Turks at the Battle of Mohacs in 1526, it became increasingly clear that the Hapsburgs' southern border needed better defences. By the end of the sixteenth century Vienna had created the Vojna Krajina, a line of forts, watchtowers and warning beacons garrisoned by German mercenaries backed up by local frontiersmen (*granicari*), designed as a buffer between Ottoman and Hapsburg lands. At its strongest, the military zone stretched like a belt of varying widths across the entire north-western border of the Ottoman Empire, from the Adriatic to Wallachia, in present-day Romania. At that time, 'Croatia' in the modern sense did not exist, being three entities: the north and eastern region ruled by the Hapsburgs; the Istria, Kvarner and Dalmatia regions ruled by Venice; and an independent Dubrovnik which gave a politic nod of allegiance to the Ottomans.

Like so many problems of the modern Balkans, the experience of Boris, Svetlana and their families is an indirect result of historical decisions made by foreign rulers. The *granicari* were largely Christian Orthodox populations of Vlachs, an enigmatic dark-skinned people from the mountainous interior of Dalmatia and Bosnia, displaced by the seemingly inexorable north-western drive by the Ottomans and granted land rights by the Hapsburgs in return for military service. From a modern Serb perspective, the Krajina was an independent region of Orthodox Christians – therefore, Serbs – who stood alone as the brave border guards of Christianity for centuries. Today, many historians see the identification of Serbs with Orthodox Vlachs as contentious and anachronistic. What does seem clear in an otherwise murky history is that the Vlachs did not identify as Serb until prompted by the nationalist movements of the nineteenth century, when 'Orthodox' and 'Serb' were united in popular thinking for political purposes. Much of the brave border-guard image is also a myth, as the region's run-down forts frequently failed to prevent the Turks from seizing more territory. In 1615 a foreign visitor to one of the Krajina's military centres reported rusting guns and starving, semi-naked soldiers.

From a Croatian perspective, the Krajina was virtually a separate state within their own shrinking borders, peopled by foreigners and outside their control. The Croat Church and nobility were particularly disturbed by the fact that the Krajina had no serfs, only soldiers who paid for liberty with service. This was seen as a threat to Croatia's harsh feudal system, a temptation to its hundreds of thousands of bonded labourers. But Vienna ignored or paid off Croatian complaints.

When the Ottoman threat receded in the seventeenth century, the Hapsburgs lost interest in the Krajina; the area became a backwater and remained so. In 1941 Ante Pavelić and his Ustaše attempted to forcibly re-Croat-ise the Krajina, resulting in the extermination of many thousands of Serbs. Tito used the strong anti-Fascist feeling among Krajina Serbs when recruiting Partisan militiamen. Under Communist rule, the region remained one of the least developed areas of Yugoslavia, with Serbs a 90 per cent majority in what they saw as 'Serbia within a foreign country'.

Between the Dinara and Svilaja mountain ranges, the valley opens into a broad, flattish plain, and we enter a land where gutted houses ripped open to the skies stand beside abandoned orchards heavy with autumn fruit; a land neither dead or alive. In one former village two women sit, knitting, outside a house with no roof; their washing hangs inside what must have been a neighbour's living room or kitchen. Chickens and goats wander between broken walls. Next door the women's family laugh and call to each other in their new house which shines bright in the sunshine. One family all alone in a village of more than twenty empty and devastated homes.

Village after village along the road to Knin is destroyed. Houses and barns are pockmarked by bullet and shrapnel holes; every building has lost its roof. Only the gardens are undamaged. After many examples of this it strikes me that the shelling must have been impossibly accurate.

'How was every house hit so precisely?' I ask.

'There's no piped gas here,' Boris says, 'everyone uses canisters. Domestic gas, that's what was used to blow the houses up, not mortars – cheap and effective.'

Not really a war then; just neighbours deciding to throw a match at your gas supply in the middle of the night. Boris describes these things with a banker's eye. Ivan stiffens slightly in the passenger seat; after his talk of Serbs being unable to confront what they have done, the tables are turned. He knows who did this and it makes for uncomfortable viewing. But even now he can't quite refrain from adding his little asides, reminding me why there are no Serbs here now and what they did before they were made to leave. Today it all rolls off me.

In 1990, when Tudjman's ultra-nationalist HDZ party won the elections, Croatia's six hundred thousand Serbs weren't happy; but most observers agree that the Serb uprising that started in the Krajina in 1990, and became full-scale aggression in 1991, was not local but largely incited and even organised from Belgrade. On the other hand, Krajina Serbs had never accepted the reality of Zagreb rule; memories of Ustaše atrocities were still raw and Serb agitators who claimed the HDZ was the new Ustaše and Tudjman the new Pavelić found willing ears. While Milošević stirred the Krajina pot, Tudjman added wood to the fire, thinking he could control the Krajina without the support of local Serb moderates. Extremists like Yugoslav Army commander Ratko Mladić, later infamous for his role in the war in Bosnia, took power, demanding autonomy for Serb Krajina. Based on the 'where there are Serbs is Serbia' notion, this ultimatum was particularly outrageous in the context of Kosovo and the equivalent demands of that region's Albanian population which Milošević had stamped on only a year earlier. Mladić grew up in Ante Pavelić's home town of Bradina in Central Bosnia and saw his own and other Serb families destroyed by Ustaše. Even monsters have reasons.

Between 1991 and 1995, the government of the self-styled Republic of Serbian Krajina attempted to eliminate any traces of Croat history from the region. The Serbian media created a new doublespeak for the murders and expulsions which took place – *čišćenje terena*, 'cleaning the land' – which the world came to know as 'ethnic cleansing'.

But not even Ante Pavelić attempted what Tudjman achieved when the Croat army retook the Krajina in 1995: the murderous expulsion of the Serbs, the largest single population movement during the nineties war. Ironically, the world was largely unaware of the atrocities committed against these refugees because all eyes were focused on the Bosnian city of Sarajevo, besieged by Bosnian Serbs.

We stop briefly for me to take advantage of the facilities offered by the shell of a Yugoslav Communist building. Over the main door, a plaque with the five-pointed star and Tito's engraved portrait is still visible. Nearby a monument to the villagers who died fighting Fascism is marked with graffiti. It reads, 'That was then, this is now'.

Knin is a grubby, provincial depot town, a kind of Balkan Crewe or Alice Springs, set in a craggy landscape dominated by broken forts. While Boris and Ivan walk cautiously down a street filled with dark, unshaven men, I make my way to the local OSCE office to find out what I can about Knin.

In a clean, bright room, Marcus, a British staff member, offers me a mug of tea and apologises for being the only available person. 'The Swedish Ambassador is coming in an hour, so our director is preparing for that. He's sorry not to be able to tell you about OSCE's work here himself.'

I wonder why an ambassador would bother coming to Knin, but say, 'I appreciate anyone talking to me. One look out there and it's clear you're very busy.'

He grins. 'The town's full of displaced Bosnian Croats. The government in Zagreb dumped them here at the end of the war to fill the empty Serb houses. They're a majority population now: more than 50 per cent of Knin is Bosnian Croat, and it's a problem that literally stretches from here to Zagreb along the main road, kilometre after kilometre of refugees sitting in empty Serb houses.'

'There's obviously no employment.'

'None, and a lot of people still need humanitarian aid which is going to be withdrawn at the end of this month. God knows what'll happen then.'

The phone rings and Marcus speaks to the caller in slow and careful Croat.

Replacing the receiver, he shakes his head. 'That's an old Serb man, one of my re-housing cases. He and his wife live in their garage because their house was burnt down. He wants me to help him, he's always calling and coming in. But there's nothing I can do, people are already living three families to a house.'

'It must be hard not being able to help.'

He grins wryly. 'You get used to it. The main problem for us is that local people are furious at the way they think the Bosnian refugees are being given preferential treatment.'

'Are all those rough types out there Bosnian Croats?'

'Yep, and they're sitting pretty in the houses of displaced Serbs. There's a Housing Commission but it does nothing – it's the local Croats who're still living three to a house because theirs were wrecked by Serbs.'

'Are there any Serbs here at all?'

'About two thousand, and more are coming back. The villages north of here are being resettled slowly. It might seem strange, but Knin's Croats and Serbs get along fine together. It's the incomers, the Bosnian Croats, that all the locals dislike. It's not surprising, a lot of them are the real dregs of Hercegovinan society – illiterate, petty criminals, that kind of thing. All the refugees with any education or oomph went to Canada, Britain or America.'

'I can see that Knin wouldn't be most people's first choice.'

He grins. 'Exactly.'

Twenty minutes north of Knin we reach the village, which Boris asks me not to name. It's not really a village, just two buildings set among beautifully lush landscape overlooking the valley and the Dinara. The modern concrete house is smashed and burnt, its rooms filled with scattered rubbish and broken furniture; his cousin's house, Boris says. The small farmhouse next door, where Boris was born and lived with three generations of his family until he went to university, is of rough stone and at least two hundred years old. Beside the double entrance gate is a sty for a single pig, empty now, the feed bowl upturned. The smoke house nearby is black-walled from years of curing hams from the pigs that lived by the gate. Stone steps lead up above the sty to the small drying house which is hung with shrivelled corn cobs. The outhouses still have barrels and great stone jars for wine from the family's vineyard and oil from their olive trees. Chicken coops and goat sheds, overgrown with grass, surround the cobbled yard.

The farmhouse is spartan and low-roofed, with no obvious bathroom or toilet. Jackets and coats, disintegrating with damp, still hang in the cupboards. In a room over the kitchen Boris hesitates, visibly moved.

'This was my room,' he says. 'These are my books.' He points to a mildewed pile of economics textbooks, and picks up a tatty, unbound manuscript.

'My MA thesis,' he says, and smiling ruefully throws it back.

As we leave the farm he pulls the tall double gates behind him, as though by this action he can protect what lies inside. What looks like graffiti is daubed across the wood and signed 'Petar'.

'What does it say?' I ask.

'It says, "Don't burn this place, the Twelfth Croatian Division lives here." Petar is my sister's son.'

'Why did he write that?' I ask, wondering why Boris's nephew would side with the Croats?

'My sister married a Croat and Petar went with them when the war started. Because of him this house is still standing.'

Boris's face is expressionless as he shows us the orchards and vineyards that surround the farmhouse. Red and white grapes hang heavily on their swaying, rotting frames. We squelch across fallen figs to view the extent of Boris's land. Meadows stretch towards wooded slopes; groves of oak and birch and trees I don't recognise are home to large emerald lizards and their prey of mantis and giant crickets.

'I used to look after the goats here, make sure they didn't stray. Over there on the edge of the woodland there's an underground room, a bunker – my grandfather made it in World War II to hide in when the Ustaše came.'

When Ivan goes for a pee in the vineyard, Boris draws me into the trees, his hand firmly placed in the small of my back. Before I can wonder at his actions we're standing beside a large, deep hole with exposed tree roots, and he's close to tears. Without Ivan to translate, how will we communicate? But somehow we do.

'The ground just fell in here in 1989, collapsed for no reason. My grandmother said it was an omen, of bad things to come. She was right.' He walks back alone, wiping quickly at his eyes.

Returning to the car, we meet three older men carrying heavy shopping bags. They greet Boris warmly, with hugging and back-slapping.

'These are friends I haven't seen in fifteen years,' he says excitedly. 'They invite us to their home for coffee. Now you will see my village!'

Ivan looks at me. 'You want to go?'

'Definitely,' I say, 'don't you?'

'We have to,' he says, 'it would be impolite to refuse.'

We follow the three men down a path overgrown with nettles and brambles. After walking in single file for ten minutes, with still no building in sight, we're suddenly in a tiny hamlet of empty houses. I peer through broken windows into scenes of destruction; clothing, broken glass and smashed furniture litter the floors. One or two houses look like they might still be lived in. We walk on until we reach a ramshackle farmhouse; its windows are covered with plastic sacking stamped with the UNHCR logo. The big, grassy yard is lined with rusting cars and car parts. A puppy and several cats of different sizes and colours play-fight with each other and with the chickens pecking around the yard. I'm introduced to Dushanka and Miroslav, a Serb couple in their forties or fifties.

We sit in the yard at a large round marble table, battered and broken on one side. Coffee comes in tiny cups decorated with eighteenth-century French ladies, chased by Miroslav's home-brewed *rakija* which makes my throat close and eyes stream, to everyone else's amusement.

'The Croats tried to destroy this table top,' Dushanka says through Ivan, 'but it was too strong and they gave up. So we can still use it. We're happy that something survived.'

'How long have you lived here?' I ask.

'This was our home for twenty-five years before the war, then in 1995 we were taken to a refugee camp in Serbia, near the border with Bulgaria. We wanted to come back, to come home, but there were men in the camp who told us we must stay, that if we came home our Croat neighbours would cut our throats. After four years we stopped believing them and came home anyway. It was the best thing we did. As you see, no-one has hurt us and why should they, we never hurt them.'

'Our two sons are in Belgrade,' Miroslav says, 'one is a journalist, the other a chemical engineer. When NATO bombed the city a few months ago they both lost their jobs – the newspaper office was blown up and the chemical factory too. But they are both well, and that is what matters.'

I shiver. There's something terrible about taking hospitality from people who barely have a home and whose children my own country has just bombed into unemployment. But there's nothing to do except take my cue from my hosts, who seem delighted to be entertaining a Croat and a Briton at their broken table . . . and from Ivan, who today embodies the very soul of Slavic brotherhood and unity, affably translating without the constant asides of yesterday.

We're joined at the table by two more men and an elderly woman who wears a headscarf and walks with a stick.

'She lost her dog, her cat, then she had a stroke,' Dushanka says. 'She couldn't do anything for months and there was no medical treatment, but she's made herself walk again.'

Now I begin to believe the stories of Serb toughness. As the talk goes on around me I take photos of the old woman, who poses repeatedly, smoothing her scarf and torn cardigan. After a few pictures she pokes at my expensive German boots, then at her broken shoes, until I realise she's asking me to swap. I almost consider it.

'This one is her husband,' Boris says, clapping his hand on the biceps of a still-handsome man, much younger than his wife. 'He was the village strongman. I remember he could carry three bales of straw – not just one, like everybody else! Her father was also a strongman, many years ago, at a time when there was a dispute between our village and the next. When this happened, two men would usually fight to resolve the matter; but her father was a gentle man who hated fighting, so when he had to shake hands before the fight he just squeezed the other man's hand very hard until he gave in and they all went home.'

Everyone laughs, remembering the story, if not the incident. The old woman preens at the memory of her father and pats her husband on his muscular arm.

All around us the cats, chickens and puppy compete politely for space and whatever they can find to eat in the dirt. The puppy drags a completely rigid cat by the ear for a few metres, drops it, then licks it all over. Watching the animals' happy co-existence, anything seems possible, but perhaps that's just the effect of three glasses of Miroslav's *rakija*.

Before we leave, Dushanka and Miroslav lead me into their orchard. They want to show me what they have – the neat rows of potatoes and cabbages, hives buzzing with bees, and the apple, plum and pear trees. Miroslav fills a big bag with fruit which he presents to me.

'I was a teacher,' Dushanka says in English, startling me, 'a teacher of English and History.'

Ashamed, I realise it never occurred to me that this woman in her torn T-shirt and someone else's trainers might understand me. I'd assumed she was uneducated because of the way she lived.

'The honey will be ready in six moons,' she says, gazing at the hives. 'Honey of your own always tastes best.'

We return to Split by a different route, through Vrbnik and Ramljane. The landscape is different, but the destruction is the same. The empty Serb houses accuse – but whom? The Serbs took too much and lost it all; the Croats have it all and are in an empty limbo. I wonder yet again how it's possible to live in a village filled with dead houses and the ghosts and memories of former neighbours and friends. Clearly, anything *is* possible.

'This was a very fascinating day for me,' Ivan says as we approach the coast. 'Boris and me, we've never spoken about the war before yesterday . . . not *really* talked about it. I've learnt a great deal.' He pauses. 'Do you believe in collective guilt?'

Uncertain of the question I hedge. 'I think there can be collective responsibility.'

'I rejoiced you know, when Belgrade was bombed. I wanted to dance. I was happy because Serbs were learning how it felt to be attacked.'

A strange admission, driving through a landscape destroyed by Croats.

'But I also rejoice that these people have come home. I'm glad that they're safe in this country. It proves to me that Croats, at least, are civilised.'

'It must be difficult for you,' I say. 'I would have confused feelings in your position. I *have* confused feelings, and I'm an outsider.'

'Oh no,' he says, 'I know what I think.'

A few kilometres further on, he says suddenly, 'When I was with those people I wanted to put my arms around them. When I see how they live I become like a snowball, I'm a very soft person inside.'

'Hmm,' I say, 'that *must* be confusing.'

'I suppose you're right,' he says grudgingly, 'it *is* confusing. But who can blame us? I must be a masochist . . . I know I say things I shouldn't and never leave anything in peace. I know my failings.'

That night, as I pack my bag and pay my bills, I feel sorry to be leaving Split, with its Mediterranean heart and Slav soul, with so much undone and unseen. I've even grown fond of the Bellevue, where everything is decrepit; everything except the service.

In the darkness, the lights from the square filter through the shutters and play on the ceiling. Tomorrow will bring another city, Sarajevo, and another country, Bosnia.

9 Tributaries

Where have you hidden your dreams,
Land without an outline . . .

from *Traces*, Ajnuša Horozovic

Rain sweeps the harbour, scouring the wooden masts of a small yacht, the twin hulls of a sleek catamaran, the decks of the Jadrolinija ferry, *Petar Hektorović* – a name that rolls awkwardly in an alien mouth. Slovenia seems far away and Rab is just a memory of warm beach and bright sun. Summer is over, even in Split.

The city slides past the wet windows of my bus in a spray of water and damp chill. The conductor, a dark-haired Bosnian with a five o'clock shadow, hands over a ticket with the word 'Sarajevo' printed on it. I hold the small piece of beige paper carefully. After years of wondering and hoping, I'm going back to Sarajevo.

There are only five passengers; the other four crowd together at the front of the bus as if believing there's safety in numbers. One woman wears enormous blue rollers on the top of her head; the rest of her hair hangs dead straight around her pale face as she stares sleepily through a window. Across the aisle a man reads a news story about killings at a rural bar called Café Belfast.

Instead of turning inland as I expect, we carry on down the coast towards Dubrovnik. The rain continues to fall, disappearing into the sea, washing away the dust of summer from leaves and branches, soaking into the thirsty brown earth. It's greener here than further north, with more trees than scrub. The sea looks close enough to touch, its low waves dashing themselves against small jetties, pebbled beaches and the side of the road. Fishing birds sit proud of the water on stumps of rotting wood, watching and waiting. Further out, a multitude of rowing boats sway with the invisible nets that dance below the surface of the water.

The road sign for the town of Duce has been changed: someone has sprayed a háček above the letter 'c'. The place has become 'Duče', pronounced 'douche'. We pass a vast empty monument to former enterprise: walls crumbling, roof spars naked as dinosaur bones, the chimney an accusing finger. This iron and steel works, silent long before the war, is reminiscent in its decay of the Welsh valleys that still echo with the death rattle of industry. There, it was called progress; here, on the Dalmatian coast, it marks the demise of a Communist labour force and the rise of tourism.

Descending towards Makarska, a bay stretches before us full of tiny yachts, their sails a riot of jewel colours brilliant against the blue of sea and sky. The horizon is filled with Hvar, home of lavender flowers and bees. The sun hits the water at the point where island and sea meet, a white underline of light, perfectly straight. As we pass the tip of Hvar, a multitude of other islands appear – Sćedro, Vis, Korčula, Pelješac – layer on layer of islands in shades of grey and blue, as delicate as a silk painting.

The road rises steeply through the cool, green gloom of a pine-tree tunnel. Manchester United footballer David Beckham glares down at passing traffic from a hoarding as we re-emerge into the light. Then the sea is suddenly hundreds of metres below the road, its surface dimpled and glazed with silver stretch-marks. A tiny cove, inaccessible except by boat, curves between towering cliffs; pale beach merges with water that changes from turquoise, to green, to darkest blue as it leaves the shore behind.

Even from this distance, the rocks on the seabed are clear; clear as the water itself.

The small town of Ploče sits on the northern edge of the Neretva delta, an area of freshwater lakes and canals. The excess of water in an otherwise dry land creates an opulent greenness and remark- able fecundity. Orchards are ripe with lemons, oranges, apples, figs and every kind of soft fruit. Greenhouses line the banks of dykes, and a masked man walks between rows of green-leafed vegetables, spraying insecticide from a chemical pack on his back. It's mostly small scale, with individual plots of land marked out by rows of native bamboo, goldenrod and water-filled ditches. Red-roofed houses line the banks of a branch of the Neretva, its water level high after the rain.

Filled with produce and shoppers, Ploče reflects its fertile hin- terland. Bunches of grapes, buckets of olives and bottles of oil; barrows of yellow maize; enormous watermelons, their crimson flesh bright against dark-green skin. This region's lush plenty contrasts with the poverty of Knin, still fresh in my mind; this plump, ripe maize a reminder of the husks in the drying shed above the gateway to Boris's house. It's hard to believe I'm in the same country, that near the start of the third millennium politics and geography are still so intertwined. Ivan's words speak in my head as if he were still at my shoulder.

'Let no-one fool you into thinking they were the only victims. Let no-one fool you into thinking the Communists did nothing for us – look at the roads, the buildings, the schools. But don't forget the Communists were also Serbs, men from Belgrade. Communists, Četniks . . . they were all the same in the end – not Croats.'

We follow the Neretva inland, past Metković, past road signs to Mostar and Sarajevo. As we cross the border into Hercegovina, heartland of Bosnia's Croats, it feels that this is where I was always headed, that all other roads led to here, the physical turning point of my journey. Somehow that's an uncomfortable thought, as though other places, other people, were less significant. But it's not about that: it's about the name, 'Sarajevo', having being carved into the psyche of anyone who ever saw or heard a news programme between 1991 and 1996.

In 1978 I travelled from Split by ship to Dubrovnik, from there by train to Mostar and Sarajevo and from Sarajevo north to Banja Luka and Zagreb; a circle of coast and mountains. This time there are no plans past Sarajevo. Anything could happen.

Of all Bosnia-Hercegovina's major rivers, only one is not a tributary of the mighty Sava, itself a tributary of the Danube. We follow the independent Neretva through villages and small towns, past bars hung defiantly with the white, blue and red chequerboard flag of Croatia. Tudjman and the HDZ cling to this place, to the Croat 'brothers' forced into submission to the Moslems in Sarajevo. 'Croatia must give up claims to Bosnian territory if it's to become part of Europe,' David Austin told me when we met in Zagreb; but following this river, it occurs to me that it may not be the land or even the 'brothers' that Croats desire, but the beautiful Neretva itself.

South-west of Mostar, the land is a flat plain ringed by the ubiquitous mountains. Destruction and modernisation have been drastic, and I recognise almost nothing. Homes stand empty while construction goes on around them; new, white houses spring from the cultivated land west of the river like a crop of red-capped mushrooms. There are no mosques, for this is Bosnian Croat territory. Close to Mostar itself, the destruction is more evident and more comprehensive – from pockmarked walls, the plaster blown away to reveal the Ottoman and Hapsburg brickwork beneath, to whole buildings now a heap of charred bricks. Restaurants without customers or roofs; road signs bullet-holed into colanders. There's little evidence of reconstruction here in Mostar's town centre – the war could have ended last week rather than four years ago. Walls with a smooth enough surface sport the same 'White Boy' graffiti I saw in Split.

In 1978, the Neretva flowed through the centre of town beneath the elegant single span of the Stari Most, the Old Bridge that linked Mostar's east and west. Blown to pieces by shelling in November 1993, the sixteenth-century bridge exists today only in memory and photographs. The single surviving record of my original journey is a small, grainy image of Mostar's Old Bridge and the stone walls and minarets surrounding it. Clear memories of 1978 are rare, but I've never forgotten leaving the train station and walking towards that bridge through the eastern part of town, past mosques and wooden houses in the company of Communist soldiers and short, dark, strong-smelling men in sheepskin jerkins. It was a hot September day. The call to prayer went out as I crossed the bridge, passing small sun-browned boys who leapt, screaming with fear and delight, into the water far below. For the first time in my life I was aware of being an alien: I was European, and this was not Europe as I knew it. It was a moment of great excitement.

Now, as the bus passes through the town centre, I can just see the temporary metal bridge that joins east to west. There's reconstruction here now, but it's slow. Two years earlier, Hungarian engineers serving as NATO peacekeepers began the salvage of the Old Bridge, watched by Bosnia's president, Alija Izetbegović. I've heard that the people of Mostar feel their needs are ignored by the international community, and are angry that their city is less well known and less well funded than Sarajevo. It's not as simple as that, of course. Mostar remains deeply divided by war: few Bosnian Moslems cross that bridge to the West and few Bosnian Croats go East.

The road pursues the Neretva through hills that gradually become mountains. The railway line clings to the cliff face, passing under tunnels blasted through rock by Hapsburg engineers; here on the valley floor there's barely enough space for river and road. The only escape from this long, narrow trap is to find a tributary and hope it leads you out. The river cutting deeply between cliffs is almost the same unnatural green as Slovenia's Soča. Its water looks pure enough to drink, but here near Mostar it has a bloody past. In June 1941 the Ustaše arrested and murdered many hundreds of Mostar Serbs, throwing their bodies into this river until the water ran red; animals fed on the bloated corpses washed up on the banks. The Serbs retaliated: after pushing back the Ustaše forces, they attacked local Croats and Moslems, whom they saw as collaborators, and murdered whole populations in their turn. In April and May 1992, history repeated itself as Croats fought to protect both themselves and their Moslem neighbours against a Yugoslav Army bent on making the Neretva the border between Serbia and the rest of the world.

Road and river repeatedly cross and intertwine. Bridges are makeshift here: brand-new structures sit beside smashed ones; others are in the process of repair; many are guarded. Crossing one part-built bridge at a bend in the river, I see the first sign that this is a country controlled by international forces. Some SFOR troops have set up an uncomfortable-looking camp at the base of a rock face, and thin cooking smoke drifts up beside a fluttering blue and yellow flag. Very young, very skinny men with white-grey faces patrol the bridge, checking trucks; I guess these teenagers are from the former Soviet Union even before seeing the Ukrainian flag.

As we move deeper into Bosnia the mountains become higher, their limestone peaks brilliantly white in the sun. Mined areas are marked with hexagonal symbols, and we pass a ruined church, its large Christian cemetery overgrown. Bizarrely neoteric buildings in pinks and purples are under construction in the midst of the destruction. Something perhaps to do with money and local politics.

Approaching Jablanica it's obvious who lives in this seemingly prosperous town. There's a factory, new buildings – and a brand-new mosque. The few burnt-out houses are Croat homes, maybe Serb. Apart from church and mosque, the only way to tell who lives where is by the headstones in the cemeteries.

We lose the Neretva after Jablanica; it disappears, merging with the dark turquoise-green waters of the Jablanica Jezero. The road passes the lake's southern edge, its mirror-like surface plump with the waters of several tributaries, reflecting rock and trees and occasionally the bus itself. The lake ends at the town of Konjić, and as if by magic the Neretva reappears, heading south towards the Republika Srpska and its source near the border with Montenegro. Our road goes north on the last stage of our journey to Sarajevo, and soon the landscape changes yet again, becoming more Alpine. Goats and cows graze in steep pastures; clusters of great rounded haystacks look like fat monks gossiping; wooden balconied houses remind me of Slovenia, Austria and southern Germany. The grass seems suddenly very green, the orchards dense with apples and plums. There's work here, and some prosperity. The small factories along the road turn logs into pallets, rock into gravel, and several of the new stone and wood houses we pass are remarkable designer-built properties. The road sign for Sarajevo Canton stands beside a garden where a woman hoes her vegetables; men tie up vines, chop wood, cart hay. Flowers hang from balconies in baskets and pots, creating a profusion of colour not seen since leaving Slovenia.

We pass a sign to Igman – Mount Igman, the high point of the range south-west of Sarajevo from where the city was shelled – then round a bend and quite suddenly Sarajevo is there, shining in the afternoon light. It's bigger than I remember, spreading across several low hills. The river running beside us now is the Bosna. It's only a small river here, nothing like the broad, mighty water-way that will enter the Sava on the border with Croatia. Men and women tend maize and cabbages in the fields of its broad, flat val-ley, and along its banks families are camping, picnicking and fishing. Somehow it's all unexpectedly civilised. In the outer suburbs I see a mixed Christian and Moslem cemetery – the first and, as it turns out, the only one I will see on my journey. There are very few ruined houses. It seems so different from Mostar . . . but then no-one disputes that this is Bosnia.

The young man sitting behind me has been looking over my shoulder for the past half-hour. He taps me politely when curiosity gets the better of him and asks if he can look at what I'm reading. It's a history of Bosnia given to me by a friend at the Bosnian Embassy in London, the same friend I'm on my way to meet.

'Is this your first time in Sarajevo?' he asks.

I repeat the now stock phrase, 'No, I was here twenty years ago.'

'Ah,' he says, 'but everything has changed since then. Now it is all new and different.' He smiles. 'Welcome to Sarajevo.'

I am oddly moved by his simple remark, which has passed into custom in this part of the world as both a greeting and an irony.

Entering the city, the rural suburbs of moments earlier seem like a false memory. Whole streets are lined with old houses in ruins, their roofs gone, walls shattered, gardens rank and cratered. The closer to the city centre, the greater the destruction; the main road into town is lined with wrecked buildings. The Bosnian passengers look out impassively, or continue to read their books or newspapers. The handful of foreigners gasp at the extent of the damage. Whole apartment blocks are devastated, but most dramatic of all is the *Oslobodjene* building, its many glass and metal storeys melted around the central lift shaft, turning what was one of the most modern publishing centres in the world into a phallic stump. Destroyed by Serb shelling in 1992, the Bosnian morning newspaper *Oslobodjene* – which the man behind tells me means 'Liberation' – continued to be produced in a nuclear shelter beneath its former offices. The newspaper came out every day, but the cost was high: five staff were killed and more than thirty were wounded in the first ten months of the war alone.

'That was an old people's home,' he says pointing to an ugly pink and blue structure that's collapsed on itself like a mouth without teeth.

We pass a fairground and the UN offices, the satellite dish on its roof dwarfing the building beneath. Reconstruction is every-where, right next to crumbled homes and offices. Sarajevo's architecture is a blend of old and new, East and West, shattered and shining new. This juxtaposition of past and present, alive and dead says something to a visitor about the nature of this city and of its inhabitants. I have a sudden feeling that this is not a place you can enter. It enters you, whether you let it or no.

The sense of opposites meeting becomes clearer as I cross the city centre; that, and a sense of recognition, of remembrance. On the taxi radio a woman sings a mournful Islamic song. Young boys rollerblade past roofless buildings. We pass the reconstructed Holiday Inn – probably the world's most famous Holiday Inn – home and office for international journalists throughout the 1992–95 siege. The pair of shattered tower blocks nearby have black polythene billowing in place of windows. I glimpse a man kneeling in the courtyard of a mosque; watched by women and children, a second man lays his hands on the other's shoulders as if in blessing. The sense of recognition is strong, but it's a strangely second-hand feeling. Am I remembering my own expe-rience, or the many hours of TV footage, documentaries and fea-ture films of the war?

There's no-one at home in the apartment on Jezero street where I'm to stay with Shahbaza Sidran, the mother of Miranda, my London friend. The guard in the sentry box outside the nearby Russian Embassy follows me into the apartment block, waving at the road and making encouraging noises. I don't have a clue what he's trying to say. Then a small, elegant woman arrives at a trot and the guard grins with relief before disappearing back into his box.

'Miranda and I are eating lunch in a restaurant around the cor-ner,' Shahbaza says in a mixture of German and Bosnian. 'We saw your taxi pass – I told this guard to look out for you.'

This must be one of the most secure places in Sarajevo, with a twenty-four-hour embassy guard – clearly in her pocket – only metres from the front door.

'I make them cups of tea,' she says by way of explanation, handing me a key to the apartment. 'There are two men also staying in my house,' she says as we walk to the nearby restaurant to rejoin the family. 'Albanian men from Priština. But they are good men, not a problem for you.'

After lunch Miranda takes me on a tour. It's *her* city, where she grew up, was educated, worked, got married, had her child. Now she shows me Sarajevo with a mixture of longing and sadness. Showing foreigners around my own country of Britain, I always learn something new, see things with a fresh eye; Miranda comes home often, but it's only in the company of a visitor that she really notices what's changed, what's gone. Mosques have been restored, while offices and shops remain wrecked. Restaurants have closed and new ones opened. A favourite café is shut down, a particular theatre changed beyond recognition.

'Sometimes I feel like a tourist,' she says sadly.

'Do you miss being here? Would you like to live here again?'

'Of course, I miss it terribly. But it will be a while before things are as they were before the war. When you talk to Bosnian people you'll find that everyone's life has been divided into before and after the war.'

'And the future?'

'The future belongs with our children. When I had my daughter Hena in 1997 I felt very strongly that I was giving something to my country, something for the future. I want her to be brought up here, in her own country, as a Bosnian.'

Miranda decides to show me the Eternal Flame, a memorial in the heart of the city to the dead of World War II, so we make our way towards it along elegant pedestrianised streets, past newly painted Austro-Hungarian buildings. There are bookshops, pharmacies and travel agents. The passers-by are well dressed despite the unfashionable clothes stores that I've come to expect. Everyone looks busy and everyone, including Miranda, ignores the foreign soldiers all around them as if they were invisible. We pass armed men from France, Spain, Russia, Italy, Sweden and Hawaii. Interestingly, they're all identifiable as what they are: the Swedes look very Swedish, the Italians very Italian. They all look unbelievably young and fresh faced; or perhaps I'm just getting older.

The road forks at the end of Maršala Tita, and there, set into the pavement, is the Eternal Flame. Or at least it should be. The gas-fired Flame is out. All the gas in Sarajevo is out. The Russian government has cut off the supply to Serbia and Montenegro because they haven't paid their bills. Miranda gazes at the monument and shakes her head before walking on along Ferhadija towards Baščaršija, the old Ottoman market district.

I have a sense of specific recognition, even before Miranda says: 'This is where the Serbs shelled people queuing for food. There was a big queue that day because the shop had ice cream and no-one had seen ice cream for a long time.'

My scalp crawls at the memory of a man being carried away from the spot where I'm standing, his left leg missing below the knee, white bone very bright among strips of hanging flesh. Of course, I didn't really see this, only the image of it in a film called *Welcome to Sarajevo*, which re-created the scene from news footage. The shop is painted a clean lemon yellow now, and there's a plaque set into the restored plasterwork that Miranda translates: 'Here seventeen people were murdered by Serbs.'

Many of the paving stones in Ferhadija are red; throughout Sarajevo, red paving stones mark the place where people fell, to shells or snipers, and there are many.

At a junction of streets, Miranda points west. 'Look, up there . . . that's where the Serb guns were, along that ridge and beyond, encircling us. You can see now that there was nowhere to hide. We were like mice in a trap.'

Many of the pine trees along the ridge are dead, burnt or snapped by the guns firing around them.

'Where was the Bosnian Army?'

'Here in the town. They couldn't do much to attack the Serbs but they defended us very well against the JNA for four years. Without the Army, Sarajevo would have fallen.'

As we continue our tour through the centre of town, it's impossible to walk more than a few hundred metres without coming across old friends of Miranda's, who seem to be mostly men. Passing the entrance to an old apartment block we literally bump into Adin Hebib, who invites us into his home. Sitting puffy-eyed across a table covered in sketches, old newspapers and a litre bottle of *rakija*, Adin epitomises my idea of a dissolute Balkan artist. He pours the alcohol into wine glasses and slugs his back.

'I'm killing myself with it,' he says, flourishing the empty glass and grinning, 'but slowly.'

Most of his work seems to depict the same repeated image of the Old Bridge at Mostar in different lurid colours and thick childlike brushstrokes. I make polite noises, which is just as well because he produces a photograph of himself and his assistants working on a large, dramatic mural at the Bosnian Embassy in Washington DC.

'That's our ambassador there,' Miranda says, pointing to a short man in the photo. 'He's Jewish.' She grins. 'And they call us a Moslem country!'

Rummaging on the littered table, Adin produces another photo and hands it to Miranda.

'Who are they?' she asks.

'My children,' he replies.

She looks confused. 'Which children?'

'My latest children! Aren't they wonderful?'

Miranda's face turns from pink to white and back again. 'Then you're not with . . .'

'No, not for a long time. How long have you been away?'

Walking back down to the street, Miranda shakes her head. 'Can you believe he's got five children by three clever and attractive women? I've known him for years and I never get used to how he carries on!'

There's something serendipitous about today. Leaving the building, we meet the historian Eleanor Weissmann, an expert on

Bosnian culture whom I'd tried unsuccessfully to reach before leaving London and had been thinking about earlier while on the bus.

'Can't talk now,' she says, handing me a business card, 'got a meeting. Why don't you come to the lecture I'm giving on Bosnian tombs for the Foreign Ladies Society of Sarajevo. We'll be talking about Bosnian history. National Museum, day after tomorrow. See you there.'

Then she's gone, her tall, stately figure disappearing into the crowd of passers-by.

The country of Bosnia was first mentioned as a separate territory by the tenth-century Byzantine emperor/historian Constantine Porphyrogenitus. The area he referred to was smaller than present-day Bosnia and based around the Bosna valley north of modern Sarajevo. In the early eleventh century, the Byzantine imperial sec-retary, John Kinnamos, wrote, 'And Bosnia is not subordinated . . . it is on its own; a nation living an independent life and governing itself.' This independence fluctuated. Bosnia, like its neighbours Croatia and Serbia, was for extended periods of time dominated by either Hungary or Byzantium, the latter ruling indirectly through governors called *bans*. All this changed in 1180 with the rise of the legendary Bosnian ruler Ban Kulin, who gave Bosnia twenty-four years of peace and economic and cultural growth. He made treaties with Ragusan (Dubrovnik) merchants to expand Bosnia's extensive mining potential and made dynastic marriages between his own family and those of neighbouring rulers. He faced religious diffi-culties from both Hungary, which wanted to control the Bosnian Church, and Rome, which regarded Bosnian Catholics as heretics. After Ban Kulin's death in 1204, these unresolved religious issues became a justification for the invasion of Bosnia by Hungary in the 1230s. But Hungary's gains were short-lived, cut off by the

Mongol invasions of 1241 in which Hungary was crushed and Bosnia left virtually untouched.

The greatest expansion of Bosnian political, economic and cultural life took place in the early fourteenth century under Ban Stjepan Kotromanić II and his nephew, Ban and later King, Tvrtko Kotromanić. Ban Stjepan, who ruled Bosnia for more than thirty years, left a powerful, territorially expanded country on his death in 1353. Tvrtko built on his uncle's gains. After contending with unruly nobles, including his own brother, he created a nation larger than modern-day Bosnia. By the late fourteenth century, his kingdom covered the region from the Sava River in the north to the Drina in the east. In the south and west, Bosnia ruled the Dalmatian coast and islands (with the exception of Ragusa), from Šibenik to the Bay of Kotor in modern Montenegro and Novi Pazar in modern Serbia. Tvrtko was crowned King of Bosnia in 1377 and before his death in 1391, decided he was King of Croatia and Dalmatia too.

Bosnian soldiers defeated a Turkish raiding party in the Neretva valley in 1388, and in 1389 those same Bosnians fought the Turks alongside the Serb Prince Lazar at the famous battle of Kosovo Polje. The battle ended in a stalemate, though Lazar was captured and executed. Serb history turned a draw into a defeat, Lazar into a Christian martyr, and expunged any mention of Bosnian or other allies. The Turks soon gained all Serbian Orthodox land and held it as overlords for the next five hundred years. It would be another hundred and fifty years before the Ottomans finally gained control of all Bosnia.

In the fourteenth century, Vrhbosna, the south-central region of Bosnia, was also the name of a village on the trade routes between the country's metal mines and the hungry metal markets at Ragusa. Bosnia's mines and decorative metalworkers were famous throughout Europe in the Middle Ages and attracted many foreign workers. Saxon metallurgists managed many of the Ragusan mining colonies dotted throughout Bosnia producing lead, copper, silver and gold. Despite being on the trade route, Vrhbosna village was still little more than a fort and a few dozen houses when the Turks invaded in 1448, but its potential was noted and the future town of Sarajevo was born.

Bosnia's metalworking tradition still exists here, and can be found among the many workshops and jeweller's stores in the narrow streets of Baščaršija. Miranda and I drink small cups of dense Turkish coffee at a small outdoor café and watch as a masked man creates something with a blowtorch in the street outside his workplace. Shops display ornate metal coffeepots, bowls and models of medieval Bosnian tombs. The many jewellery shops are filled with gold – red, white and yellow. I buy a pair of exquisitely crafted earrings at a more than reasonable price. The small box is wrapped in shiny paper and gold ribbon, and placed in a gold and purple bag. It feels as if I've bought something of great value.

Given the city's recent history, I'm surprised at the number of early Ottoman buildings remaining in Baščaršija. Mosques, bathhouses and inns branch off the main market streets of wooden shops and cafés. Miranda explains that aid money has gone into restoring this part of the city. In the courtyard of a sixteenth-century mosque, men wash their feet at a fountain under a decorated pavilion while doves flutter and perch in the trees. Graveyards with their distinctive Turkish stele surround the courtyard, with the tombs of the famous or especially holy closest to the mosque. Young men seated on carpets pore over the Qur'an under the entrance porch of the mosque.

'Do many people go to the mosque these days?' I ask.

'Bosnia was not a religious country – we grew up under Communism – but it's *become* a religious place since the war. To be a practising moslem is a political statement these days. When I was young I never saw a woman wearing a *burqa*; on this visit I've seen several.' She shakes her head. 'I don't like it, it's not the Sarajevo I knew. We were proud of being one of the most culturally diverse cities in Europe. Diversity was Bosnia's wealth

and we valued it. But now religion has divided us from our neighbours and we are divided even among ourselves. Did you know
that "Moslem" spelt with a lower case represents religion and
with a capital it's an ethnic group?'

'How did that happen?'

'Until the 1961 census everyone here was seen as ethnic Serb
or Croat because there was no way any other group could be
defined. It wasn't until the 1971 census that my father, for example, could refer to himself as a Moslem in the sense of "nationality", and then in 1974 constitutional change in Yugoslavia
allowed Bosnia's non-Serb/Croat population to really declare
themselves for the first time.'

'And what about people calling themselves Bosnian?'

Her eyes flash with unexpected passion. 'No-one could call
themselves that because there *was* no Bosnia and therefore no
Bosnians as far as Belgrade was concerned. That's the one thing
to come from this terrible war: Bosnia exists again.'

At the end of a short alleyway we enter an Ottoman inn, called
a *han*. Like many of the buildings in the Baščaršija, the *han* is
wooden from the first floor up and has been burnt down and rebuilt
many times in its three hundred years of life. Almost invisible from
the street, inside it's vast: a series of galleries lead off a central
courtyard which in the past would have been open to the sky; long
beams support the roof, lending a dizzying sense of space overhead. The guests slept in cubicles along the gallery. The cubicles
are businesses now; one door has a travel company poster on it.

'It was the custom in Ottoman territory that each guest receive
the first three nights lodging and food for himself and his horse
for free,' Miranda says. 'That was Ottoman hospitality.' She
looks around the echoing, empty space and sighs. 'We Bosnians
are proud of our heritage, and rightly so. The Ottomans were
civilised – more tolerant and intellectually advanced than most
European countries. It's strange isn't it, how things change.'

Two men are sitting in the living room of the apartment wrapped in a fug of cigarette smoke and watching football at high volume. The Albanians. We smile diffidently at each other as Adem Villasi and Xhaver Demaqi introduce themselves. I ask if they expect Shahbaza.

'She doesn't stay here,' Adem says. 'She comes in to make breakfast and tidy, but she doesn't stay . . . it wouldn't be proper.'

Does this mean it's improper for *me* to be here? Or maybe such strictures don't apply to a non-Moslem woman. Perhaps northern European women have no virtue to lose?

Adem is an attractive, slender man in his early thirties. Xhaver is older, with a seemingly permanent grin which has little to do with humour. We talk about Kosovo and NATO, and they tell me they're attending an internationally funded course which will equip them to create a computerised survey of Kosovo's geo-physical phenomena.

'How did you feel when NATO started bombing Priština?' I ask after everyone's relaxed and we've swapped cigarettes for *rakija*.

Xhaver grins ambiguously. 'Delighted!'

'Really happy,' Adem says.

'Even though you knew you might be killed?'

'In these situations you weigh up the risks. The chance of being murdered by a Serb was much greater than being hit by a bomb. Anything that made it less likely we'd be murdered was a good thing. We would listen for the sounds of the planes and the noise of the bombs falling. Sometimes when we heard these things we would stop hiding and go outside. Usually it was impossible to go out and there was always at least one person on look-out in our building. I kept a suitcase packed, in case we had to leave very fast. When the war started it was winter, and the clothes in the case were thick and warm. As the seasons changed, the clothes in the case changed too, until it ended just now, in the summer.'

Xhaver nods. 'My family couldn't leave the house because the Serbs were out there, waiting for us. When NATO dropped the bombs, all the Serbs ran and hid under the ground. Then the streets were OK. This was the only time we could be free. One day a neighbour, a friend, was murdered. The Serbs came and demanded all his money and gave him time to sell things and get more money for them. After he gave it all to them they killed him. They cut his throat.'

'The Serbs tried to get into my building,' Adem says, 'my wife and two-year-old daughter were there. The soldiers tried to smash in the front door but it was made of steel and wouldn't break, but they kept on pushing and banging. We had no weapons . . . Can you imagine everyone in the building just waiting to see if they would be killed in the next few minutes? Can you imagine what that was like?'

I shake my head. I can imagine it, but there's that yawning gap between imagination and reality.

'My wife put her hands over our daughter's ears so she wouldn't hear the banging noise. The door opened outwards, not inwards, but they couldn't work that out, so eventually they left.' He draws hard on his cigarette. 'My daughter was afraid all the time, afraid of the noise of the bombs. We put cotton wool in her ears every night but she still heard and she cried a lot, asking over and over, "What's happening, what's happening?" She still cries, but she was lucky. Other children were killed or hurt, or saw their family blown to pieces around them. Those children will never recover.'

As Adem speaks, I think of the Serb couple I met the previous day, Dushanka and Miroslav, their children bombed into unemployment and hunger by NATO. Is it only twenty-four hours since I sat at that broken table in the Krajina?

I ask about democracy in Kosovo. How is it that with a 90 per cent majority population, Albanians lack power in Yugoslav politics? Do they not vote?

Adem looks at me as if I'm stupid, which in respect of Kosovan politics is probably true, and answers irritably.

'Do you think one person, one vote means democracy? Where have you been all your life? We are almost two million Albanians in Kosovo, but we are allowed only three or four deputies in the

Belgrade parliament and they are too few to have any power. Of course we all vote for Albanian deputies, but it's meaningless when the number of our representatives is already decided.'

Xhaver's grin is even more fixed. 'Democracy has many forms: ours is a sham, Belgrade has made sure of that for many years.'

The conversation lapses, as each man draws in on his own thoughts. On TV, an overweight, middle-aged man in shades, his collar and tie askew, sings modern Moslem songs in the courtyard of a *han*. It's so cold that his breath hangs white in the air; his feet shift on the cobbles, not in time with the music, but to keep warm. Behind him, frozen-looking women jiggle stiffly. Xhaver and Adem chuckle, and comment in Albanian. I ask about the origins of the Albanian language.

'It's a Latin language, similar to Romanian and Italian. Albanians are Illyrians, the original inhabitants of this part of Europe – you know about that?'

I nod, glad to seem not entirely ignorant, but then make a cultural *faux pas* anyway.

'Strange,' I say, thinking aloud.

'How strange?' Adem asks suspiciously.

'I always thought Albanian would be like Turkish,' but at the look on his face I hastily add, 'but then I know nothing.'

'You're right,' he answers tartly, 'you *don't* know anything if you think the Albanian language is anything like Turkish.'

There are red geraniums on the windowsill outside my room, which I have to avoid crushing as I close the shutters. It's a sitting room, with a small bed, two large black leather sofas surrounded by paintings and drawings, and a wall covered in bookcases, full of academic tomes on history, culture and criticism. I've never met the man whose room this once was, Miranda's father, Shahbaza's former husband. It feels that nothing has been changed, nothing moved since he last lived here. The desk where he worked looks undisturbed, though that's probably just my fantasy. Abdulah Sidran is Bosnia's leading screenwriter and poet. At that desk he created some of Europe's finest moments in film, works which won him the Palme d'Or at Cannes and prizes beyond count in the Former Yugoslavia.

I get into bed with his most recent book of poems, open a page and read:

> *Poslušajte*
> *Kako diše*
> *Planeta Sarajevo*
>
> Listen
> to the breathing
> of Planet Sarajevo

I close my eyes and listen, as the poem demands, to the sounds of the city beyond the closed shutters and the geraniums.

10   The History of Acronymia

T HE NEXT day is Saturday, and the international forces are taking the day off. Italian *carabiniere* strut in their tight black.
Greeks and Russians wave, smiling, as I photograph them. Black
and white American soldiers, gun in one hand, camera in the
other, take photos of rugs, coffeepots and the mountains surrounding us. Restaurants are filled with uniformed men, each
nationality claiming its own territory. In one café, some French
boys order ice cream then prop automatic weapons beside their
chairs like umbrellas; but the guns slide on the tiled floor and drop
with a metallic crash. There are uniformed women too, but not, it
would seem, with the Russians, the Ukrainians or any of the other
south or east European nationalities represented here.

Baščaršija is only a small area of the city, but its mosques and
shops and cafés draw me as easily as any tourist. This is a place
where things happen. Beside the troop-filled cafés, bridges are
being rebuilt to the sounds of hammering. Plasterers stand on high
wooden planks filling in bullet holes and shrapnel scars. Tattooed
men drill and dig and shovel cement. Outside an old wooden
house a young man splits logs with an axe, then hurls them onto
a growing pile; split, hurl, split, hurl – the motion is hypnotic.

At the far end of the district, beside the *čevapčići* and *burek*
shops, is the *Sebilj* fountain; around it, elderly men and women sit
on upturned Coke crates and sell paper bags of bird corn. The sun
warms red roofs and glitters along the white of minarets; beyond

the vendors and the soldiers are mountains and poplar trees. I buy some corn, and immediately a cloud of birds descends, their wings brushing my face and hair. Handfuls of bird food rattle on the pavement, and as the fat, glossy pigeons scuffle I have a *déjà vu* . . . not of an actual past experience, but a creative one. I wrote this scene – the birds, the minarets, the soldiers, the mountains – in a novel. Only, that city was different; not Sarajevo but Mazar-i-Sharif, Afghanistan.

In the courtyard of an early Ottoman building that houses a small museum, I meet Jasmin, the curator. The building is exquisite, a small jewel, its simple elegance and symmetry a reminder of the wonders of Islamic architecture, yet the scale is human and homely. Jasmin tells me it used to be a theological school, and it's easy to imagine an elderly imam warming himself in front of the fire, his feet on a stool, attentive pupils around him.

The museum's octagonal main chamber displays the city's minarets, bathhouses, markets and *hans* in a remarkable model of nineteenth-century Sarajevo.

'It was made many years ago by a famous man,' Jasmin says. 'He loved the city, you can tell this because everything in the model is so perfect. It took all his life to make, there is more of it in these other rooms. I will show you.'

Individual rooms surround a small fountain courtyard, each echoing the form of the central chamber, even down to the fireplace. Smaller models are on display here: close-ups of Sarajevo; specific locations; three-dimensional images for everyone to look at, made at a time when photography was an expensive private hobby. Poplars seem to grow from the bright green of painted grass and streams to flow under tiny bridges. With its trees and pastures, houses and *hans*, the model makes me believe that old

Sarajevo too was like that – a comfortable, yet vibrant place, created on a very human scale.

Most perfect is the curator himself. Tall, narrow-hipped and broad-shouldered, with shining black hair and eyes, Jasmin is a very beautiful young man. He smiles, showing large white teeth, and tells me he's nineteen and a student. His gaze is open and innocent, as if he's never had an improper thought in his life. From a café beyond the walls, what sounds like local jazz is replaced by the Rolling Stones. Jasmin looks down at me, smiling, waiting perhaps for me to ask a question. I decide, reluctantly, that a theological school, even a former one, is not the most suitable spot for a pick-up. Not by a woman, anyway.

Walking to the main market I stop briefly at an office on Ferhadija and am invited to meet a highly respected Bosnian cultural historian the following day, which means missing the medieval tombs and Sarajevo's Foreign Ladies.

'I'm in the office this morning anyway,' Eleanor Weissmann says when I call to let her know that I can't make the Ladies Circle. 'Come in the next hour and I'll be here, we can chat then.'

Yellow trams rumble along Mula Mustafe Bašeskije, past the old synagogue, past a new health-food shop and past a large green and white building, the shop on its ground floor selling vacuum cleaners and other electrical goods. From the first floor upwards, the elegant nineteenth-century building is a shell of walls and broken roof spars.

In a space between old apartment blocks and faceless sixties buildings, the green-painted market stalls are bowed with produce. Women in Moslem *šamija* and floral headscarves offer bags of dried herbs for tea and medicines, none of which I recognise. Vendors bundle spinach, cucumbers and large golden onions onto scales to be weighed. Pomegranates, tomatoes and heaps of red, white and yellow peppers shine as the sun catches their glossy skin. Many of the stallholders are young and smile for the camera. A small boy with glasses hangs by the wrists from the roof of a stall, trying to do a chin-up. Compared to a London market, it's very quiet. No-one shouts the price of carrots or yells an offer on apples. Men and women move between the stalls with a minimum of noise or bodily contact. Many of the shoppers are male, some with disabilities: scars, a missing limb, a limp. Elderly people, just a few items in their bags, walk slowly away, heads bent, looking at the ground. In early February 1994, more than seventy people died here in one of the most shocking incidents of a shocking war. After many thousands of deaths, the shelling of Sarajevo's central market stunned the world. It was images of this market, with its bleeding victims, corpses and body parts, that prompted the mobilisation of NATO forces against the Serbs, up there on the hills.

I buy a bag of dried mint and something that looks like catnip, in return for photos of the wrinkled stallholder. As I walk away, I glance past the Catholic cathedral in its pleasant, café-filled square, and peer in the direction of the river and the hills looming hazily in the sunshine, their crown of broken trees a reminder, if one were necessary, that there's nowhere in this city not overlooked.

In an office near Maršala Tita, the imposing Eleanor Weissmann is ready to talk.

'A pity you can't make the lecture this afternoon,' she says from behind her desk, 'and the Foreign Ladies are very interesting too.'

'Who exactly are these Foreign Ladies?'

'Oh, diplomats, wives of diplomats or international community staff. They're enormously powerful because they're able to raise huge sums of money for charitable causes and because they've got lots of influence. I'm hoping they'll be useful in raising money for the preservation of _stećci_ – that's what the medieval Bosnian tombs are called.'

'Are they in need of preservation?'

'Oh God, yes. This country has already lost so much of its heritage; years of war, and now thugs are trying to get rich quick. There was an old English guy – he died quite recently, I think, must have been nearly a hundred – he spent a lot of time in this country in the twenties and took remarkable photos of things that have completely disappeared: wooden watermills, bridges, houses hundreds of years old, and even tombs. The carving on some of the *stećci* is exquisite and unique, and now they're disappearing.'

'I read some Bosnian history before coming here, but it's pretty complicated and . . .'

'Not at all! Not if you're a historian, anyway. There are just lots of ridiculous theories around. Once you get past those, it's perfectly straightforward.'

Right.

'The main theory, which few real historians give much credence to these days, is about Bosnian Bogomilism. You know about Bogomils?'

'Uh, vaguely.'

For the next hour, Dr Weissmann lectures me on Bogomilism, a Christian heresy based on the Manichean dualist teaching which believed that God and the Devil, Good and Evil, have almost equal power, and that as the Devil rules the world and the flesh, all things material should be rejected as far as possible. Named after a tenth-century Bulgarian priest, Bogomilism spread through the eastern Balkans in the centuries that followed. The origins of the Bosnian Catholic Church are vague and barely documented, and this vagueness has allowed the imposition of theories and agendas, mostly around Bogomilism.

'Historians since the nineteenth century have been keen to prove that the medieval Bosnian Church was Bogomil,' Eleanor explains from behind her desk. 'It suited the political purposes of many groups, even the Bosnians themselves, to believe that this was a non-Bosnian belief, something from outside. Some Croat historians have wanted to prove the Bogomil theory because it strengthens their proposal that there was no independent Bosnian

Church, and therefore no independent Bosnia. Serb historians have tried to prove the opposite, that the Bosnian Church wasn't Catholic at all, but Orthodox – which of course would make Bosnia just an adjunct to Serbia. When Austro-Hungary took control of this region from the Ottomans in 1878, *their* historians were also eager to prove that Bosnia had never really been an independent state – but then they also made the mistake of imagining the Bosnians would welcome them as liberators, when in fact the majority of Bosnians wanted to stay within the Ottoman Empire . . . just with a bit more autonomy.'

'Like the Slovenes and Croats with the Austro-Hungarians?'

'Exactly.'

'And the Bosnians themselves, what do . . .'

'Bosniaks, Bosnian Moslems, *like* the idea of Bogomil religious ancestry because it means they were never Catholic or Orthodox, neither Croat or Serb, though of course those national–religious distinctions are quite modern. Some Bosniaks and others have used Bogomilism as a reason to explain why so many Bosnians converted to Islam, compared to Serbs or Croats. Having been persecuted for years as heretics by Catholics and Orthodox alike, it was easy for Bosnians to embrace a different religion, or so the theory goes. That's always been a big issue in this part of the world – the Bosnians as traitors to Christianity.'

'And what do *you* think?'

'Having studied many tombs, everything points away from Bogomilism . . . though there are reputable people around who are still convinced Bosnia was Bogomil. Dualism hates the material world, but the carvings on the stones are full of positive physical symbolism. They're more likely to be left-over paganism than Christian dualism. Then, of course, there are no comparable tombs in any known Bogomil regions, such as Thrace or Bulgaria itself. Bosnia must have been a remote and difficult place to reach, and medieval priests were probably still half pagan, possibly illiterate, and didn't follow Catholic practice precisely enough for Rome, which interpreted laxity as heresy . . .'

The phone rings, interrupting her flow. 'I've got a woman with me, some writer or other. I'll call you later.

'But I think the most interesting thing about it all is the political dimension,' she continues. 'The way in which an independent Bosnia was seen as being related to an independent Church. Bosnia was a large and powerful kingdom up until the mid-fifteenth century when the last king was beheaded by the Turks. His mother was in Rome at the time and she *donated* Bosnia to the Papacy, hoping this would force the Papacy to save her country. It didn't, of course.'

As I listen, it strikes me that a refutation of the Bogomil theory is as clear a political statement as the acceptance of it. There's another, more current theory about Bosnia, fuelled by the work of historians like Dr Weissmann, one which I imagine has gathered strength since the war: namely that because Bosnia was politically and theologically independent five hundred years ago, it therefore should and must be a nation. Precisely the same arguments are used by Bosnia's neighbours to justify their claims. By extension, peoples who ever lived anywhere within human memory retain territorial rights, regardless of who might live on that territory today. On this basis, my own family are Romano-Celts and the Anglo-Saxons should bugger off where they came from fifteen hundred years ago. Or rather, we're British Celts and the Romans should go back to Rome. Or perhaps we're descended from those Indo-European invaders who overwhelmed the aboriginal inhabitants of Britain in the mists of pre-history, in which case I should bugger off myself.

Finishing with Bosnian history, Eleanor moves on to her own. Over the next forty minutes we cover Abingdon, a small town in southern England; Abu Simbel, a lost culture in southern Egypt; and her acquaintance with Anthony Blunt, a British spy and art critic. Before I can guess her age, we pass on to childhood, paternal relationship and a past life as the murdered concubine of a Babylonian ruler; all topped off by mystery religions and shamanism, studied with a bizarre-sounding individual in Belgium. By the time we leave the office, mental exhaustion has set in.

As I emerge, blinking, into the daylight, Eleanor views me critically and eyes a cosmetics store across the street.

'It's remarkable what you can buy these days,' she says. 'I look a great deal younger than I am.'

Two words cross my mind. Virgin's blood.

Back at the apartment on Jezero, there are messages for me. One from the Dispatch Centre of the Office of the High Representative, the international community 'government' of Bosnia, offers a lift to Mostar; another is from the Deputy Head of Mission at the British Embassy. 'Leaving for Banja Luka Friday,' it says, 'let me know if you want to come.'

The Albanians are out and Shabaza's tidying up. She wants to know how the two men are behaving.

'They're great,' I say. 'Good company, and the only Balkan men I've met here who use anti-perspirant.'

Language is a hindrance to communication, but over coffee we breach the linguistic barriers between us. On the TV four foreign diplomats sit around a table. The translation blocks the original English, but I just catch the US representative saying, 'There's no other way, Bosnia must have a purely Bosnian solution to its problems, sometimes we forget this . . .'

Shabaza nods at the TV then shows me a poem hanging on the wall, it's called *Osmijeh* ('Smile').

'Smile,' she says, translating, 'smile, it costs nothing. A smile is more valuable than money . . .'

It reminds me of the sentimental rhymes inside greeting cards, but I smile anyway.

'A smile is more valuable than business, a smile brings joy to all who see it.' She turns to me, her face taut. 'Slovenes don't smile. Croats don't smile. Serbs smile, but who knows what it means? Only Bosnians smile and really mean it.'

Surprised, and wondering who is meant by 'Bosnian', I finish my cup of strong sweet coffee and disappear into my room, closing the padded door. On the wall near the sofa is a drawing of a young girl; I can't tell if it's Miranda or her sister who died less than a year ago in a car crash. I look at Abdulah Sidran's empty chair and the small scars in the plasterwork where a stray bullet ricocheted around the room sometime between 1992 and 1995. It's so easy, almost automatic, to stand back and feel surprise or even aversion, at something said or not said. But this isn't the place for that; not this house, not this city; maybe not even this country.

The next day it rains, warm sunshine replaced by chill and damp. In the morning I follow up leads and contacts, arrange meetings and ring organisations. The list of acronyms in my notebook gets longer, as the extent to which this country is directed by outside agencies becomes clearer: OHR, SFOR, UN, UNHCR, UNPROFOR, OSCE, ICTY, PHR. The list sounds like a secret litany.

It's not far from Jezero to the middle of town, but rain has lowered the spirit of the city and my own has sunk with it. Walking through the small park between Jezero and Maršala Tita, I watch damp leaves fall among the old Turkish-style gravestones and the new, coffin-shaped boards marked with the fleur-de-lis of Bosnia. A grave covered with fresh lilies carries the inscription 'Jasmin Čamdija 1968–1993'. Nothing more.

I feel tired as I walk to Ferhadija for my appointment with Rusmir Mahmutćehajić, the Bosnian cultural historian and polymath who began his academic career in Theoretical Physics and Ergonomics. In London, Dr Mahmutćehajić's name was always mentioned to me in hushed tones of respect. Bearing that in mind, I walk up the stone steps to his office with some trepidation and a feeling of visiting the headmaster. The reality is quite different.

I'm greeted by an elegant and urbane man in his early fifties. The hand that's offered is very slightly off-centre, and taking it I realise that Dr Mahmutćehajić can see me only dimly.

Over tea I'm asked about myself, a rare thing for a travel writer. I mention being daunted at the prospect of writing about Bosnia, even through the medium of my own experience.

'No-one is qualified to write about Bosnia.' This is not meant to be off-putting; the Doctor includes himself in the remark. 'How can anyone write about such loss of pluriformity?' He shakes his head slightly. 'As you know, we have four different traditions in this country – Catholicism, Orthodoxy, Islam and Judaism – and the similarities of these prevail over their differences. The striving towards perfection that all these traditions represent is the same . . . historically all four descend from Abraham. Today, of course, these differences are seen as the source of contention in Bosnia, but it is the *absence* of religion in this country that has led to the state of affairs that we have now.'

'You mean the absence of the spiritual aspects of religion?'

'Yes. We have too much of the outer forms of religion, but sadly little of its meaning any more. Since the breakdown of the totalitarian state, people have moved towards religions which represent national ideologies and idealised histories, rewriting events to suit the political moment. The same is true of cultural individuality. The more the Serbs, Croats and Bosniaks strive to be separate, the more we lose the truth of what it means to be Bosnian. Even the medieval Bosnian kingdom was pluriform and tolerant of differences – that was why the Bosnian Church was considered heretical and also why the Jews who came to this country established themselves in harmony with the Christian culture.'

'What is your tradition?'

'I am a moslem and a Bosnian, and the essence of *that* tradition confirms my responsibility towards others. You must understand that it's only since the nineteenth century that there has been a sense of "the other" in this country. The Bosnian model, where it was acted upon, acknowledged that central to the identity of Bosnia was the recognition and protection of the rights of others.

This was the thing that made Bosnia different, a model for co-existence.'

I drink my tea and listen carefully, wanting to remember.

'When I was a child I was taught to honour Christians, especially Christian women, even above my moslem neighbours.'

'And was that respect reciprocated?'

He hesitates for a moment. 'Yes, I believe it was. You see, the honour that the true Bosnian tradition taught was grounded in rationality, in the intellect, the Holy Spirit if you like. Since the nineteenth century and the rise of nationalism, there's been a corresponding rise in sentimentalism and moralism – the two lowest traditions, which have nothing to do with the spirit. *Real* tradition comes from the intellect, from the practice of thoughtfulness.'

'But in the past most people would have been uneducated and illiterate,' I say. 'How could they have grasped a tradition grounded in the intellect?'

'Very often the most respected men, the holiest men, were simple people who fed cats and dogs, who gave away half of everything they had to those who had less. We have lost that. We live in a place of ideologies which believe only in rationalism, materialism and homogeneity – the lowest aspects of the intellect. Ideology cannot resolve the problems of Bosnia, the issues of pluriformity, of how we can all live together once again with respect and mutuality. The rise of nationalism in Serbia in the nineteenth century caused a reaction among the Orthodox populations in Bosnia. No-one who did not live in Serbia called themselves Serb before that time; they called themselves Orthodox. People could come from Cairo or from Athens or Moscow and be received here as brothers and sisters in the Orthodox faith. When that was lost to Serb nationalism, the Catholic Bosnian population reacted by accepting the ideology of Croatian nationalism, Croathood. The result of that was the question, "How can I protect myself from my brother?" '

'And the Moslems?'

'The actions of Serbia and Croatia in trying to create buffers between their own states by using Bosnia as the dividing line has

encouraged, even forced, Moslems to seek their own national programme of establishing a Moslem state. That, of course, would
destroy any remaining hope of Bosnian unity. We live in a condition of religious hypocrisy you see, all of us – Orthodox, Catholics
and moslems – and many people suffer under this, including atheists. I no longer call myself a Bosniak. I say that I am Bosnian.'

'By Bosniak you mean a Bosnian moslem?'

'Yes. I am a Bosnian and a moslem, but not a Bosniak. That
used to be a good word, one that applied to everyone who lived in
this country, to the plurality and diversity that was Bosnia. To be
a practising moslem means to recognise the rightness of all others, but the word "Bosniak" has become perverted. It is an ideological term that is intended to exclude. It's a tool of the ruling
oligarchy, a tool of national expression, just like the terms
"Orthodox" or "Catholic".' He pauses momentarily, slender fingers stroking the handle of his teacup. 'I would not say on TV that
I am not a Bosniak, as it would produce confusion. Since losing
our sense of the rightness of others we are easily confused.'

'Should *I* not repeat it?'

'I cannot say it, but you can say it. That's not a problem.'

The young woman sitting at reception in the outer office
knocks politely on the door and reminds the doctor that he has
another meeting in half an hour. As she returns to her desk I ask,
'What do you think will happen in the next few years?'

'It is clear what *should* happen . . . what *will* happen, only God
can know. The Serb, Croat and Bosniak entities that are preventing the return of refugees and denying unity claim that "everything can be divided". This is evil. The need of the Bosnian peoples is to understand that "everything can be joined". Without this
belief, we are dependent on the presence of the international community which is giving us an increasingly dependent mentality.
The results of this are easy to see – our young people have little
faith in the future of this country and many are leaving.' He
shakes his head and smiles at me. 'We are waiting for changes,
waiting for dialogue. I believe that we *will* have pluriformity and
mutual acknowledgement once again. The question is when.'

I take my leave of Rusmir Mahmutćehajić with conflicting feelings. I want very much to believe in the Bosnia of his tradition, the utopian state where all co-existed happily, but something tells me it just wasn't so. Not that it wasn't so here in Bosnia, but that it wasn't so anywhere, ever. At the same time, I know I've just met a unique man of great intellect and spirituality.

On Ferhadija I walk on the red flagstones, past young men in wheelchairs and the plaque about 'murdering Serbs', and it occurs to me that a bit of utopian idealism might be a good thing and that Rusmir Mahmutćehajić should be in the Bosnian government. Later, I learn that he had been and resigned.

Late that night, when the Albanians are already in bed, I walk to the bottom of Jezero to the Labyrint Club, which is run by Miranda's husband. It's discreetly situated at the bottom of a quiet residential street, and no-one would guess that a subterranean party was going on underfoot.

The most obvious thing about Labyrint is that it could be almost anywhere in the world. Large men in dark clothes line the entrance and nod, maybe expecting me. A long ramp followed by steps leads down and down, and the music gets louder and closer and the air hotter and damper. Inside, the small club is stylish, with clean sharp lines, trendy bottled beers, Escheresque levels and state-of-the-art dance music. The young men and women dancing sweatily on the stage look little different from clubbers in London or New York, except perhaps that they're wearing more clothes and, I'm told, are not using drugs. Clubs were called discos in 1978, and if I'd visited any in Yugoslavia they would have seemed very different from the UK variety. Joining Miranda and her friends, I look around and recall Rusmir Mahmutćehajić's thoughts on homogeneity.

Miranda tells me that the foreign nationals are good customers here, but tonight I'm the only stranger; there are no foreign soldiers relaxing out of uniform, none of the thousands of international officials who live and work in Sarajevo. There's a private feeling to the place, a sense that this is a family party where relatives, however distant, are welcome and everyone else is not. Being an honorary member of the family I'm offered drink and cigarettes, and despite the noise, people are surprisingly willing to make serious conversation.

'You like it here?' Miranda asks.

'It's great.'

'During the war the club was closed,' she says. 'Soldiers were based in here because it was safer under the ground. They had some kind of equipment – radio, radar, something like that.' She waves to a couple just arriving. 'You can imagine the mess when they left. It took a long time to clean the place up and open again. Alex!' She calls to a man nearby, and introducing us says, 'This is the man with four passports!'

Alex, a tall attractive man, shakes my hand. Bosnians are at once formal and tactile, and physical contact is frequent, regardless of gender and age.

'It's true I have four passports,' he says, grinning. 'My father is Serbian, my mother Macedonian,' he numbers them off on his fingers, 'so I have these two. Then I have my old Yugoslav passport and because I lived for a long time in Canada I have a Canadian passport. It's good, no?'

I grin and shout, 'Do you live in Sarajevo now?'

He shakes his head. 'No, I'm visiting friends. I couldn't live here, it's too hard. Now I'm used to Canada and the West . . . it's hard to be here, always reminded of history.'

'Was it good before the war?'

'It was paradise! We had everything. All the advantages of Communism – free education, health, security – and many of the freedoms of capitalism – money, holidays, travel. Those ten years after Tito died were the best ten years this country ever had. The worst of Communism was over by the 1970s. Did you know we had a gulag? It was on a Croatian island called Dugi Otok.'

I shake my head. Listening is hard enough, speaking even harder.

'When the gulag was shut down, it marked the end of real

repression in Yugoslavia. We were getting closer to the West, tourism was really high, things were good.'

'What spoilt it?'

'The old people, the ones from the time before Yugoslavia became Communist, it was them. These old ones still had pains in their heads, always nervous, always worrying about their neighbours' intentions, never relaxing. That was what politicians like Tudjman and Milošević were able to use, that fear of each other. I heard recently that the mayor of Dubrovnik, a hard-line Croat nationalist, has called for all the Bosnian Moslems living in Dubrovnik to be rounded up and put on an island. "Mopping up", he called it. Can you believe it? After everything that's happened.'

His partner leans towards me, her arms draped around his shoulders.

'We are all prisoners of our past,' she says. 'Bosniaks, Croats, everyone. Prisoners of the system our parents lived under and of the system we have now.'

'Elena is from Sarajevo,' Alex says, 'she lived here during the war.'

The woman looks at me, her eyes loud over the noise of the music and the shouts of the dancing youths. I feel I'm expected to say something, ask something. To fill the non-existent silence, she says, 'Sarajevo was raped before the war started, raped by people from the country. Farmers, peasants. We call them "pig's trotters". These people used to take off their farm shoes at the edge of the town and put on proper shoes, so no-one would recognise them.'

I stare, glad that it's semi-dark.

'The "trotters" would come here and sell a cow, then change the money in the streets to make more money. Gradually, they began to infiltrate even the government. Everything got changed to their way of thinking, perverted into their way of working and seeing the world, always about money.'

'And these, uh, trotters,' I say, 'are they mostly men?'

'Oh no!' she laughs. 'Anyone can be a pig's trotter!'

The next day I bake garlic in Shabaza's oven. The gas is back on; someone has paid the bill, and the Eternal Flame is burning once again. The garlic sends a wonderful, rich scent through the house. Shabaza nods approvingly when she comes in to tidy up after the Albanians. She has a routine: wash the dishes, then sit and relax with a coffee and cigarette beside an open window, thinking. She watches as I unwrap the soft cloves from their silver foil.

'The Jewish way,' she says.

As we drink coffee together, she looks at a list of names and photos of foreign reporters working in Sarajevo lying on the table.

'Who are they?'

I explain, pointing to the man I'm meeting later in the day.

'Hmm.' She pores over the names and faces, her finger tracing each one. 'Which one are you meeting?'

'This one.'

'A Moslem,' she says, 'he's a Moslem. All these others are not Moslem. This one is a Croat, and this one here. This one's a Serb. That one's foreign, not Bosnian at all.'

'You can tell this just from their names?'

She nods.

'But maybe this one's mother was Moslem . . . or the Moslem one has a Serb mother?'

She shakes her head, stroking the sheet of paper. 'Your name is your job.'

'Is your name your job?' I ask journalist Atif Muhić later that day.

'No. Not any more, though of course I work for an international organisation and that makes a difference.'

At six foot four or five, with blond hair and ice-blue eyes, Atif gives the lie to racial stereotyping based on appearance. He looks more Scandinavian than any Scandinavian I've ever seen.

'Are you tired of people thinking you're Swedish?' I ask, craning my neck.

He shrugs. 'I look Slavic, that's all.'

We sit in an outdoor café near the Holiday Inn.

'I'm trying to come to grips with Bosnian history,' I say. 'I've had the past and the present, I was hoping you might tell me about the future.' I expect him to smile at this, but instead he just tells me that things have calmed down a lot.

'Most of what I write is about politics and sport and finance, of course. Corruption is the big thing. Today I wrote about a deputation which has just arrived from the US to look into the allegations of corruption over international funding here. The other main story was football. We still have three leagues, Bosniak, Croat and Serb, though only the Bosniak league represents the country. Sport just reflects the divisions here in BiH. Croats and Serbs will eventually realise that if they want to play international-standard games and get paid for it, they'll have to join the other league.'

He seems uptight, but maybe it's just nerves at being the interviewee rather than the interviewer.

'We used to have three education systems too. We still do, but at least they've agreed to throw out the most inflammatory teaching.'

'What kind of inflammatory teaching?'

'Oh, getting classrooms full of kids to repeat things like, "I'm a little Croat," or "I'm a little Moslem." The government tried to get the schools to merge, but they all refused.'

'Are you a moslem with a small "m"?'

He shakes his head.

'So what it does it mean to be an atheist Moslem in Bosnia today?'

He hesitates, thinking. 'Tradition. That's all. It's about tradition, the traditions that fifty years of Communism squashed. People wanted to express their differences, their traditions; Tito died, they got their chance, they took it.'

'I asked Serbs I met in Croatia that question – they gave me the same answer.'

He shrugs. 'Of course. What else is there when it's not possible to separate religion from nationalism any more? If I'm not a nationalist or religious then it must be tradition.'

'And what about the future? Do you think things will change much in the short term?'

'I think they're changing already, and for the better. Working for an international organisation has given me an insight into economics. People talk about politics and ideals, but in the end it's money and the material things that affect people's everyday lives . . . that's what will make the difference.'

He's loosening up as he talks, becoming more relaxed.

'For example, in Republika Srpska some people still use the Yugoslav dinar as a political statement. Now that its value has dropped, they have to make a decision: keep using dinars for emotional reasons, or take Bosnian marks, which are stable and solid because they're tied to the Deutschmark. The answer is clear.' He pauses. 'This is a unique place, things happen that seem to have no explanation. A few months ago I couldn't go to Banja Luka, to the RS. Now I can. On the other hand, my father's cousin lived there all through the war. She was harassed and her husband beaten, but they stayed and now they're glad they stayed.'

He turns his small cup round and round on its saucer, making a high squeaking sound. 'This was never a Bosnian problem, or even a Balkan one. It's a Yugoslav problem, by which I mean a Serb problem, and it must be resolved by Serbs. I think that Montenegro will be a turning point for all the Balkans. People there are beginning to realise that it's more important to be Montenegrin than to be Montenegrin Serb. The Serbs and Croats need to sort out their attitudes to each other, but once Tudjman and Milošević have gone, that will start to happen anyway.'

'So money and materialism are the answer?'

He smiles for the first time. 'Part of the answer. It's about honesty and trust, too. Seventy per cent of all business done in this city, in this country, is black market. That's bad. But at the same time, the government has managed to increase the amount of customs and duties received, up from almost nothing after the war to

80 per cent this year. Another part of the answer is justice. There
are too many war criminals leading normal lives out there, and
too many refugees still unable to go back to their homes despite
Dayton, the UN, SFOR and all the rest. There are thousands of
refugees from eastern Bosnia living in Sarajevo now, and they're
being told to leave their homes here because the original Croat
and Serb owners want to come back. The Serbs in the RS won't
let Bosniak refugees back, but the Serbs *here* expect to be able to
return – and they do, because they know they can and that they'll
be safe. I did a story on refugee returns a year ago and it's still one
of our biggest problems. So, improvement is a logical progression
but we're aware of the worst possible scenarios too.'

There's a question I want to ask, but it's a hard one and I hesitate. It didn't need to be asked in Slovenia or Croatia, but here it
seems crucial to an understanding of things.

'Is there any sense of embarrassment in this country about
being held together by the international community, any sense of
injured national pride?'

After all my hesitation he just looks at me, his answer shock-
ingly simple.

'If there'd been a *Bosnian* sense of pride the war could never
have happened. How can you injure what doesn't exist?'

I'm the one embarrassed, by the stupidity of my question.

'I expect individual people might feel a sense of shame or
dependency, but everyone's different.' He smiles reassuringly.
'We were made into children by Communism, so that when
nationalism arrived we couldn't tell the difference. Someone was
telling us what was right and wrong, that was all that mattered.
We were robbed of our sense of political possibilities – that's
what we should feel injured about.'

When we part, I stand for a moment and watch him striding
away towards his office in the ruins of one of the twin UNIS buildings. Maybe his vision of the future is right, that normality will
emerge out of soccer and marks; but it's hard to believe that these
things can 'skin and film' the ulcers of nationalism without the
justice that he also mentioned, which seems in short supply just

now. The variety of opinions held by Bosnians is intriguing and depressing. Intriguing because of the fierce individuality it expresses, and depressing because it's all too clear what difference of opinion can mean here. I consider the almost mystical reverence with which some people recall Sarajevo and Bosnia itself; but was there ever true multi-culturalism here, or was it simply a cosmopolitan place where people of different faiths and traditions went about their business undisturbed by each other? Was the conflict about an animosity between rural and urban that evidently still exists, or was it started by nationalist intellectuals who used the less educated and informed to spread their malice? Such questions have a great many answers, all different.

The early-evening sky is cobalt blue, the sun low and half-moon high over the surrounding hills. Building sites are deserted, the long-necked cranes silent and still among the rubble and the windowless houses. Here the new and the destroyed stand side by side in their own kind of brotherhood. There are many Sarajevos, many Bosnias; so many hopes and desires, and different ways to achieve them. Right and wrong are more relative here than anywhere I've ever been. And even that thought's debatable as I look up at the damaged twin towers. Before the war, the towers were called Momo and Uzeir, characters from well-loved Sarajevo jokes. The names had different national origins, and being of equal height, the towers were said to symbolise Sarajevo's unity. The Serbs shelling the city during the siege didn't know which tower was Momo and which was Uzeir, so they destroyed both.

11   Republika Srpska

(You know nothing about the town in which I dwell
You've no idea about the house in which I eat
You know nothing
About the icy well
From which
I drink)

                    Message (Stone Sleeper), Mak Dizdar

The map in the office of the Deputy Head of the UK Mission to
Bosnia-Hercegovina is covered in red spots. Along disputed
boundaries and around towns with familiar names like
Srebrenica, Goražde, the spots are dense as smallpox, each one a
potential death or mutilation.

'Those are uncleared mines,' Janet Rogan says. 'This map's a
couple of years old, but clearing is slow so essentially the picture's the same. Bosnia's a giant minefield. The map over there
shows the SFOR sectors. Sarajevo has the multi-national headquarters. South and east of here is the French sector, north and
east the Americans, north and west, British.'

She steps sideways. 'And this is Sarajevo . . .'

Following her gaze, I realise that in getting here I'd passed
booby-trapped buildings and mined verges. Being slightly early
for the meeting, I'd considered clambering over a fence and

scrabbling around inside the beautiful, ruined and possibly mined Olympic museum next door to the embassy.

'The red spots are mines; the yellow stars show where someone's been killed or injured by one.' Taking her eyes from the bland horror of the map, she looks at me. 'Never, and I mean *never,* walk off tarmac in the countryside – and not even here in town, if you can avoid it. Forget modesty . . . if you're in the middle of nowhere and you need to pee, do it on the road, don't wander off into long grass or inside buildings. Look,' she points to the map, 'there are mines in the middle of cemeteries, in parks, along the river . . .'

I think of the families I'd seen picnicking on the outskirts of town on the day I arrived; how relaxed and pastoral it had seemed.

'Everyone who comes here gets shown this map, the state of the place. It's best to realise that Sarajevo isn't safe. A lot of clearing work's been done, of course, but we're still in one of the most heavily mined cities in the world.'

'I've noticed that the best restored buildings are the mosques and churches,' I say as we sit down.

'Because that's where some donors choose to put their money, which is bizarre when you think that the schools and hospitals are a mess.'

'Not an easy place to work.'

'A strange place. There's this idea that before the war, Sarajevo was a melting pot, a place where all the groups lived happily together – but it wasn't like that. Even in Sarajevo, which all sides agree was the most open, tolerant city, different areas of town were dominated by different groups. And in the rural areas, different ethnic groups *really* intermingled only rarely. You tend to see strings of mono-ethnic villages down a valley; for example, first a Croat village, then a Bosniak one. It's particularly evident in areas where there was "ethnic cleansing".'

'That's very interesting,' I say, thinking of recent discussions.

'I've been here eighteen months and it seems to me that the only way to look at what happened, and is still happening, is to accept that *all* sides did terrible things, abused their neighbours, committed crimes. To say that this or that lot started it just doesn't help anyone, because even if it's true, it only prolongs things. The position we take when we talk to local people is that everyone needs to look for similarities with the other groups, not differences. Everyone suffered, lost someone, so we encourage people to work together *because* of that.'

'And do they?'

'Not often. Two hundred thousand people of all sides died in the conflict here, and despite or maybe because of that, politics is still driven by inflexibility and lack of compassion.' She grins wryly. 'I've sat in meetings with politicians who simply refuse to budge on what seems a perfectly straightforward issue. "Look," I say, "this position is just plain stupid, it's preventing the international community being able to give you financial assistance." "Of course," they reply, not entirely disingenuously, "didn't you know . . . we *are* stupid! We'd rather eat grass and suck stones than do what you suggest!" In the end, there's nothing much you can do. The number of times I've wanted to say, bugger off then and suck your bloody stones!' Another grin. 'I usually manage to bite my tongue. Just.'

'The one thing everyone seems to agree on, is that things were great materially between Tito's death and Milošević's rise . . .'

'It was an illusion. It was all propped up by borrowing from the West. The reckoning was coming soon, and educated people knew that. The political gaps between the various republics were widening. Most saw decentralisation as the answer, especially in Kosovo, where there were problems within a year of Tito's death. Belgrade's solution to everything was to consolidate its own power and centralise even more.'

An assistant appears with documents to be signed. When she leaves, Janet says, 'So you're coming to Banja Luka with me tomorrow?'

'Definitely.'

'Good. We'll meet here at about eleven. Banja Luka is in the British sector and our SFOR headquarters is outside the town in an old metal factory. I've got a meeting in the afternoon, but I'll ask someone to show you around. Is there anything else you'd like to see while you're here?'

I hesitate briefly, not wanting to appear ghoulish. 'There was a news report on the mortuary at Tuzla a few months ago, the tunnel where the bodies are stored. I'd like to see it, if possible.'

'I don't know anyone at Tuzla mortuary personally, but I'll see what I can do,' she says, as if wanting to visit a morgue were the most natural thing in the world. Perhaps, in Bosnia, it is.

As I take a last look at the mine maps, at the roads and towns between Sarajevo and Banja Luka, Janet says, 'Bosnia's an unusual place. Apart from the East–West culture clash, there's also a rural–urban debate over unresolved issues between city and country people, regardless of religion. That's true of the whole Balkan region, and much of the world, of course. But here the problems are so complex; class, education, religion – a whole unending tangle, in a way, like Northern Ireland. Do you know the joke about the peasant and the genie?'

'No, but if it's anything like the other "jokes" I've been told here, I don't suppose it's very funny.'

She smiles. 'Definitely more black humour than comedy! Anyway, this farmer finds a magic lamp, rubs it, genie comes out. "You have one wish," the genie says. The farmer spends ages thinking and the genie gets impatient, "Come on, come on, I haven't got all day!" Hmm! the farmer thinks to himself, I could wish to be the richest man in the world, that would be nice . . . but then again, my neighbour might get a wish too and wish for more money than me, so that's no good. "Hurry up," says the genie, "it's only one wish after all!" Then the farmer thinks he could wish for the most beautiful woman in the world for his wife. That would be nice, he thinks, until it occurs to him that his neighbour might seduce his wife. Hmm, that's no good either. Just as the genie's about to get really cross, the farmer decides. "I know my wish!" he shouts. "Kill my neighbour's cow!" '*

In the corridor we meet the Ambassador, who shakes my hand as Janet introduces us.

* Andrej Blatnik told me a codicil to this story in Ljubljana a few weeks later. 'Kill my neighbour's cow,' the farmer says, 'and kill my cow too, in case my neighbour asks me for milk.'

'Writing about being in Bosnia?' he says, smiling. 'Well, when you know everything, maybe you could tell me about it.'

Walking back towards Jezero, meetings and conversations echo in my head. What's becoming increasingly clear is that nothing here is clear, and Sarajevo is at the heart of the opacity. Yet after a relatively short time I feel a bizarre sense of belonging in this place, of being completely at home. I already know quite a few people, get phone calls, use the trams, the public phones, visit offices and health-food shops, live in a house. Sarajevo sucks you in, offering an apparent sense of purpose. At the same time, being surrounded by complex, damaged people who've received little or no help for the traumas they've suffered is deeply uncomfortable. Despite the evident damage, it's surprisingly easy to forget that Sarajevo is a place where appalling things happened and, in different ways, are happening still. And the physical sense of being watched, of the hills crowding the city, gets stronger over time. I'm glad to leave for a few days, though there's no illusion that things will be more comfortable anywhere else I'm likely to go.

Central Bosnia is far more beautiful and dramatic than I remember. The road from Sarajevo to Zenica follows the Bosna through green hills, past villages and hamlets. The river is a ribbon of weathered copper; a similar green to Slovenia's Soća, but altogether darker. The hamlets are often empty, the villages deserted.

Zenica to Travnik. These names are part of a litany that was repeated daily on world news between 1992 and 1995, with details of ethnic groups and casualty figures; the movements of soldiers, refugees; images of crying children, lifting helicopters, hospitals, blood and guns. The names of these places lodged in my mind, and now, driving through them, I blink . . .

and they're gone. Small places to have such large and bloody reputations.

Driving with Janet Rogan is an informative and entertaining experience. Between singing along to Verdi and conducting Mozart one-handed, she asks me to see if I can find 'God Save the Queen' in the tape box.

'What cover does it have?' I ask, rooting among the tapes and thinking privately that it's beyond the call of duty to listen to the British national anthem while driving through a foreign country.

'Sex Pistols,' she replies. 'I'm regressing to my youth. Soon as I arrived in Sarajevo I played "God Save the Queen" with all the windows open.'

'That's one way to let the neighbours know you're not stuffy.'

The roadside fields are dotted with rotund haystacks, but mostly the Bosnian countryside appears as a vast interruption of prosperity and rural life; homes wrecked, population fled. At a particularly stunning bend in the river, a single house, its roof a tangle of spars, is reflected in the still water. We pass village after village, some intact and new, many others ruined. From time to time we pass men walking a single cow on a leash, like a dog.

'The Dutch paid for villagers to be given a cow, apparently on the principle that if they're looking after the cow they won't have time to plot mischief.'

The lone cows look desperate for their herds and the men look acutely bored – a perfect combination for mischief of all sorts, I'd have thought.

'After a while you can tell which villages or towns are Bosniak or Croat, by the architecture,' Janet says, pointing to a number of houses between the road and the river. 'Look, that's a Croat village over there . . . the differences are quite subtle.'

Far too subtle for me. All I can see as we pass trucks laden with logs, and farm carts piled high with hay, is the legacy of war and the struggle to assume normality. This country *was* the paradise its people claim, but it's been turned into a desert of mines and ruins. Mozart's *Requiem* blasting from the car stereo is a strangely fitting accompaniment to shattered homes and acres of cemeteries, moslem, Catholic and Orthodox. Yet the insistent fertility of this land in the absence of humans is both an irony and a cause for hope.

Between Travnik and Jajce, the road narrows, squeezing between high cliffs topped with dark pine, a Gothic landscape that reminds me of travelling through Kobarid, Cerkno and Idrija. Approaching Jajce, we pass a working industrial site, maybe a foundry. Flames leap from the open sides of the building, smoke belches from three chimneys. It's not an attractive sight, but it's the only real industry I've seen in many weeks, and must be welcome here. Not everyone wants to be a farmer or cow minder.

Jajce sits on a leafy hill, topped by a medieval castle. It's a place of waterfalls, elegant towers and houses that nestle among the many trees. From up there, the little town has witnessed good and bad for many centuries, and survived. In the of autumn 1992, Jajce fell to the Serbs; today, it's predominantly Croat, though many Bosniaks are starting to return.

Beyond the town, the road climbs to provide an almost one hundred and eighty degree view north as far as the eye can see. King Stephen Tomačević probably came this way in May 1463, racing ahead of the pursuing Turks. Due west of here, in the fortress of Ključ, he finally surrendered himself and his companions on a promise of safety. As we wind down into the valley of the Vrbas, one of Bosnia's most beautiful rivers, I think about the young man forced by circumstance to trust the word of an enemy. Stephen Tomačević and his followers were promptly beheaded by their captors. The last king of Bosnia was not the last Bosnian to find that things didn't turn out as agreed.

Banja Luka is a small, pleasant city, with parks and tree-lined avenues. Janet drives on to her meeting, leaving me to stroll through the pedestrianised shopping areas, past cafés hidden in cul-de-sacs and courtyards. The sun is shining, and the air is warm and fresh; in a region with relatively little traffic or industry, it would be. But there's a strange feeling to the place, as though I've entered a different country without crossing a border. The locals might say I have crossed one, that this is Serbia. I visited Banja Luka only briefly in 1978, but long enough to remember how it looked and felt; and it was not like this. The strangeness lies mostly in the difference between the place itself, its buildings, streets and parks, and the people who inhabit them. Something's not right. The wide avenues and elegant buildings speak of a prosperous, populous city, but Banja Luka's citizens look tired, anxious and, above all, poor.

During the Ottoman period, Banja Luka was for a time the 'capital' city of Bosnia and seat of the Turkish administration. It became a thriving Moslem town, with a Jewish community, an Orthodox monastery, Catholic churches and one of the Balkans' most beautiful mosques, the Ferhadija. By 1991, following hundreds of years of East–West migrations, the majority population of Banja Luka was Bosnian Serb. With the outbreak of war, the city became the centre of Bosnian Serb independence, the heart of a new 'Krajina', a military borderland defended by Četnik paramilitaries from Serbia itself. Men like Zeljko Raznjatovic, who'd belonged to Europe's criminal underworld for years before the Bosnian war, and who used the conflict to reinvent himself as the infamous 'warlord', Arkan. His paramilitary unit, the 'Tigers', committed some of the worst atrocities of the war, which included forcing elderly women to walk through minefields.

There are few Bosniaks or Croats in Banja Luka today, and none of the thirteen mosques; they were all destroyed by Serbs after 1993. The modern Catholic cathedral is run-down, its paint peeling. An unfinished office block is graffitied with 'NATO Go Home' and covered with posters of election candidates; a nearby department store sells little more than out-of-date cosmetics and acrylic jumpers from China. This isn't a place foreigners come to, except on diplomatic business, and people look at me curiously. It's a strange feeling, wondering if you're an intruder, the enemy, or simply an object of surprise.

At the British Embassy office in a small, suburban road, I'm met by Vesna Ravic, the embassy's Political and Commercial Assistant. A green-eyed Serb beauty, with very good English, Vesna has everything under control.

'I'll just call my boyfriend to come and meet us, then we can go out and eat, have a drink, do something fun!'

When the boyfriend arrives, it's as though I've stepped into an Oscars Award ceremony. Boris, a Hungarian-Serb from Belgrade, is tall and darkly handsome, and together he and Vesna look like a Hollywood couple, only real. Walking the few blocks to a local Chinese restaurant, they seem a difference species from the other people in the street; and a different species from me.

'I lived in London for seven years,' Vesna says over our Bosnian Serb Chinese meal. 'I worked in Selfridges, Harvey Nichols – lots of places. It was great.'

'That waiter!' Boris hisses.

'What?' I ask.

'Didn't you notice how he grovels with you?' Boris says, grinding his teeth. 'He ignores us, even though he can't speak English. And look! He's given you chopsticks, and us knives and forks!'

It's true, and any minute now the waiter, who struts like a government official, is going to get thumped.

'Why does he behave like that?'

'Because he thinks we're ignorant Serbian peasants!'

Vesna nods, saying little.

'But surely he's Serbian too?'

'Of course!' Boris splutters. 'That's exactly why he treats us so badly!'

'Perhaps he's new?' I suggest. 'He seems very nervous.'

'I don't care if he's a virgin!' Boris says. 'No-one treats us like that without explaining themselves.'

And explain the waiter does. Confronted, he crumbles sadly, literally to the wall. It's his first day and he knows nothing. He apologises. Honour is appeased, and Boris is all graciousness.

After dinner we walk through the main streets, which seem busier in the dark of late evening. People sit on low walls, chatting with friends; most are male, many probably refugees from those parts of Bosnia now Bosniak or Croat dominated. As we drink coffee and beer at an outdoor café, we talk about politics; about Serbia, which they're for, and Milošević, whom they're against. Boris tells me what it was like to be in Belgrade during the NATO bombing.

'You remember strange things – like cutting tomatoes. Lots of memories of being bombed are connected with food. Strange!'

'He didn't want me to visit him in Belgrade while it was going on. He actually forbade me!' Vesna interrupts, grinning. 'As though that would stop me!'

'One time the bombs were dropping, we could hear them nearby, and I carried on making the dinner. Vesna thought I was mad. She told me to stop, to get out of the house.'

'And do you know what he said?' she laughs. 'He said, "I don't want to die hungry." '

'I did say that, didn't I,' Boris grins. 'But actually, it's a line from a film.'

The next morning I find an Orthodox 'holy picture' in the dirt beside Janet's car. A rather smug St George is killing a crocodile with wings. I pick it up without thinking.

'Best not to get into the habit of picking things up,' Janet says briskly. 'During the war that might have been a lot more than just a picture.'

I dust it off and put it in my pocket. God! How did anyone survive here?

The morning is spent photographing the Orthodox cathedral and the wonderful produce market. Of all the markets I've visited on my journey, Banja Luka's is the most exotic and foreign, with its mustard-coloured church candles, caged birds and live river fish. It's a strange oasis of brightness and warm scents, and the only people who seem offended by my photographing are the ones who don't get their picture taken. The Serbs here laugh and joke, and are shyly self-deprecating around the camera. I remember my conversation with Andrej and Nataša in Ljubljana about the charm and charisma of the Serbs, and the dangers of national stereotyping. It's hard to square this place and these people with the horrors that I know took place. Perhaps it's hard for them too.

'They're expecting you at the "Metal Factory" around lunchtime,' Janet had said as we'd parted earlier in the morning. So around noon I walk past the busy café tables of the Hotel Bosna, past the local gangsters and dealers, to find a taxi and head north out of the city.

The Gurkha soldiers manning the gates to the 'Metal Factory' are pleasant, smiling and utterly inflexible when no-one comes to claim me. I'm kilometres from anywhere and the Gurkhas have my passport, so there's nothing for it but to sit on a sandbag and eavesdrop on the flow of radio communication from a nearby hut.

After about half an hour, a stocky young man in British uniform appears.

'You're waiting for the Polad?'

'Sorry?'

'The Political Advisor, Mr Inett?'

I nod.

'Sends his apologies, he's tied up in a meeting. I'm the

General's aide, I'll bring you in. They won't be long,' he looks at his watch, 'it's almost lunchtime.'

The Gurkhas smirk politely as I'm swept into the compound and through a door marked 'Headquarters, Multi-National Division (South West)'. The British SFOR contingent based in Banja Luka live and work around what used to be a large factory, built in the heyday of Communist expansion; now it sits in a sea of camouflage green.

As we arrive, General Viggers and his Polad, Graham Inett, emerge together from the conference room. Never having met a general in context before, it strikes me as we shake hands that Freddie Viggers, a slight man with sprightly energy, is both pleasantly normal and the heart of a highly efficient hive.

'Let's go to lunch,' he says, and everyone moves as a body, exactly a pace behind.

I can smell Britain before we reach the canteen. Bacon, chips, baked beans and hamburgers. And salad, the first edible greens in days. Graham and I chat as we queue.

'Where would you like to go this afternoon?' he asks.

'Where do you suggest?'

'We could try Kožarac, that's roughly between here and Prijedor. Things are going on in the village there. Janet suggested I take you to Omarska, but I'm not too sure about that – the last time we went there we were threatened with automatic weapons and told to piss off and not come back.'

'Threatened by whom?'

'Some local bandit in a Mercedes with blacked-out windows . . . thinks he's important. "Fuck off out of my village!" he said, as if he owned the place.'

'Were you scared?'

'Just a bit!'

'Maybe we should go then, confront the fear . . . ?'

Graham looks at me over his lunch tray. 'I'm from Watford,' he says, as though that explained everything.

The cutlery in the officers' mess is plastic; only the senior

command table has stainless steel. That, and a plate of untempt-
ing cakes, is the only difference between the General and the least
lieutenant. I wonder if Wellington nibbled hardtack and slopped
gruel with the lower orders. I'm asked about myself and what I'm
doing, and it feels odd to be answering, rather than asking the
questions.

'Omarska, is it?' General Viggers asks as we finish coffee.

'Yes,' I say.

'Not sure,' Graham says.

'It'll be OK,' the General says, 'it's quiet enough now.'

The Omarska iron-ore mine looks clean and bright in the afternoon sun. Thin grass covers the ground between the railway lines
and surrounds the rusting boxcars that carried the ore away in
Tito's day. After local Serbs set up a concentration camp here in
1992, the cars carried a different kind of freight: Bosniaks and
Croats from across the region; intellectuals, professionals and
political leaders from the towns of Prijedor and Kožarac; farmers
and labourers from the predominantly Bosniak hill-villages of the
Brdo – all were brought here to Omarska. Many of them never
left alive.

In 1992 Omarska was a place of horror, where women and men
were raped, tortured, humiliated or murdered by their military and
police guards. But it wasn't only the guards who committed these
acts; outsiders observed or took part in what became a form of
local entertainment. Prisoners were kept without sanitation, bed-
ding, clothing or any medical help in what must have been utter
physical and mental desolation. Men were castrated, starved,
beaten – often to death – with metal rods and tools, industrial
cable, rifle butts and batons; some were thrown alive into bonfires
of blazing tyres. Women washed away the blood of murdered fellow prisoners. Many of the dead who were driven away each day

to mass graves are among the unknown disappeared victims of a brutality not seen since in Europe since the Holocaust.

Survivors tell of a small building, known as the 'red house', where prisoners were taken and from which very few returned . . . but I can't see it, or much else, from the safety of Graham's locked car.

'It looks OK, you can get out if you want.'

The interpreter stands stiffly beside the vehicle. Very thin, very blonde and very upright, Mira exudes the prickly dignity of a Bosniak obliged to rub shoulders daily with those Bosnian Serbs who tolerated, if not participated in, the vileness of Omarska and the other camps in the region.

We hover on the outskirts of the mine; Graham and Mira clearly don't want to go far from the car. There's no intrinsic sense of evil here, the place itself doesn't shout 'horror'; the evil was the people, and they're long gone. Looking towards the village, which is little more than a single street, I'm struck by how close it is: the homes and the mine are only a few hundred metres apart. Omarska camp didn't exist in a remote, uninhabited spot. It happened on the edge of a village full of people.

'They saw nothing,' Mira says, jerking her head towards the houses and cafés. 'They heard nothing. Nothing happened here.' Her voice is level, with even a touch of irony; but her body is rigid.

The villagers stare silently at the car as we drive away, doors locked once again. Graham relaxes visibly as the square box of the mine tower disappears behind us.

'It still goes on, you know. Only last week a Bosniak guy returned from abroad and went into a bar near here and killed two local Serbs. Most of the killings these days are done with grenades and are pretty indiscriminate, but he was very precise, knew exactly who he wanted. The two men had raped his wife and killed members of his family. He gave himself up immediately, then hanged himself in prison.'

This seems to be a story about justice, which makes the ending seem particularly cruel; an archetypal tragedy of Greek proportions. Plan revenge, carry it out, then have nothing to live for. But these events must surely have been more complex than that?

Before the war, the town of Kožarac had a predominantly Bosniak population of over twenty-seven thousand. In May 1992, Kožarac's Bosniaks were either murdered or terrified out of their homes by minority Bosnian Serbs, who, apparently believing there was about to be an Islamic uprising against them, attacked first. Whatever the evidence or lack of it, many Serbs clearly believed they were at risk from their former friends and neighbours. The 'cleansing' of Kožarac turned out to be an inciting incident of the Bosnian war.

Today there are one hundred and twenty Bosniaks in Kožarac, most of them elderly returnees trying to prepare a home for families scattered in centres and camps across Bosnia and much of Europe.

We leave the car near the small military post run by Czech peacekeepers.

'The Czechs are great,' Graham says. 'Everyone likes them because they're Slavs, but they're NATO too. Without them being here, without *someone* being here, none of the returns to this town could have happened.'

With its many trees and wide streets, it must have been pretty here once. Now Kožarac looks like all the Bosnian war pictures I've ever seen, rolled into one. Stumps of breeze block and pillars of brick are all that's left of the houses we pass. Orchards are full of trees laden with apples and plums, the ground littered with rotting fruit. The domed entrance porch of the mosque looks intact, belying the devastation within. Remembering Janet's advice, I walk only on tarmac or well-trodden paths.

'There's a fair bit of reconstruction going on,' Graham says. 'The Germans and Norwegians have done most of the building work. Mira, can you ask those people there if we can talk to them?'

The couple, in their seventies, seem happy to chat and show us around their newly rebuilt home. It's a big, family house and might be good if the plaster and mortar weren't already crumbling. The pine ceilings look OK and hint at Scandinavia, but most of the work is rubbish.

'We're waiting for electricity,' Mira translates, 'recently we have water.'

'How do they get food?' I ask, as there's no sign of any kind of store or shop.

'From the internationals.'

'And will their family join them here?'

'God willing.'

The old man's weathered face is shaded by a baseball cap bearing the logo of some US sports team; his younger, plumper wife wears a big yellow apron. They pose for photos unselfconsciously, arms around each other. After, the woman smiles, pointing at me and the camera.

'She says to tell you her husband is a Moslem and she's a Serb from Montenegro. When you show these photographs to people in England, you must tell them that not all Serbs and Moslems are enemies.'

Further along the road, Graham talks to a Bosniak man he's met before, who tells us how his house was rebuilt by the Norwegians, then burnt down again. Now the Germans have fixed it. His eyes fill with tears as he says that he's alone, without family here and with no money. He's not a young man, not young enough to start a new life. I listen to his story with a profound sense of shame. Why does he tell us about his life, his pain, just because we ask him? I feel shame for him, for his helplessness, but more for myself. Why am I listening? I can do nothing for him *but* listen and repeat what he tells me, and that won't stop his house being burnt down again, or put food in his belly, or bring his family home.

Near the town's only bar, we chat with a Serb woman of about my age. Most of her teeth are missing, from lack of food she says. She has no means to keep herself.

'I lived in Croatia,' she says, 'near Knin. I would like to go back, but I can't, it's not safe there.'

I tell her that I met Serbs in the Krajina who had returned and said they were glad of it. She looks uncomfortable.

'It's not bad here,' she says. 'I quite like it really.'

'How do you live?' I ask.

'I have my ways and means,' she says, winking and showing her gums.

Her ways and means become clear when we reach the bar and sit at one of the outdoor tables. She's lolling around inside, trying to look enticing, and there's plenty of potential trade. Four Serb men who look like well-fed thugs are playing cards and drinking heavily at a nearby table. Opposite us, a Bosnian Moslem with a cast in one eye and a purple and pink scarf tied pirate-fashion round his head is also drinking heavily. The Serbs talk and make jokes which only Mira understands; she assumes an even cooler and more dignified air.

'I'll buy you all a drink,' the Bosniak slurs.

'Thanks, but no,' Graham says.

'Do you think we can't afford to buy drinks for our visitors?'

'Let me buy you one,' Graham offers diplomatically.

'Oh no,' the Bosniak says, '*you* are the guests, *I* will buy.'

There's sniggering from the Serb table, and Mira becomes paler and even more rigid, clutching her handbag to her stomach like a shield. She drinks nothing and seems to resent even sitting in such company. Not in the least afraid, she seems angry and mortified, a semi-permanent condition which is expressed in vicious banter between herself and Graham.

'What are they saying?' I ask.

'Rude things,' she replies.

One of the Serbs turns around and asks Mira what I do. When she tells him, he says he knows a good romantic story; he'll tell it to me and I can write it and make a lot of money.

'Why don't you tell the story and make the money yourself?' I ask.

'I don't know how to,' he says, grinning. They all laugh.

I resist the urge to say try picking up a pen.

'Give me an oven,' one of the other men says. 'I don't have an oven and I need one. Why doesn't SFOR give me one?'

They all laugh at what must be a private joke.

'We don't do ovens,' Graham says, smiling.

More beers appear on the table, ordered by the pink and purple pirate in the corner.

'Will you have some of mine?' I ask Mira.

She shakes her head vehemently, though it's a very hot day.

'Aren't you thirsty?' I ask.

'No,' she snaps.

She's desperate to leave this place, but won't or can't say so. The atmosphere is becoming unpleasant, with a subtle menace quite new to me.

'Shall we go?' I say, and she leaps to her feet as Graham pays for us all.

The atmosphere lifts as we walk away; even Mira seems to breathe more freely. Graham, on the other hand, seems perfectly relaxed, perhaps a result of two large beers. A horse and cart races past us at great speed, and for the first time I notice that there are no cars here.

'That's a Serb refugee centre over there in the school,' Graham says, pointing to a dilapidated, modern building.

'What's it like inside?' I ask.

He shakes his head. 'I don't know, I've never been in there.'

'Shall we take a look?'

We walk across what would have been the school yard and up the steps to where a semi-circle of little old ladies are knitting intricate patterns in brightly coloured wools. We smile, and they smile back. The caretaker's cubicle, beside the main door, is lined with soft porn and there's a camp-bed with soiled and crumpled sheets. Inside it's much the same: poorly dressed women of all ages sit around the walls of an echoing hall, knitting. The smells of cooked cabbage and unwashed bodies wafting through the hall remind me of prisons I've visited, and the constant click of needles takes on a sinister air.

Mira introduces us and all goes well for a few minutes. The women knit; most smile and tell us they've lived here for five years. They seem very different from each other: some look resigned, others angry; a few older women seem almost happy. But I'm rapidly learning that my own understanding of emotion and that of the people around me can be very different indeed. The atmosphere changes abruptly as men appear. A short, black-bearded man with a vast belly and high voice says he's the caretaker and demands to know what we want; his small, shrivelled side-kick repeats the demand. More men appear and we're quickly encircled. One of the younger women starts shrieking loudly.

'What she's saying?' I ask Mira, who's perfectly white.

'That we come here looking, but it's not to help. No-one helps them . . . no-one cares about them.'

'It's true,' the caretaker says, stepping closer to Graham, then stepping back again when he's forced to look up at the taller man. 'We've been here for five years . . . five years!' His raised voice brings yet more men from the depths of the building. Most of the women continue to knit nervously, except for the one whose voice climbs higher and higher, winding everything up a notch. 'We get nothing and the Moslems get everything. Look how we live, look how long we've been here!'

Graham attempts to calm the situation, but without much success. Bodies are starting to press in on us and my heart begins to pump faster. This, I realise with detached surprise, is a very unpleasant situation. Perspiration stands out on our translator's stony face and at this moment her dignified separation of the personal and professional seems incredible.

Graham and the Serbs are involved in a discussion of local politics which the Serbs are winning by sheer weight of numbers.

'I can't agree with you there,' Graham is saying, 'I'm sure the last mayor tried to do his best for everyone.'

Loud shouts of disagreement follow Mira's translation, fingers are jabbed and fists shaken.

Suddenly, I have a burst of inspiration. 'Tell them I'm a researcher, that I'm a writer. Tell them we came here because I'm interested to know how they live, how things are for them.'

She repeats this, and the noise quietens a little.

'Tell them we're here because we're just as interested in them and their lives as in the Moslems. We came here to get as fair a picture as possible. I will write what they say to me, just the same as I'll write what any Bosniak says.'

By the time this is translated, the room is almost silent. The crowd draws back from us; a few of the men look uncomfortable.

'Right, let's go,' Graham says after shaking hands with the caretaker and smiling politely all round. We walk away, followed by Mira, muttering under her breath in Bosnian.

'Fuck!' Graham and I say simultaneously once we're clear of the building. 'Fuck!'

'Does that sort of thing happen all the time round here?'

'Never seen anything like it before, thank God.'

On the way back to the 'Metal Factory', Graham says, 'Not a comfortable place, is it? And the more you learn, the worse it gets. There have been over a hundred bodies exhumed around Kožarac since the war ended, and there's probably a lot more, just waiting to be found.'

'Do you really think the last mayor did his best for those people?' I ask Graham as we smile and nod at the Czech soldiers who've been keeping an eye on the car.

'Of course not, he was a complete fuckwit.'

'Enjoy your day?' General Viggers asks as we drive into Banja Luka that evening for a concert of the Band of the Blues and Royals at the city's National Theatre.

'It was extremely interesting.'

'We saw things today you've probably never seen, General,'

Graham says from the front seat, and he reports the afternoon's events.

'I can believe it,' the General says, 'the more guards you have around you, the less you see. I like to be able to talk to people and shake hands without intimidating anyone, that's why I have only two bodyguards most of the time – my counterpart in the American sector has fourteen.'

'Does that mean he's seven times more important than you?' I ask jokingly. At which the General has the good humour to laugh.

'Seriously though,' he says, 'during the NATO bombings it was very tense here. We tried to calm things locally by saying "Yugoslavia's a different country," etc. But then we stepped up our own security and the locals were understandably annoyed, complaining that we told them to calm down but didn't follow our own advice. They were right, of course.'

Driving along at a sedate sixty kilometres an hour, I remember Graham's words on grenades rather than guns being the weapon of choice for local assassins, and it occurs to me that sitting beside General Viggers in a relatively slow-moving vehicle might not be the safest place in the world.

Outside the theatre, the car doors fly open as the General's aides and bodyguard rush him inside. Something round and fist-sized falls to the ground beside me, and I experience a single second of absolute horror before recognising a very large conker in its green protective shell. Above us is one of the tallest horse-chestnut trees I've ever seen, with hundreds of conkers poised, ready to drop on the unsuspecting. The General's already inside the building and no-one else has noticed a thing.

As we round the sweeping staircase to the first landing of the theatre, two bagpipers – a Gurkha and a Scots pipe major – stand to attention as the General passes. A couple of British bobbies, seconded here from their jobs back home, chat in a corner, their dark-blue uniforms bizarrely familiar. Only local civilian staff and British military and police personnel are invited to the concert. Here in the heart of the Republika Srpska, the feeling of home from home is odd and unsettling. Janet appears, but has to rush off in the interval, called unexpectedly to a late-night meeting some-where deep in the countryside.

It's very hot in the auditorium, at least it is in the front row of the circle. I feel rather sorry for the band sitting on the stage under bright lights in full dress uniform. One or two of the trumpeters are in the full gear – gleaming helmet and thigh-high boots. The rest of the theatre is a sea of camouflage green, dotted with spots of local colour. These musicians play for the Queen's parades and the tunes that echo across the deserted streets of Banja Luka are mostly military and British. Almost invisible among the men of the horn section, a tiny British Asian woman blasts away on a trombone. The General surreptitiously brushes at his eyes during a particularly moving solo by the pipe major, and claps and shouts 'Bravo!' at the end of every piece.

Sitting in the hot, semi-darkness of the Republika Srpska's National Theatre, there's plenty of time to think about the day. From Omarska and Kožarac to the Band of the Queen's guard requires a surreal leap of the imagination that I'm still struggling to make. The soldier-musicians' uniforms and instruments glitter in time with the Irish melody 'Danny Boy', a song about war and music and people who don't return. Perhaps, after all, that leap is not so great as it seemed.

12   The Last of Sarajevo

A FTER Banja Luka, Sarajevo seems a bright metropolis. It's early evening when Janet drives through the city centre to show me the Latin Bridge, formerly called the Gavrilo Princip Bridge, site of the assassination of Archduke Franz Ferdinand. It was renamed the Latin Bridge after the Bosnian war because Princip was a Serbian nationalist, though in 1914 Sarajevo viewed his action as a liberating one. Now he's seen as just another violent Serb. In 1978 I measured my own feet against the impression of Princip's, which marked the spot where he stood to fire the fatal shot. The impression is no longer there, and the bridge isn't named on any of the available maps; no-one I asked could point it out.

Heading towards Jezero, we pass the central market, silent and empty.

'You know about the famous explosion here in the market place?'

'Yes.'

'There was a lot of talk at the time that it wasn't a Serb shell at all, that the Bosnian Army fired the mortar.'

'I heard that. What was behind it?'

'The people who believed the rumour argued that things were dragging on, that the West was losing focus on Sarajevo – that the killing of ordinary people drew world attention like nothing else before, and forced NATO to take action.'

'And now?'

She shrugs. 'Both sides denied firing that particular shell. It's another one of those things we'll never know.'

How could anyone plan that, let alone do it? But who's to know what's possible in such a war, except those who experienced it?

'I haven't been able to do much about Tuzla for you,' Janet says as we pull up near Jezero, 'but I've been in touch with Ken Corlett, a British policeman working for the ICTY in Sarajevo. He's the guy who knows what's going on with exhumations here. I've talked to him and he's expecting you to call.'

'I'm amazed you remembered!' I say, genuinely surprised.

Janet grins. 'That's British diplomacy for you.'

A few hours later I meet Mela Telalbašić, Sarajevo representative of the London-based Bosnian Institute. An attractive, middle-aged woman, Mela appears relaxed and comfortable as we order octopus salad in a restaurant on Ferhadija. After initial pleasantries, however, the conversation takes a less comfortable turn.

'All my family have died since the war started, of natural causes . . . though what's natural after what we've been through? Stress, malnutrition, they take a toll on the body. My sister died quite recently, then my mother-in-law and later my father too. My husband died only last month, and about three weeks after his funeral I read a notice in the newspapers asking for relatives of a person with my mother's name to come forward.'

'Your mother's also dead?'

'She died early in the war, while she was visiting my sister in Grbavica, in Srpsko Sarajevo. My sister wasn't allowed to go to the cemetery to bury her because she was a Bosniak, and the Serbs didn't want us in their graveyards.' She pauses, as the waiter brings the salad. 'The notice asked for someone to identify my mother's body.'

'But she was buried . . . ?'

Mela smiles, grimly. 'Oh yes, she was buried – but where? We assumed the Serbs buried her in a coffin, in a cemetery. Now we don't know what happened. Either way, her body ended up in a mass grave in Republika Srpska. Even the dead have been ethnically cleansed. My mother is in a mortuary, in a bag.'

'You had to go there and identify her?'

For the first time she looks less than relaxed. 'Before my sister died, she told me how our mother left her house to be buried – what she was wearing, what jewellery, the coffin. But none of the things she described were found in the mass grave. So I had no means of identifying her.' She pauses. 'The mortuary was a terrible place. The smell was unbelievable, and the dirt.'

She's silent for a while, but soon looks up and smiles brightly. 'Do you like the octopus? It's very good here, I often come to this restaurant just for the octopus salad.'

Nothing in Mela's conversation suggests an ethnicity, despite having said her family were Moslem. 'Are you Moslem?' I ask finally.

'I'm none of those groups that people talk about,' she says. 'I'm a Bosnian.'

'What does that mean?'

'It means what it says. But if you really want to know, I'm of mixed Bosniak, Croat and Mongol heritage.'

'You mean the Mongols who invaded hundreds of years ago?'

She nods. 'Did you think there were only three peoples in this country?'

As Mela walks with me to the tram stop, she tells me that she lives with her brother and his second wife because her own house was damaged during the siege.

'The Serbs made a mess of it, then the Bosniaks finished it off. It still looks like Hiroshima and there's nothing much I can do. The internationals have offered me money to restore the interior, but what good is that when the roof needs replacing?' She smiles. 'I expect you've noticed, nothing is straightforward here.'

That night I develop a chest infection that keeps me in bed for a day.

'Look what happens!' Shabaza says. 'You go to the RS, you give them your money, and look what you get in return – a disease!'

Her treatments – animal fat on thick rags applied to the chest and pungent herbal tea with honey and lemon – though homely, are effective, particularly the grease.

'During the war we had no medicines here, so we used what we had . . . *rakija* and garlic, they cure many things.'

Thanks to Shabaza's ministrations, by the second day I'm able, with only partial loss of concentration, to meet up with Ken Corlett in a local bar. Formerly of the Lancashire Police in north-west England, Ken tells me he's been working for the International Criminal Tribunal for Yugoslavia at the Hague since June 1998. While driving us to the ICTY office in his UN vehicle, he outlines his career fighting crime.

'When I started work with the Lancashire Constabulary as a bobby on the beat in 1974, I never dreamt that my police career would bring me somewhere like this, working on an international stage. I considered working for Interpol at Scotland Yard, as I'd done some investigative work abroad, but it was suggested that I work for the Hague Tribunal . . . and the rest is history. It's great work. I really enjoy it, most of the time at least. That feeling that you really are doing something for individuals and making a contribution towards lasting peace here.'

'What kind of things do you do?'

'Investigation mostly. Statement taking, interviewing victims of crimes. I take statements from people who've been in concentration camps, for example, and also from witnesses. I really believe that telling someone like me, someone they feel can actually help bring the perpetrators to justice, helps people get on with their lives.'

'Isn't it horrible listening to vile stories over and over again?'

He nods. 'Yep, but they're no more vile than crime in Lancashire or London . . . there's just more of it here. It's the scale that makes the difference, that's all.'

'How long do you think you'll stay here?'

'Until the job's done.'

Ken shares the ICTY team office with an Irish policewoman and a Sri Lankan policeman. Posters of People Indicted for War Crimes (known as PIFWC's) cover the walls, hazy photographs of rough-looking Serb and Croat men peering out from above lists of those already captured and others already acquitted. Ken rolls up a poster and gives it to me. There's a shillelagh on the wall too, along with a Mountie's hat, a Welsh policeman's helmet and a French police kepi. Reminders of old colleagues and of the outside world.

'This is an introductory presentation about the ICTY work at the mortuary in Visoko,' Ken says, opening his laptop. With a few clicks of the mouse we're looking at Bosnia's criminal investigation mortuary, a low, white building, its front open to the air. With my brain dulled by infection, the only image that really registers with me are the racks outside the mortuary building, where clothes and shoes are drying in the open air.

As Ken drives me back to Jezero after dinner, we pass the *Oslobodjene* building and the pink and blue ruin beside it.

'Has anyone told you that was an old people's home?' Ken asks, pointing to the pink and blue building.

'Actually yes, as I was arriving a guy on the bus told me it was.'

Ken shakes his head. 'Don't believe everything you hear.'

When we arrive at Visoko mortuary the next morning in bright sunshine, the clothes racks are lined up around the entrance, just as in the computer images. Cheap trainers hang by their laces beside ragged pullovers, knitted bedroom slippers, thin green fatigues and matching socks. Just inside the door to the main building, I avoid stepping on a purple jumper stretched out on a large sheet of numbered paper. The jumper's hand-made, the stitching idiosyncratic – perhaps the wearer knitted it herself – but the most striking thing about it is how clean it looks; you'd never think it had lain for years on a rotting corpse in a mass grave.

What Ken's computer couldn't convey is the all-pervading stench. I thought I'd prepared myself, but it's not only worse than I'd imagined, it's completely different. The mortuary is filled with an acrid, ammonia smell that lingers weakly in the entrance and gets progressively stronger inside the building. The scent of old death disturbed.

Ken introduces Dr John Clark, the mortuary's senior patholo-gist. A tall, grey-haired Scotsman, Dr Clark smiles as he shakes my hand and asks if I'm a medical doctor.

'No,' I say.

'Ah,' he says, and immediately offers to show me the latest batch of bodies just arrived from an exhumation site. 'We were just about to unload these when you arrived.'

I follow him towards the large refrigerated container standing in the open entrance to the building. But for the mud stains and the letters 'UN' printed in black on the sides, the big metal box could contain anything. It's all rather sudden, and wondering whether to decline and seem feeble, or follow and risk horrors, I lag a few steps behind.

'You wanted to come here,' a stern inner voice says. 'What did you think you'd see? It's just a job to these people . . . don't be pathetic.' 'But how will I react?' another voice asks. 'How can anyone guess that sort of thing in advance?'

'It's still locked,' the pathologist announces, 'maybe I can find the key.'

At that moment a member of his staff comes over to ask a question, and to my relief the container is forgotten. Instead, I'm introduced to the various forensic scientists, many working on computers in the big, white-tiled entrance room. This building on the edge of a small town north of Sarajevo is the nerve centre of criminal forensics for the ICTY and attracts scientists from around the world, among them Canadians, Australians, Sri Lankans, British and South Africans.

'This is where we store the information we gather,' Dr Clark says, pointing to rows of scientists sitting at laptops. 'And over here is where we examine the remains and establish cause of death, if we can.'

Most of a skeleton is laid out on a long metal table draped in green cloth; jaw and teeth are in one pile, and the small bones of hands and feet are heaped neatly at the end of each limb. The missing part, the skull, is being painstakingly glued together by a young Canadian woman. There's a faint, earthy smell from the remains, but it's almost lost in the general stink of decay that fills the place and which no-one else seems to notice. Despite such evidence of death, it's almost impossible in this white, quiet environment to grasp that the person who lived in these bones died in terrified despair, probably screaming or cursing.

'See . . . here,' the pathologist points to the skull taking shape in his colleague's hands. 'There's the exit hole of the bullet, probably what killed him.'

'It's a man?'

'Yes,' the woman says, 'you can tell from the pelvis, among other things.'

'Why is the skull fragmented?' I ask.

'Could be that it shattered from the bullet impact, or maybe from the pressure of bodies thrown on top of it. Sometimes there are pockets of air in the graves and then body parts, usually the head, fall away, making identification even harder.'

As the skull takes final shape I think of the Celje family in their illuminated coffin boxes, and of the last lord, Ulrich II, killed by a blow that split his face.

We pass more tables with more remains, some of them with tissue still adhering.

'It's much easier dealing with skeletons,' Dr Clark says, 'but in the larger, deeper graves, where the pressure is greatest, you find more tissue on the bodies, which makes our work of establishing cause of death more difficult. But most of the bodies we get are just bones held together by clothes. If you come this way, I'll show you the cold-storage room.'

As the heavy door swings open, I realise the horrors of the container are here after all. White, mud-stained bags lie in discrete heaps around the long, dimly lit room. If the stench had seemed bad before, in here most of the senses are affected. The chill air tastes of decomposition, and my eyes sting. My hand moves involuntarily to pull my T-shirt up over my nose and mouth, but stops halfway as I catch a slight, amused glance from the Scotsman beside me. Like everyone I've met in here, he seems interested in my reaction to what I'm seeing.

'Those bags over there are from Srebrenica,' he says, 'those from Omarska, and these here from Tuzla. None of them have been examined yet, but they were all from mass graves. The bodies in the container outside will join them.'

With its piles of corpses so neatly contained in their white, unmarked plastic, this is the kind of room nightmares are made of.

'Zoë was interested in seeing the tunnel at Tuzla,' Ken says.

The pathologist shakes his head. 'We're lucky, these are civilised conditions here. Tuzla has thousands on thousands of unrefrigerated bodies piled on rows of shelves. Not a good place.'

We seem to have been standing in this room far longer than necessary and the smell is becoming unbearable.

'Let's have a look at the ammunition,' Dr Clark says, finally closing the steel door.

In the next room several men sit at a large table covered in bags of bullets and shell cases.

'We're all having coffee,' a bearded Australian says. 'Do you want one?'

'Thanks,' I say, and look wonderingly at the mug of coffee that someone hands me. There's a definite culture among the staff here; it's what makes them observe outsiders like me and even Ken. They watch, smiling, as I drink the coffee and pretend the ammonia smell isn't there.

The Australian lifts one of the many bags on the table. 'These bullets are from the grave we're unearthing near Tuzla. The execution site was a large building quite close to the grave, it's still covered with blood and bits of human tissue inside. The victims were shot and then grenaded. It's very interesting,' he says earnestly, 'you should go there. Maybe Ken will take you?'

I glance at Ken, who looks disapproving.

'Maybe I could go on the bus?' I say, at which they all laugh.

'Did anyone tell you about secondary and tertiary sites?' the Australian asks.

'What are they?'

'The Serbs dug up original grave sites and reburied the bodies to make locating them more difficult.' He walks to a large notice board, uncovers a concealed, hand-drawn map and points to the different symbols on it.

'These are the sites of executions and burials, and these are secondary and tertiary burials. This one here,' his finger rests on an 'X' on the map, 'we thought there were only thirty bodies in it, but as we were finishing up we discovered another three hundred underneath.'

He goes back to the table and picks up a bullet, turning it over in his fingers. 'All of these are going to the United States for forensic examination, then that information goes to the courts at the Hague as evidence.' He looks around the room, and there's real passion in his eyes as he says, 'We all want to find the people who did these things, and this . . .' he points at the ammunition, the map, 'is the only way we have. But we *will* find them – otherwise there's no justice for the guys in those bags in there.'

His colleagues nod, silently.

Ken looks at his watch and I finish my coffee. We all shake hands as we leave, and the Australian laughs: 'Didn't anyone tell you to never shake hands with a pathologist?'

This must be what they mean by morgue humour.

At seven the next morning Ken meets me outside Arrivals and Departures at Sarajevo airport; through his OHR contacts, he's arranged for us to observe a local exhumation. My chest infection has now spread to my nose, a day too late; breathing is difficult and I feel like crap. Bosnia is not a good place to be ill, not just because medical care, even in Sarajevo, is limited, but because anything short of a double amputation or death would seem like mere whingeing. But Ken's enthusiasm for his work is infectious too, and makes it easy to forget feeling rough. On the positive side, I won't be able to smell anything.

'It's the Bosnian Serbs today,' he says, as we sit near the Interentity Border which runs beside the airport; the place where Moslem Bosnia and the Republika Srpska meet. We're part of a line of vehicles belonging to OHR officials, the Bosnian Exhumation Commissioner, the police. Across the road on a disused stretch of tarmac, a Belorussian airplane, abandoned during the war, crouches forlornly.

'Serb burials?'

'Yes. They're looking for Serb bodies today. Each ethnic group has the same access to exhumation procedures.'

'Who are we waiting for now?'

'The Serbs.'

The Serbs arrive half an hour later than everyone else. Their Commissioner, a dark, stocky man, is accompanied by a thin, black-haired woman in denims who someone says is a judge and someone else, a journalist. The Bosniaks line up along the road beside their cars and there's a tense shaking of hands. Not for the first time, I look at these people standing together and think that they all look exactly the same. If anything, these Serbs look more eastern, more 'Turkish', than the Bosniaks. At least they do to me. What exactly do people here mean when they claim to be able to distinguish ethnicity at a glance? How does a naked Serb look different from a naked Croat? A Serb woman from a Bosniak? But the answer is as vague as so much else here: 'We just do.'

When the Serbs turn their backs, the Bosniaks glance at each other and grimace. This whole business of looking for evidence of killing in the presence of the alleged 'killers' strikes me as very odd and unhelpful.

We drive to an open patch of ground beside a shelled apartment block in the suburb of Dobrinja. From a distance the modern building looks ruined, but close up I see it's hung with satellite dishes and drying laundry. The roof is in shreds and the walls are pockmarked with bullet and shrapnel holes, but the two lower storeys are home to refugees from parts of Bosnia now under Croat or Serb control. As the Serb workmen begin marking out the site under the windows with scythes and tape, several generations gather on the dodgy-looking balconies above and start drinking coffee among flowering geraniums.

But whatever they hope to see, they're disappointed. Four hours and four trenches later, the earthmover drives off, having undermined the foundations of the building, killed several small trees and exposed nothing more than several bags of domestic rubbish. Ken's left for a meeting in Banja Luka and I've met Josephine Cookson, an Australian forensic anthropologist working with Physicians for Human Rights.

'What made them think this was a good place to dig,' I ask her.

'They get tip-offs. People say they saw something . . . someone remembers something. This wasn't a likely spot, too open, and the soil's not right. You can tell quite soon if there's a burial because of chemical colour changes in the soil.'

'Don't they do tests before all this digging?' I ask.

'Sometimes,' she says, and grins.

At lunchtime we move to a site beside a bridge over the Miljacka River. It's on the Bulevar Meše Selimovića, the main east–west road into Sarajevo, which used to be called Sniper Alley. The fair I passed coming into the city from Mostar is just across the road; its empty wheels, rides and stalls, silent observers of the activity fifty metres away. The handful of fairground workers turn away; they've seen this all before.

'Why this place?' I ask Selma, the OHR official.

'Someone claims to have seen bodies thrown from a mini-van on the corner of a bridge during the war. Apparently there's photographic evidence and the bridge in the photo might be this one.' She shrugs. 'They've already dug up the other three corners, this is the last.'

The earth is soft and the driver of the earthmover sets to, ripping into the riverbank without preliminaries. The original group of observers has swelled to more than twenty, all men, now leaning idly on the parapet of the bridge. Selma, a very attractive young Bosniak, is the object of what in the West would be considered gross sexual harassment. I watch her smile and wince as the Serb Commissioner sinks hard, hairy fingers into her upper arm when she tries to escape his attentions.

'You're an OHR official, why do you put up with it?' Josephine and I ask when we're alone.

'I have to work with these people every day,' Selma moans. 'What else can I do?'

'Smile politely and say "fuck off"?'

Selma grins and wriggles uncomfortably.

'Women work and men watch in this country,' Josephine says, 'it's just like the rest of the world.'

'It's true that the Devil makes work for idle hands,' I say, thinking of the farmers with their lone cows.

Josephine laughs and continues taking notes in a little book. Among other things, she's here as an advisor and witness to the scientific nature, or otherwise, of the proceedings.

'It doesn't *look* very scientific,' I say.

'They have their own way of doing things,' she replies. 'Some of them, like the Bosnian Commissioner, have been at it for years, even before the war ended . . . not an easy job.'

The Bosnian Commissioner is a heavy man, still young but with white streaking his dense moustache. He doesn't immediately look the stuff of heroes, but from what Selma tells me, he's dedicated to the retrieval of Bosniak dead. With twenty thousand people still unaccounted for in Bosnia, his commitment will be needed for many years to come.

An hour and two trenches later, the riverbank is pretty much destroyed and the Miljacka runs red with mud. Plastic rubbish from the churned earth washes downstream, just a fraction of the many ugly and terrible things buried beneath the surface of this country. The only organic item turned up is a hibernating tortoise, which all the men, Serb and Bosniak alike, rush, oohing and aahing, to examine before it's carried gently to a leafy allotment on the other side of the river.

We move back to Dobrinja once again, to a patch of dirt beside a disused car park. Below the main road and hidden on three sides, this spot looks a far more likely place for secret burials. But I'm beginning to suspect that none of this is about results.

There's no room for the earthmover here, so they dig by hand. At five o'clock it starts to drizzle, and the sides of the trench turn slick. Then there's a sudden commotion as pieces of a coffin emerge out of the dirt. The Serbs leap into action, photographing, measuring, waving me forward to the edge of the hole to take photos myself. Their excitement is palpable. Continuing to dig, they turn up a few bits of wood, two pairs of rubber gloves and a pair of trousers.

'The gloves suggest the bodies have been removed,' Josephine tells me. 'There could be any number of reasons for that.'

The trousers cause the most commotion, as the Serb Commissioner leaps dramatically into the trench and starts looking for a label.

'*Serb* trousers?' I whisper to Josephine, who giggles quietly and whispers back, 'Made in Taiwan.'

Bits of wood from a second coffin appear, then a third pair of rubber gloves; but the Bosniaks, including the Commissioner, have got bored in the rain and are drinking coffee in a nearby café. There's no sense of gravitas here, and the situation turns to farce when yellow marker flags are laid around the trench and the Serb Commissioner declares it a mass grave.

'But there's nothing here to suggest a crime,' Josephine says to me in amazement as we leave the site. 'Murder victims don't usually get buried in coffins, and you require at last three bodies to declare a mass grave. We don't have one body, or even fragments of one.'

'Are you going to say that to them?' I ask.

'I've tried saying things in the past but they just ignore me. They only want scientific opinions or evidence if it backs them up.'

Returning to town we pass a woman in a long, colourful dress. Close up, I notice the darkness of her skin; she could be from anywhere in India.

'Gypsy,' our driver almost spits. 'They get everywhere here . . . into bombed houses with no water, no toilet. They live like animals.'

No-one says anything, though Josephine breathes out heavily. What is it about human nature, I wonder, that makes the victims of brutality so capable of brutalising others? And looking back at the woman who looks so exotic in this grey landscape, I remember Mela Telalbašić's words: 'Did you think there were only three peoples in this country?'

Mela is waiting for me under a striped umbrella. The small square beside the Catholic cathedral is lively, the café pleasant.

'Tell me what you've been doing since we last met,' she says.

When I mention Visoko, she hesitates.

'That's where my mother's body is.'

'I thought you'd identified your mother?'

'I couldn't find her. How can you know someone from a rotting skeleton? She's still there.'

I feel guilty, embarrassed, as if I've trespassed on someone's territory of grief. 'What will happen?'

'I remembered recently that my mother broke her arm once, so there may be a fracture mark that would show up on an x-ray. I'll get in touch with the people at the mortuary and tell them. Maybe it will help.' She smiles at me. 'At least you know what's it's like there now.'

'Only as an outsider,' I say, 'not as you know it.'

As we finish our coffee she asks me, 'This is your last day here, yes? Is there anything you'd like to see before you leave?'

'I'd like to go to the cemetery across the river . . . for the view from up there.'

Mela looks at her watch. 'It'll be dark soon, if we're going we should go now.'

And with that she hails a passing taxi.

The sun is resting on the horizon as we walk between the slender white gravestones of the Alifakovac Cemetery. It's bitingly cold up here, several degrees colder than in the town only a few hundred metres below us.

'Did you know that the plain stones mark a woman's grave and the ones with "hats" indicate a man's?'

'No, I didn't. Are they all like that?'

'Moslem graves usually are, it's a Turkish style.'

The stones are crowded together, but there's room for an occasional tree and many of the graves are planted with flowers. Below us, the winding streets and red-brown roofs of this old part of town reach down towards Baščaršija across the river. Domes and minarets, cathedral spires and breweries, office blocks and hotels glow as if on fire.

The sun slides behind a distant hill, faster and faster. I look at Sarajevo, lovely and frail, strong and damaged. Here is the end point, from which my homeward journey begins, though there are other places still to see, other cities to visit. The sun disappears, its last gleam of light brushing the tallest buildings, distant Momo and Uzeir pointing like two broken fingers towards the sky.

The bus station is thick with fog, the young refugee beggars blurred in the early light. It's October now and true autumn in Sarajevo, though leaves are still green and some days still warm. Fog clings to the tower blocks of Sniper Alley, to the fairground wheels and the garden where a tortoise sleeps. The city is part imaginary as we start south-west for Mostar and Metković, cross-ing the Miljacka, the Željenica and finally, the Bosna. For me, the Bosna is the last of Sarajevo; but as the bus rattles across the bridge, the river is hidden by rising vapour. I'm leaving an invis-ible city, marked by an unseen boundary, and I don't know what to feel. Like a funeral without a coffin, it's hard to say goodbye.

Only a few weeks ago I travelled this same road, marvelling at the beauty, the wonders of this place. It's still a wonder, with its towering crags, dark lakes and tree-lined hills. But now each patch of green has many possible interpretations – a garden, a minefield, a mass grave. I think of that statement of stubborn resistance: 'Eat grass and suck stones'. There's a lot of stone here in Bosnia, and a lot of grass too. As we cross the Neretva, I hope that some will remain unsucked and uneaten when Bosnia is whole again. Closing my eyes, I let myself be carried towards the sea.

Metković and the Croatian border. The bus falls into line behind a dozen others as each passenger's passport is collected by the conductor and handed over to the border guards. This is always an unpleasant moment; it arouses old fears of losing offi-cial identity, and reminds me of being thrown off buses in other parts of the world for no reason other than idle curiosity or avarice. After twenty minutes or so, a young woman in uniform appears and starts returning the passports; reaching me she stops and flicks through mine slowly and deliberately. Irritated and tired I wait for the problem to be stated. Her fingers turn page after page until, almost reluctantly, she hands it back.

'You travel such a lot,' she says in a small and wistful voice.

From Metković we turn south into the heart of the Neretva delta. Travelling from Split to Sarajevo I only touched the northern edge of this fertile marshland region which is famous for its freshwater eels, black hens and tangerines. The road rises above the plain, the bus chugging and grinding. Far below, karst and sea, lakes and marshes, meet in a tapestry of blue, gold and green; of canals dividing narrow strips of cultivated land. Local fishermen hunt eels and frogs in *trupica*, traditional wooden canoes, though this is a protected area, a key region in the cycle of migration, hibernation and nesting, and a hatching ground for many varieties of fish. The Neretva's green waterways meet Adriatic turquoise among red roofs, cypresses and limestone. From up here the delta has a timeless quality, as if nothing has changed since Diocletian's times.

South of Metković we make a brief return to Bosnia at Neum. This town, and the twelve kilometres of coastline around it, is Bosnia's only access to the sea.

'We're not really welcome in Croatia,' Bosnian friends told me in Sarajevo. 'We spend our money there but they don't want us and they don't treat us well. Neum at least is ours.'

Croatians may or may not want Bosnian tourists and their money in Croatia, but they definitely enjoy the tax-free benefits of Neum, where everything from olive oil to perfume costs a fraction of Croatian prices. The grey economists of Bosnia and Hercegovina sun their outsize bellies on private yachts here in the daytime and stroke concealed weapons with gold-heavy fingers in the evenings.

With its beaches, tennis courts, modern hotels and apartment buildings piled on top of each other, Neum looks like Stalinism hits Las Vegas. Everywhere there are flowers, and the sharp angles of new buildings. Kids are brown from playing in the sun, and men and women look relaxed and casual. Squashed between mountains, the sea and Croatia, sun and air give tiny Neum a comforting illusion of space. The bright Mediterranean light is almost shocking, and makes a sharp contrast with Bosnia's deep mountain valleys. It's hard to believe that the ruined buildings, minefields and graves of Mostar are only forty kilometres away.

There are no border crossings at Neum, but as the bus swings down the coast road towards Dubrovnik there's no doubt where Bosnia ends. Croatian territory is signified by a gigantic cross, a marker between 'good' Christians and the circumcised teenage boys playing basketball on Neum's concrete beaches.

13   Stone and Light

> *If there were several Dubrovniks in the world only one would be the real Dubrovnik; this genuine, authentic and only city made of stone and light . . . Incomparable Dubrovnik.*
>
> Jure Kaštelan

From my window in the annexe of the Hotel Imperial, I can see trees, the sea and the thick walls of the Stari Grad, Dubrovnik's Old Town. The Hotel Imperial itself, closed since it was shelled by the JNA in the winter of 1991–92, stands forlorn and dignified across the parking lot. I can see the melted lead of the Imperial's roof, the hole where the shell hit still gaping like a wound in the head.

It's many degrees warmer here than in Sarajevo, more like late summer. What Shabaza called my 'Serbian disease' is still hanging on, and I'm glad of the softness of the Mediterranean climate as I walk the short distance to the Pile Gate. I pass beneath a statue of the city's patron, Sv. Vlaha, St Blaise, and enter a gateway so vast and elegantly constructed I pause in mid-stride. Grey stonework dating from 1460 towers overhead, making the individual feel at once insignificant and protected, presumably a normal state for the ordinary citizen of fifteenth-century Ragusa, as Dubrovnik was once known.

Beyond the inner gate, the city's marble-tiled main street stretches ahead, a pale, honey-coloured confection of Gothic, Renaissance and Baroque architecture. My first thought is that of all the places I've revisited on this journey, this is the only one to have remained absolutely unchanged. But of course, that isn't true. Nearly 70 per cent of Dubrovnik's buildings were affected by Serb shelling between 1991 and 1992. Some buildings were totally destroyed and more than 20 per cent were gravely damaged. But my initial impression is superficially accurate. The restoration of historical Dubrovnik is a wonder, second only to the city itself. Huge international funding went into the reconstruction. Stonemasons, carpenters and architects from all over the world worked on a project few ever thought they would experience: the repair of a medieval town.

The Placa runs into Luža Trg, a small square lined with churches, palaces, cafés and galleries. It's four in the afternoon, and the Old Town is quite empty. An hour and a coffee later, everything changes; shops open, kids appear from nowhere eating ice cream, playing ball and shouting loudly. Nuns in pale-grey habits scurry from this church to that convent. Polite, well-kept dogs sniff each other then trot after their owners, heads high. This is one of the most perfect places for socialising I've ever seen. Small children run loose as their parents chat, eat and drink in a setting of exquisite beauty and historical significance that's not big enough to get lost in. There are no cars, no bicycles, and everyone looks relaxed.

A little girl attempts to climb the Orlando Column in the middle of the square. The column supports the statue of a knight, carved in 1417 on the order of King Sigismond of Hungary and Croatia. 'Orlando', or 'Roland', was a well-known figure both literally and metaphorically in late-medieval art, and statues of him were common across Central Europe. Ragusa's Orlando had a practical use too: his forearm was used as a statutory measure in the Republic – the Ragusan ell, measuring 51.1 centimetres.

The statue's wide appeal lay in its representation of Roland, anti-Islamic hero of the *Chanson de Roland*, an early-medieval poem. The hero is described as a nephew of Charlemagne killed by Saracens while defending Christian Europe's western border at Roncevaux in the western Pyrenees in August 778. This version of the story emerged around the time of the First Crusade, a time when Europe first grasped the extent of the threat to Christendom. The real Roland/Orlando was the Duke of Brittany, and though a leader in Charlemagne's army – which entered Spain to fight *for* the ruling Moorish princes against invading Maghribians – he was no relation of the great man. Neither was he foully done to death by Arabs, as the poem states, but killed by Basque robbers while guarding the Franks' rear and baggage train.

The child clutching Orlando's legs on a pleasant evening in Dubrovnik knows none of these things, but when she's old enough, I wonder which story she'll believe. Will she follow the tradition which fears her Moslem neighbours, less than fifteen kilometres away?

The next morning I meet the Director of Tourism for Dubrovnik, an attractive, smartly dressed woman who tells me without any hesitation that Dubrovnik's tourism is a mess.

'It's only in the last few years that the restoration has been completed,' she says, as we drink coffee in her pleasant office overlooking Luža Trg. 'Hotels, shops and tourist agencies were all affected by the war here and in Bosnia.' She walks to the window. 'Come and look . . . the extent of the damage is clearer from up here than on the ground. Many of the buildings you can see are empty inside – they're merely façades, to make everything look OK. Can you see the difference in the roof tiles?'

I can. The warm honey and ochre tones of tiles many hundreds of years old contrast with the brick-red and orange shades of the new tiles used to repair the damage done by shelling.

'They tried to match the tiles but it was impossible. The original factory closed many years ago. In the old days, Dubrovnik's tiles were shaped on the tile-maker's thigh . . . who can make such things today?' She shrugs resignedly and returns to her seat. 'So, we started to recover, and many people took out big loans to repair and upgrade their services and facilities. Then this year we have the war in Kosovo and Yugoslavia, and everything crashes again because the rest of the world imagines we are still one country, or at least neighbours. Many people here have very serious financial problems because they can't repay their debts. People don't eat well, don't dress properly . . .'

I comment truthfully on how very smart she looks. She laughs, pleased by the compliment, but finding it humorous too.

'This,' she holds her skirt between finger and thumb, 'is ten years old . . . and this,' she points to her shirt, 'is seven. We've all learnt how to make everything seem better than it really is, even our wardrobes!'

She stands up and shakes my hand. 'Please, feel free to use my computer if you have emails to write, and in a moment a guide will be here to meet you. I hope you enjoy your stay with us.'

Sitting at the desk of the Director of Tourism, I think how extraordinarily different north and south Croatia are from each other. Quite how different I only discover after meeting Dubravka Vrenko.

My rare experiences with guides have never been very successful, so Dubravka, an attractive older woman, is a pleasant surprise; her positive enthusiasm for her own city is informed and measured. We get on immediately and find we have much in common, from food to astrology. Sensing my general tiredness, Dubravka is torn between wanting to show me her city and indulging me by sitting and talking over wine and seafood.

' "Dubravka" is a female variant on "Dubrovnik",' she says. 'It's a common name in this part of the world. But I'm a true citizen.' She smiles. 'Do you know anything about Dubrovnik's humanitarian and social welfare history?'

'Nothing at all,' I say.

'It was always ahead of its time. For example, the city governors understood that clean running water was vital for public health and so the Onophrio and Little Onophrio fountains were built in 1438 to bring water from a well many kilometres away. In 1437 an institution was set up to care for elderly men, and in that passage over there . . .' she points behind me, 'you can see a place in the wall that used to be a special window to the orphanage, built in 1432. There was a horizontal wheel on which the unwanted baby would be placed . . . the wheel would be turned and the baby would disappear inside the orphanage without anyone seeing who left it there. This was done to protect women, rich or poor, who couldn't care for their babies or were in trouble. It was against the law to accost anyone leaving a baby.'

'I heard they recently introduced that same idea somewhere in Germany,' I say. 'They must have got the idea from here! But what happened to the children?'

'They were all brought up together until they were old enough to be sent to rich houses as servants, or to the convents and monasteries.' She lifts her wineglass and tastes the wine. 'It's good wine, my favourite. Good for the blood.' We clink glasses.

'One of the most important decrees passed here, or anywhere for that matter, was the abolition of slavery in 1416 – four hundred years before it was stopped in your country.' She shrugs. 'Maybe the Republic didn't need the trade. With the exception of Venice, we were the greatest power in the Adriatic in every sense. One result of the good living, wealth and stability that Ragusa enjoyed before the earthquake of 1667 was a great upsurge in creativity.' Her face lights up as she speaks. 'We had poets and dramatists, musicians, composers and scientists. And not only men, there were famous women here too.' She pauses to watch as a grey-haired man makes his way slowly past us. 'You see that man?'

I nod. He looks vaguely familiar.

'He's a goldsmith, he has a small shop in one of the streets off the Placa.'

I remember seeing him at work, his hair sticking untidily up from behind large goggles and a blowtorch.

'His family have been goldsmiths in Dubrovnik for over seven hundred years.'

The man's heading home for the afternoon meal, maybe a siesta, his feet treading the same marble tiles as his father and generations of fathers with his name. Such an unbroken family history is almost inconceivable to me, who experienced a sense of achievement on tracing one of my own family lines back to 1830. Perhaps this is the secret of Dubrovnik's success down the ages; not its buildings, or even its good works, but the real tradition, the long, long history of families and individuals who make up a citizenry. This is what most of former Communist Europe lost after generations of war and internal strife; and what the West has surrendered without a fight.

'There are several families living in the city today who can trace their lineage back to the earliest records, and at least one person has a named ancestor who signed a decree in 1023. Of course, a lot was lost in the earthquake and fire of 1667. Nearly all the beautiful Renaissance palaces and churches were destroyed, and more than five thousand people died. It's hard to imagine, but this city is only a shadow of how it would have looked before 1667. But if you like, I'll show you what we have. Some of it is very beautiful indeed.'

Of the handful of pre-earthquake buildings and public amenities like the Onophrio fountains, the structure that for me best illustrates Jure Kaštelan's description of 'stone and light' is the cloister of the Franciscan monastery near the Pile Gate. The Franciscans first came to Dubrovnik in 1235, and work began on the cloister before 1350. The friary church was destroyed in the earthquake; all that remains is the main door surmounted by a *pietà* sculpted in 1498 by local masters.

The side entrance to the friary is dark and covered in scaffolding, and the overhead sun dazzles as we enter the cloister. At the heart of the quadrangle is a semi-tropical garden of palms and flowering trees. Sunlight illuminates the pale limestone walls and slender double-columned arches so they appear to glow as if from within. This effect of light on stone, reflected in the lush central garden, is the nearest thing I've seen to the subtleties of medieval Islamic architecture. But the cloister's beauty lies in detail as much as overall effect; each of the dual columns is topped with a different animal head, a floral arrangement, a human face.

'Look, up there . . . can you see? A man with toothache, his face is swollen on one side. Maybe this is the only sculpture of toothache in the world!'

'It's incredibly beautiful,' I say. 'I've seen quite a few cloisters, but none as marvellous as this.'

'The Dominican cloister here is very beautiful too,' Dubravka says, smiling as she leads me into the monastery's treasury. 'There was some rivalry between the Dominicans and Franciscans. They tried to outdo each other in many ways . . . perhaps all this beauty was one result.'

The treasury houses a vast wealth of precious crosses, statues and other religious artifacts. I stare, fascinated and repulsed at the ornate gold and silver reliquaries containing pieces of saints and martyrs. The adjacent library is closed, but Dubravka tells me it contains over two hundred incunabula and many manuscripts.

'One of the manuscripts is a kind of journal, written by a friar apothecary. It has a very interesting entry which states, "Today in the afternoon at about five we were watching a line of lights in the sky and we were watching them for an hour." It may be one of the earliest recorded UFO sightings!'

'They were apothecaries,' I say. 'Maybe they'd been testing draughts and potions!'

She laughs and we walk on to the pharmacy, where to my surprise a white-coated woman is counting pills in an electronic counter among all the paraphernalia of a modern chemist shop.

'The friars opened this pharmacy in 1391. It's one of the oldest working pharmacies in the world – I get my own prescriptions here sometimes.'

'Why is it so very different here from the rest of Croatia,' I ask, as we sit in the small market square off Luža Trg, drinking wonderful, soft red wine from the nearby island of Pelješac.

'Most people here feel they're Dubrovnikers first, and Croats second,' Dubravka says. 'After all, we've been part of Croatia for less than two hundred years. Until the twelfth century, we were part of the Byzantine Empire. Then the mainland settlement of Dubrovnik and the islet city of Ragusa merged and became a very prosperous place. The Venetians soon became nervous of Ragusa's mercantile power, and for about a hundred and fifty years, from the mid-thirteenth century, they controlled the Ragusan Republic. But as with Byzantium, Ragusa always managed to remain independent despite outside interference.'

The tiny fried fish and whole baby squid Dubravka has ordered for us to share arrive on giant plates brought by a smiling, efficient woman.

'After Venice,' Dubravka continues, 'Ragusa paid tribute to the King of Croatia. By that time the Republic owned land up and down the coast, and islands too. Ragusa's leaders must have been some of the wisest politicians the world has known! Even when the Ottomans seized Bosnia, Serbia and most of Croatia, Ragusa remained independent.' She grins. 'We just changed who we paid tribute to.'

Modern Dubrovnik is a slow and elegant place. I find it difficult to imagine it at its height in the sixteenth century, the docks clustered with ships, the groups of bankers and merchants from across Europe dealing and haggling in its streets and behind its heavy doors. The city's decline began with the financial and social disaster that followed the 1667 earthquake, and it was all over by 1806 when the French army entered Dubrovnik during their 'Illyrian' campaign and declared the Republic at an end. With Napoleon's defeat, Dubrovnik was handed to Vienna and it remained part of the Austro-Hungarian Empire until the creation of the Kingdom of Yugoslavia after World War I. At the end, it seems, outside interference proved too much, even for the wily and long-lived Ragusan Republic.

Across the square I notice a carp of black-clad crones sitting outside the Rector's Palace. Dubravka smiles when I mention what Marina had said to me on Rab, about widows and suffering.

'It's true,' she says. 'These women's lives are so restricted they have no life at all.'

'I wonder what they think when they look at us enjoying ourselves, eating and drinking in public?'

'I expect they think we're going to hell.'

That evening I visit a gallery where a British artist is showing his sketches and drawings of the city. Foreign artists have long been attracted to Dubrovnik and its inspirational environment. John, a tall slender man with a beard, has been coming here every summer for years.

'I live in Pembrokeshire most of the year,' he says. 'I'm a psychotherapist in that other life.'

He seems to be with a vibrant, colourful woman called Jana, who says she was once a tour guide in Dubrovnik and now lives in Italy with her daughter.

'You're writing about your experience in our country? Ask me anything you like, anything at all. I studied philosophy at Belgrade University, then I ran a chain of art galleries all over the Former Yugoslavia. Ask me whatever you like . . . I will answer anything.'

'When you were in Belgrade, did you ever think there could be a war between Croats and Serbs?'

'Never, never did such a thing even enter my consciousness.'

It's been a while since I last asked my 'question'. Boris and his wife were Croatian Serbs; Atif Muhić a Bosniak. Finally, I'll ask a Croat.

But unlike the others, Jana is not atheist but a staunch Catholic. Undeterred, I press on.

'When you lived in Belgrade in the 1970s, did you think of yourself as a Croat or as a Yugoslav?'

'As a Croat.'

'Even then?'

'Of course, because I was born in Croatia.'

'What if you had been born in Belgrade, of the same parents.'

'I would still be Croatian, of course. Actually, only one of my parents is Croatian.'

'But you were born in *Yugoslavia*, had a Yugoslav passport, Yugoslav parents, only one of whom is Croat. I'm trying to understand what it means to you when you say you're a Croat.'

'Look,' she says with evident irritation, 'it's a very complex thing.'

'I understand that, I've asked this same question of different people with different backgrounds. But all I've really been able to grasp is a *feeling* that people have, which they usually call a "tradition", but I've never quite grasped what they mean by that. You told me I could ask any question, so I'm asking: what is this *feeling* that people can't explain but have been ready to kill and die for?'

She shuffles on her seat and continues to look angry. It seems as if I've cornered her, but she is an intelligent, educated woman, able, I assume, to look after herself.

'It's about Dubrovnik too,' she says, avoiding my question entirely. I glance at John, the psychotherapist, but he's looking at his sandals.

'Dubrovnik is not Croatia, just as Sarajevo is not Bosnia. But Sarajevo *represents* Bosnia, and this is not true of Dubrovnik and Croatia.'

I seem to have lost the plot somewhere.

'Dubrovnik is separate, freer, prouder; our people are quite different. But Dubrovnik is scarred by war. My daughter is scarred too. When we first moved to Italy during the war, people would say what a happy child she was, how you would never think she'd been in a war. She was six years old then. Now she is eleven.' She pauses, breathing hard. 'She's a pupil at the La

Scala ballet school. Recently, her class was asked to make drawings of Peace. The other kids drew doves, globes. My daughter
drew a grey picture of ruined buildings and a river full of bodies.' Almost in tears, she says, 'All those years I thought she
was OK, but it wasn't true. She's scarred, just like our beautiful
city.'

Walking back to my hotel which, I've discovered, is government
owned like the Bellevue in Split and run by equally depressed and
unpaid staff, I think back over the conversation. While speaking
to her, I'd known that Jana's aggravation was not directed at me
but at her pain, her daughter's pain, Dubrovnik's pain. Pain, it
seems, has affected people's ability to answer a question like,
'How do you feel you're different from Croats or Serbs or
Bosniaks?' and by extension the question, 'Who are you?' As the
hotel lift chugs and jerks to the third floor, it occurs to me that
many of the people I've met on my journey seem far clearer about
who they are not, than about who they are.

Outside the closed and silent main building of the Imperial,
a fair-haired man less than a metre tall is guarding the
entrance. There's always someone on guard and I wonder what
goes on inside, away from the public gaze. For some reason,
my thoughts wander to Visoko and what I saw there. It's not a
subject for the dark or for sleep, but it's there, persistent and
clear. I think of Mela Telalbašić's mother; the broken skull of
an unknown man revealing the truth of how he died; heaps of
soiled white bags called 'Omarska', 'Srebrenica', 'Tuzla'.
Then I think of Dubrovnik's reconstructed wounds and hidden
scars, of Jana's story, and my own lack of compassion. In 1978
I visited Dubrovnik before Sarajevo. Making this final part of
the journey in reverse has coloured everything I see and hear.
Even three weeks earlier I might, listening, have been nearly
as choked with feeling as Jana herself. Tonight I felt almost
nothing; perhaps because of Visoko, because of Kožarac.
Jana's daughter is alive and so is Dubrovnik. How quickly

pain's effects can be graded and pigeon-holed: Severe, Less Severe, Not Really Bad At All. It's probably a good thing that I'll be leaving soon.

The next day, Dubravka drives us down the coast towards the Montenegrin border and the town of Cavtat. For a few kilometres Croatia is no more than the road itself. Just over the steep cliff that cuts down to the sea is Hercegovina.

After coffee in a café near the tree-lined beach, we visit an art gallery dedicated to the work of a scion of Cavtat, the great Croatian painter Vlaho Bukovac, born here in 1855. The gallery is bursting with colour and sweeping brushstrokes; the work is astonishingly flowing and grand, yet with little of the sentimentality of so much British work of the same period. Large canvases describe ancient Slav and Croat myths and legends, while the portraits of beautiful women and rich men are vibrant yet soft. The scale and breadth of the work is humbling, and as we walk around the gallery together I can see that Dubravka is proud to introduce a foreigner to Bukovac's achievements.

'Do you like this work?' she asks as we walk back to her car.

'Very much,' I say. 'It's grand but not over-romantic. There are so many wonderful writers and artists from this part of the world that we in Western Europe never read and never see. It's a great pity, I think we miss a lot.'

From Cavtat we drive inland, along the brief strip of Croatia between the sea and that other country beyond. Dubravka shows me her home among maize fields and lakes, the places where she walks and relaxes with her husband, a sea captain in the Ragusan tradition. Driving back towards Dubrovnik, we round a steep uphill bend in the road.

'Look there,' she says, 'at the rock . . . do you see?'

'What is it?'

'Eight years ago to this day, the war started here. I was at home with my husband when the shelling started; it was Serbs from Montenegro, up there on the hills. We grabbed some bags, got into our car and drove as fast we could towards Dubrovnik because we thought they'd never shell that. Most of the way along the road from my house we were hidden by trees – only that one part of the road, that bend back there, was exposed. But they were waiting. The shell missed us by a metre and hit the rock. Now, every time I pass it, I remember that moment, and how we survived.' She smiles cheerfully. 'My husband returned to his oil tankers and I was alone in a strange borrowed house. We'd planned everything so carefully for our retirement and we were already in our fifties. Our house was beautiful, filled with every comfort, every gadget, and pieces of art collected from around the world. Our children were married and secure. But in all our calculations and investments we never planned for war. For eight months I didn't know if we even had a home, if it had been shelled, or if soldiers had taken it over. It's less than ten kilometres from here to the city, but all the land between was occupied, so it was impossible to learn anything.'

We reach the road above Dubrovnik and park so I can have a last look. The view is spectacular: the Stari Grad sits on its small rocky peninsula jutting into bright-blue sea amid a sprawl of villas and houses that curves along the shore. Dubravka leans on a stone wall and gazes out across her beloved city.

'It was horrible, not knowing if we'd lost everything, our home, our possessions, security in old age. But after a while I began to have a different attitude. No-one in our family had died; no-one we knew had died. I realised then how lucky we were, that safety and survival of family and friends was the *only* thing that mattered. When I understood this, my whole attitude to life and to material things changed.

'As soon as it was reasonably safe, I went back to my house. It was damaged, but it was still standing. There was no electricity, no gas, but I lived there for five months, alone, cooking on wood. Every night I lit a candle so people would know the house was occupied and they would stay away.'

'Weren't you afraid on your own.'

'In the beginning of the war I would have been, but by that time, no. I was alive, everyone close to me was alive. Anything more was a blessing.'

Early the next morning I board the *Liburnia* once again, this time for the long haul back to Rijeka. There's a busy mix of passengers and the ship seems oddly full of people who look like someone else; there's an Anthony Blunt, a couple of rather good Hemingways, a Proust, a Zorba and a few personalities whose names I can't remember. But with my boat pass and a cabin with a porthole, a washbasin and a desk all to myself, I can avoid the general on this particular trip and be delightfully alone. It's exciting too, perhaps because the last time I slept on this ship it was on the hard boards of the upper deck with a hundred other people.

We pass island after island until we reach Korčula, where I spent some time in 1978; on this journey I get no closer than the ship's rails. Then, I stayed in the outhouse of a woman who kept chickens under the vines behind her kitchen. She's probably dead now, the house filled with grandchildren, or maybe it's been abandoned in favour of a new, whitewashed box.

We reach Split in the early evening. From our berth in the harbour I can see Diocletian's city and the Bellevue Hotel in its nest of colonnades. Lights are coming on all along the Obala, winking among the tall palm trees. But the works of men, even an emperor's, are forgotten as the sun sets in a dazzlingly surreal display. Above the mainland mountains, the clouds are iron grey, waiting to discharge. A perfect line of puffy charcoal hangs over the chain of small, offshore islands. The cherry sun drops very slowly into the sea in a glory of cyan and salmon, yellow and azure, cobalt and turquoise, pink and green.

Most of the passengers are on deck, gazing at the sunset as the *Liburnia* pulls away from Split. To head north we must first round the coast by sailing west, directly into the spectacle that seems to be on the point of fading, only to re-emerge in new shapes and colours.

The crowd of passengers parts as two crew members appear, and with respect but no ceremony, the Croatian flag is lowered to the deck, folded and put away for the night.

Afterword

WHEN I started this journey, it was with a sense of looking for the past in the present. I soon realised, however, that little of what I experienced in 1978 was rediscoverable or even relevant twenty years on. The pleasant journey begun in Ljubljana in August 1999 changed over the weeks as I found myself following the decline of the Former Yugoslavia from its beginning in new, vibrant Slovenia, through beautiful but troubled Croatia, to the tragedy of Bosnia, itself touched by the events in Kosovo and the Federal Republic of Yugoslavia. Particular events and meetings that appeared remote or unimportant while travelling, have on reflection gained a greater resonance for me. It is as though I witnessed a moment in the lives of three countries.

In the six months since the *Liburnia* discharged its passengers into a cold, wet Rijeka dawn, much and little has changed in the Former Yugoslavia. The death of President Tudjman in December 1999 and the subsequent election, sometimes referred to as a 'revolution', has brought dramatic change to Croatia. President Racan has little time for his hard-line opponents; married to a Serb, he strongly supports the work of the ICTY. His government's moves towards democratisation and away from nationalism have already brought tangible benefits to Croatia in the form of foreign investment and economic co-operation. Observers anticipate Croatia becoming a positive example for other countries in the region, exemplifying the benefits of international co-operation and liberal government. Franjo Tudjman, the forgotten man of Croatian politics, is now barely mentioned. Shortly after the new government was elected, the country's leading football team, NK Croatia, was renamed to become once again Dinamo Zagreb.

Bosnia too has held national elections, but the results were neither as revolutionary nor as positive as those in Croatia. Bosnian Serbs remain anti-Western and hard-line in their voting, despite the moderate attitudes of the present leadership of the Republika Srpska. Bosnian Croat nationalists were not influenced by the political changes across the border, and voted for the HDZ, perhaps because they lacked a true alternative. However, the Bosniak-controlled areas showed a strong move away from nationalism, with the multi-ethnic Social Democratic Party ousting the nationalist party of Alija Izetbegović from power in several urban centres, most notably Sarajevo. These national results suggest that a majority of the population still see their destiny linked to their ethnicity and not to the Bosnian state. To some observers, this seems to confirm their nagging doubts about the viability of Bosnia itself, which they continue to regard as a Western artifice. To others, in and outside of Bosnia, the results suggest that although it will take a long time to restore the pluriformity that existed before 1991, it is already happening.

In the spring of 2000, fifteen Bosnians of all ethnic groups joined the International Police Force in East Timor. When asked about their inclusion in the Force, a Bosnian spokesman said that Bosnia was glad it could repay some of the help received from the international community and use its experience of conflict to help others. On 13 August 2000, the Croat and Moslem football teams of Mostar played each other for the first time since the war. The match was played without incident, though some of the buses carrying Moslem spectators were stoned as they left the ground. For every leap forward in Bosnia, there always seems to be that small step back, as if the possibility of happiness is too much to bear.

Slovenia is currently experiencing political turmoil, caused partly by a parliament too finely balanced between Left and

Right. The balance of power can be swung by even one individual member of parliament changing their political allegiance, and it's hoped that the next elections will resolve this. President Milan Kučan sits above the petty day-to-day wranglings of government and is, if anything, more popular than ever. His second term of office expires in 2002, and the constitution does not allow a third term. Slovenes are already wondering who, if anyone, is fit to succeed him.

Though my experience in 1978 often seemed very remote in 1999, I was made aware of the extent to which the past informs the present for all the people I met, even in Slovenia, where few people refer to past events. On the day I returned to London to begin writing this book, the news in Ljubljana was of the trial of an elderly Croat Ustaše officer. Five years after the end of the Bosnian war, the net is slowly closing around those who perpetrated some of the worst crimes. Dragolub Prcać, the Deputy Commander of Omarska camp, was arrested in the spring of 2000, within weeks of the murder of the infamous Arkan, shot through the eye by a gunman in a Belgrade hotel. Justice comes in many forms. It's rumoured that even Radovan Karadžić is considering surrender.

The people I met on my journey are often on my mind, many because of continuing contact. Andrej and Nataša have given Brin a sibling and Slovenia a new citizen; his name is Lan. The first Hrvoje has opened a new multi-media centre in Split, helped by an American grant. Miriana, who liked my honest eyes, sends wonderful cards and writes longingly of Ladbroke Grove. When he has time, Ken Corlett lets me know when to cross the names and faces of People Indicted for War Crimes off the PIFWC poster he gave me.

I saw many wonderful and beautiful things in the Former Yugoslavia, both natural and man-made, but perhaps it is human nature to remember the worst most vividly. My experience of Visoko was brief, but I'll never forget what I saw there – death and decay at its most vile, but also the dedication and skill of those who work to make some kind of justice possible. The war, and the search for the missing of Bosnia and Kosovo which resulted, feature regularly on British TV as fiction and documentary. It seems the West has a continuing fascination with the outcome of the war, perhaps a kind of guilt that it tries to assuage by remembrance. Strangely, I find looking at images of Visoko on screen even worse than actually being there. Now it has sunk in.

As I was finishing this book, a final and poignant reminder of my journey came by chance through a phone conversation with Mela Telalbašić. She told me that on 2 March 2000, her mother was buried in Sarajevo's Bare Cemetery.

'In the end,' Mela said, 'there were several things that identified her: the old fracture in her arm, a piece of fabric and the shoes she was wearing, which had belonged to my sister. It was so wonderful to know she was gone from that terrible place. Ever since I first heard she was there, I couldn't think of anything else.'

The connection between London and Sarajevo isn't the clearest, but I could hear an uncharacteristic quaver in the voice at the other end of the phone line.

'The day we went to the cemetery was cold and grey with heavy, heavy rain, but the next day . . . oh, it was so warm and bright, and I said to my brother, "It's over. *Now* she's free." '

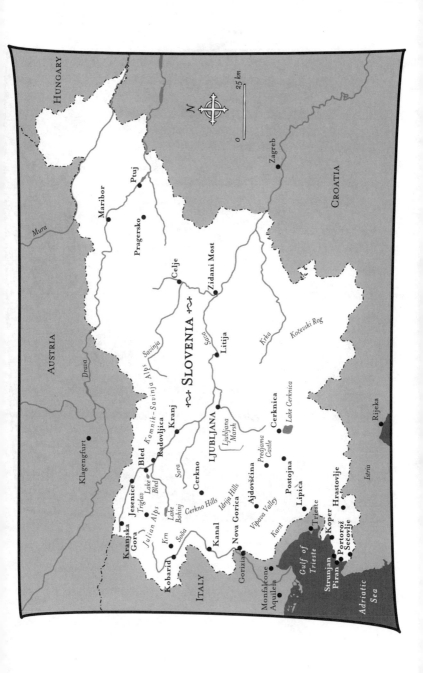

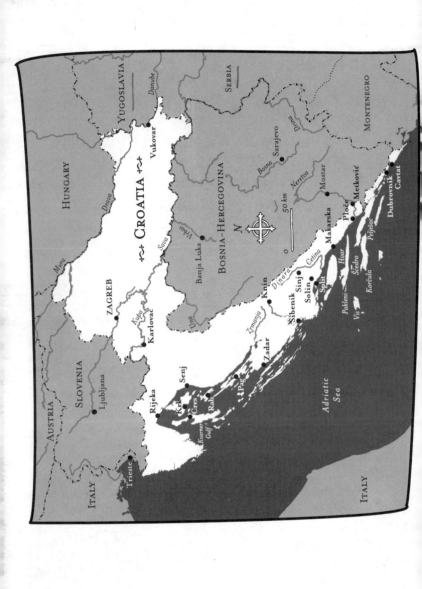

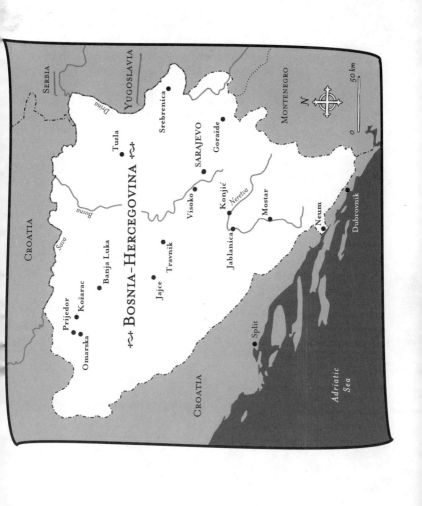

SERBIA

YUGOSLAVIA

MONTENEGRO

CROATIA

Drina

Srebrenica

Tuzla

Goražde

SARAJEVO

Visoko

Konjić

Neretva

Mostar

Bosna

Banja Luka

Jablanica

Neum

Prijedor

Kožarac

Travnik

Dubrovnik

Omarska

Jajce

Sava

↬ BOSNIA-HERCEGOVINA ↫

Split

CROATIA

Adriatic
Sea

N

50 km

0

LONELY PLANET JOURNEYS

JOURNEYS is a unique collection of travel writing – published by the company that understands travel better than anyone else.

It is a series for anyone who has ever experienced – or dreamed of – the magical moment when they encountered a strange culture or saw a place for the first time. They are tales to read while you're planning a trip, while you're on the road or while you're in an armchair, in front of a fire.

These outstanding titles explore our planet through the eyes of a diverse group of international writers. JOURNEYS books catch the spirit of a place, illuminate a culture, recount an adventure, or introduce a fascinating way of life. They always entertain, and always enrich the experience of travel.

'Lively, intelligent and varied . . . an important contribution to travel literature' – *Age (Melbourne)*

MALI BLUES
Traveling to an African Beat
Lieve Joris
(translated by Sam Garrett)

Drought, rebel uprisings, ethnic conflict: these are the predominant images of West Africa. But as Lieve Joris travels in Senegal, Mauritania and Mali, she meets survivors, fascinating individuals charting new ways of living between tradition and modernity. With her remarkable gift for drawing out people's stories, Joris brilliantly captures the rhythms of a world that refuses to give in.

THE LONELY PLANET STORY

Lonely Planet published its first book in 1973 in response to the numerous 'How did you do it?' questions Maureen and Tony Wheeler were asked after driving, busing, hitching, sailing and railing their way from England to Australia.

Written at a kitchen table and hand collated, trimmed and stapled, *Across Asia on the Cheap* became an instant local bestseller, inspiring thoughts of another book.

Eighteen months in South-East Asia resulted in their second guide, *South-East Asia on a shoestring*, which they put together in a backstreet Chinese hotel in Singapore in 1975. The 'yellow bible', as it quickly became known to backpackers around the world, soon became *the* guide to the region. It has sold well over half a million copies and is now in its 9th edition, still retaining its familiar yellow cover.

Today there are over 350 titles, including travel guides, walking guides, language kits and phrasebooks, travel atlases and travel literature. The company is the largest independent travel publisher in the world. Although Lonely Planet initially specialised in guides to Asia, today there are few corners of the globe that have not been covered.

The emphasis continues to be on travel for independent travellers. Tony and Maureen still travel for several months of each year and play an active part in the writing, updating and quality control of Lonely Planet's guides.

They have been joined by over 80 authors and 200 staff at our offices in Melbourne (Australia), Oakland (USA), London (UK) and Paris (France). Travellers themselves also make a valuable contribution to the guides through the feedback we receive in thousands of letters each year and on our web site.

The people at Lonely Planet strongly believe that travellers can make a positive contribution to the countries they visit, both through their appreciation of the countries' culture, wildlife and natural features, and through the money they spend. In addition, the company makes a direct contribution to the countries and regions it covers. Since 1986 a percentage of the income from each book has been donated to ventures such as famine relief in Africa; aid projects in India; agricultural projects in Central America; Greenpeace's efforts to halt French nuclear testing in the Pacific; and Amnesty International.

'I hope we send people out with the right attitude about travel. You realise when you travel that there are so many different perspectives about the world, so we hope these books will make people more interested in what they see.'

– *Tony Wheeler*